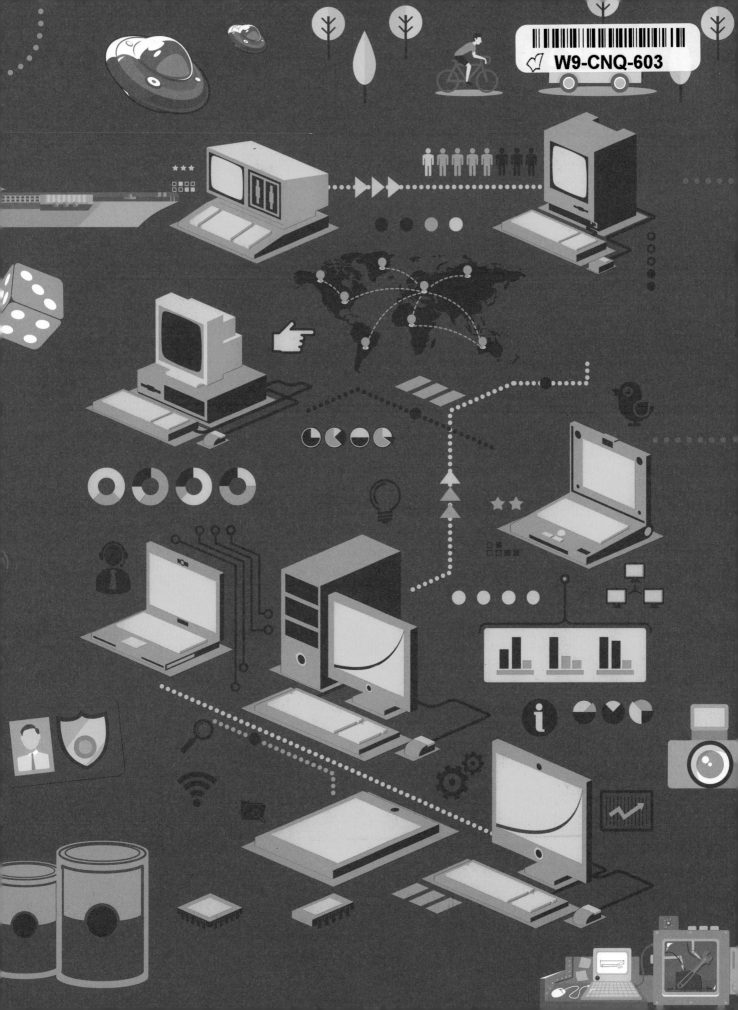

W9-CNQ-603

INFOMANIAC

INFOMANIAC
BECOME AN EXPERT IN AN HOUR

STUART DERRICK &
CHARLOTTE GODDARD

PaRragon

Bath · New York · Cologne · Melbourne · Delhi
Hong Kong · Shenzhen · Singapore · Amsterdam

SCIENCE & INVENTIONS 8

WINGS, WHEELS & RAILS 102

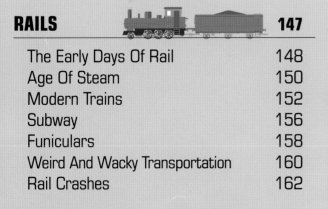

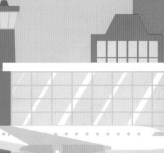

CONTENTS

CRIME & PUNISHMENT 196

WAR & BATTLES 290

SCIENCE & INVENTIONS

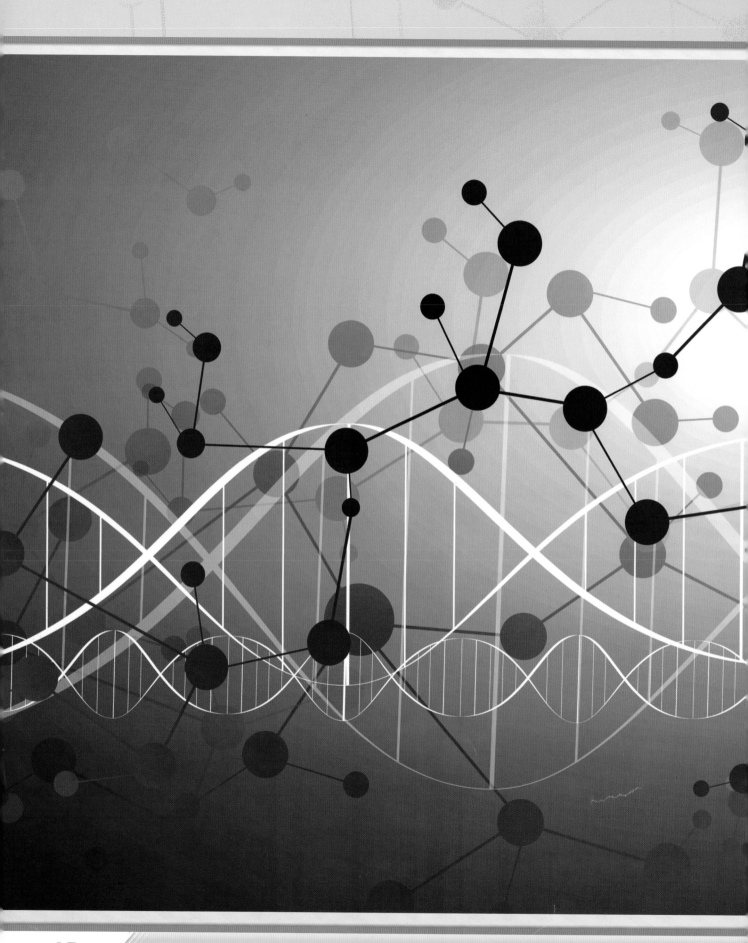

INTRODUCTION

For as long as mankind has been around on planet Earth (about 200,000 years), he has sought to understand his world and improve on it. From the earliest days of working out that some plants and animals were tasty while others could kill you, man's relentlessly inquiring mind set him apart from the other livings things with which he shared the planet.

The stories on these pages celebrate and record some of mankind's greatest and strangest discoveries, as well as some of the truly astonishing facts about our planet and the universe.

The pages are packed with amazing facts, lists, and statistics to amaze and perplex your friends. It is said that a little knowledge is a dangerous thing, but an intriguing nugget of knowledge can also

be the start of a fascinating voyage of discovery that will last a lifetime ... or maybe just for the duration of a road trip to keep your friends amused.

Each section covers a different area of scientific endeavor and innovation. Starting with "Inventions Through History," we examine how the inventive ancients were cleverer than we sometimes give them credit for, and often came up with items thousands of year ago that we still use today—razors, toothpaste, and concrete being just some of them.

Standing on the shoulders of these giants, subsequent pioneers have produced insights and devices that have gradually improved the lives of mankind. Renaissance figures like Leonardo da Vinci devised some amazing inventions, although they didn't always have the means to build them in their lifetimes. Nevertheless, this knowledge has trickled down the ages through the Industrial Revolution and into our modern times.

It's often hard to imagine how different our lives would be without some of the everyday inventions that we take for granted, but this book raises its hat to the amazing inventors of such essentials as the can opener, the lightbulb, and the flushing toilet.

Our modern age has seen no letup in our inventiveness, with the computer age ushering in a new world where communication is faster and more compelling than ever before. Just as Gutenberg's printing press made knowledge available to one and all, everyone can now be in command of more computing power than was available to the first men on the Moon, in the shape of a smartphone.

Space has not proved to be the final frontier for man, as he has sent men and machines into it, as well as exploding things and generally cluttering it up. Technology has also helped us to understand that humans are not the center of the universe. Who knows what is out there? Our best scientific brains are doing their best to uncover the mysteries of places we can never actually visit but which fascinate us nonetheless.

By working to discover the intricacies of physics and chemistry, we have a better understanding of our own relatively small planet, as well as the inner space of our own bodies. In fact, there are hundreds of facts that will astonish your friends and family, and turn you into an Infomaniac.

INVENTIONS
THROUGH HISTORY

1000000 years BCE
man tames fire

70000 years BCE
invention of the bow and arrow

INVENTIVE ANCIENTS

Moldy medicine

Alexander Fleming may be famously associated with the discovery of penicillin, after he noticed a mold on a Petri dish that killed bacteria, but the ancient Greeks, Serbians, and Indians all record the deliberate use of moldy bread to staunch wounds. Sri Lankan soldiers in the army of King Dutugamunu (161–137 BCE) would take moldy cakes into battle to be used as field dressings.

Smooth operators

The first shaving razors were invented by the ancient Egyptians, and were a set of sharp stone blades set in wooden handles, later replaced with copper-bladed razors. For much of their history, being clean-shaven was considered fashionable, and being stubbly came to be considered a mark of poor social status.

Ring of confidence

The Egyptians invented toothpaste. Early ingredients included the powder of ox hooves, ashes, charred eggshells, and pumice. They also invented marshmallows, so dental hygiene was probably a top priority.

Magnetic magic

The magnetic compass was not employed for navigation purposes when it was first invented during China's Han Dynasty (from around 206 BCE). Instead, it was used for fortune-telling purposes, possibly to order and harmonize buildings in accordance with the principles of feng shui.

Ancient pictures

The Arabic scientist and inventor Alhazen made one of the first cameras in around 1020 CE, nearly 1,000 years ago. It was a dark chamber with a tiny hole in one wall to let in light, causing an upside-down image to appear on the wall opposite the hole.

210 years BCE
Archimedes' screw allows water to be raised

1500 years BCE
sundials tell the time

40000 years BCE
cave paintings

20000 years BCE
first pottery

12000 years BCE
animals domesticated

Wake up
Greek inventor Tesibius, who lived in Egypt, devised a water clock with an alarm system, which could be made to drop pebbles on a gong, or blow trumpets at preset times.

Holy inventions!
The world's first vending machine dispensed a set amount of holy water when a coin was put into a slot, and was invented by Hero of Alexandria who was born around 10 CE. Hero's many inventions included the first recorded steam engine and a wind wheel, which operated an organ.

Concrete idea
The Romans invented a form of concrete, made of lime and volcanic rock, and used it in famous buildings including the Colosseum, many aqueducts, and the sewers of Rome. After the fall of the Roman Empire the idea of concrete disappeared for centuries, only to be rediscovered in the early 1800s.

Robot waitress
Al-Jazari (1136–1206) was an Arabic inventor and engineer whose machines included an automated waitress who could serve drinks, a musical robot band, and five machines for raising water. He also developed the camshaft and suction pump.

6000 years BCE
irrigation in the Middle East

5000 years BCE
copper smelted

3200 years BCE
earliest writing systems

1449

John of Utynam, from Flanders, was awarded a 20-year patent by King Henry VI for a glass-making process previously unknown in England. This is the first recorded patent of invention, although the patent system was first developed in Renaissance Italy.

RENAISSANCE

All-rounder

In addition to his art, Leonardo da Vinci (1452–1519) is famed for his work in civil engineering, chemistry, geology, geometry, hydrodynamics, mathematics, mechanical engineering, optics, physics, pyrotechnics, and zoology. His inventions included a diving suit, a parachute, a glider, a helicopter, an armored fighting vehicle, a calculator, and the use of solar power. Most of his devices were left unmade, often because the materials required to create them had not yet been discovered.

Top invention

The printing press, invented by German goldsmith Johannes Gutenberg (c1398–1468), is widely regarded as the most important invention of the last thousand years. The machine, which could print 3,600 pages a day, was the catalyst for a sharp rise in education. By the start of the 16th century, printing presses in more than 200 European cities had produced more than 20 million volumes; by 1600, output had risen tenfold to an estimated 150–200 million copies.

The write stuff

So-called "lead pencils" have never contained lead. Some time in the early 14th century a large deposit of graphite was discovered in Cumbria, England, and locals found it was easy to saw into sticks and make marks with. Everyone thought it was a previously undiscovered form of lead, and England had the monopoly on pencil making until scientists worked out how to make pencils from powdered graphite later that century. Before wood was used, the graphite was wrapped in string or sheepskin.

Cheers for beers

Dr. Alexander Nowell, Dean of St. Paul's Cathedral in London in the reign of Queen Elizabeth I, is credited with the invention of bottled beer. In his days as parish priest in Hertfordshire he decanted some beer into a bottle to sustain him on a fishing trip and lost it—when he discovered it again some days later it was still drinkable, and rather fizzy.

4,000

years ago the ancient Indians and Minoans had flushing toilets, but the first modern flushing toilet was built by Sir John Harington in 1596. He built two—one for himself, one for Queen Elizabeth I.

1589

The world's first piece of industrial machinery was invented by English curate William Lee in Nottinghamshire. Lee is said to have designed the first knitting machine because the woman he loved paid more attention to her knitting than to him. Queen Elizabeth I refused a patent for the **stocking frame** on the prescient grounds that the machine could damage the handknitting trade, but it became an established part of stocking making.

Far sighted

Italian scientist Galileo Galilei (1564–1642) was a man of many talents. He developed an improved telescope that enabled him to identify Jupiter's four largest moons. He also invented a superior compass and thermometer, and defended Copernicus's theory of heliocentrism—that the Sun, and not the Earth, was the center of the universe. His theories often fell foul of the church and he spent his later years under house arrest.

Frozen fowl

While on a carriage journey in 1626 Sir Francis Bacon came up with the idea of freezing chicken to preserve it by stuffing it with snow. According to the account of a friend, he leapt out of the carriage, bought a fowl, and got on with the experiment then and there. He then contracted pneumonia and died, which may or may not have been related to the fowl-freezing shenanigans.

43,000

in 1884

650

stocking frames in Britain in 1660

"Mary had a little lamb"

The first words to be recorded and played back, spoken by Thomas Edison, inventor of the phonograph in 1877. The sound was recorded and played back by a needle on foil.

INDUSTRIAL REVOLUTION

Flushed away

Despite the name, British toilet supplier Thomas Crapper did not invent the flushing toilet in the late 1800s, although he claimed he did in his business brochures. He just came up with a few improvements.

No laughing matter

American dentist Horace Wells was a pioneer in the field of anesthesia, experimenting with the use of laughing gas. He did not attempt to patent the discovery because he stated that pain relief should be "as free as the air." Wells became addicted to chloroform in the course of his research. Increasingly deranged, he was committed to New York's infamous Tombs prison, having thrown sulfuric acid over the clothes of two women, and later committed suicide.

Dash it

Samuel Morse was inspired to develop Morse code and the telegraph system when, away from home in 1825, he received a letter telling him that his wife was ill—and the next day a letter saying she was dead. By the time he got back she was already buried, so he decided to explore a means of rapid long-distance communication.

First time

The first U.S. patent issued was to American inventor Samuel Hopkins in 1790, for an improved way of making potash—a chemical used, among other things, in textile production.

In a spin

The spinning jenny, patented in 1770 by James Hargreaves, massively boosted productivity in the cotton industry. Legend has it the device was named after Hargreaves' wife or one of his daughters—but none of them was called Jenny. The name is more likely to be a contraction of "engine."

Hold your horses

Horsepower as a measurement was the idea of steam-engine pioneer James Watt as a way of charging his customers. He started out by basing his prices on the amount of coal clients were saving by using his newer engines, but many were looking to replace horses. Watt was overoptimistic in his calculations—

8

It would have taken at least eight hours and possibly several days to develop the oldest photograph that is still in existence. It showed the view from the window of French scientist Joseph Niépce in 1826.

few if any horses can replicate his estimated power over a sustained period—but we still use his measurement today.

Weird science

Not all 19th-century inventions caught on. Some that failed to make the grade were the antigarrotting cravat, invented in 1862, and a top hat that transformed into a derby, courtesy of hidden springs (1878). The diving suit fitted with a bath plug at crotch level, which allowed the diver to urinate without taking off his entire suit (invented in 1870) was not a huge success either.

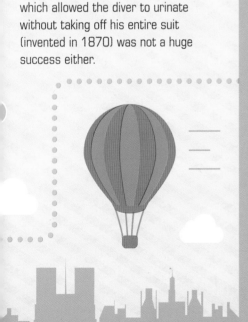

Key Innovations

1733
John Kay's flying shuttle

1769
Richard Arkwright's water frame

1779
Samuel Crompton's spinning mule

1793
Eli Whitney's cotton gin

1856
Henry Bessemer's process ushers in the Age of Steel

1884
Linotype machine makes printing cheaper

1760
John Smeaton uses air pumps to smelt iron

1769
James Watt improves the steam engine

1783
Henry Cort's puddling process strengthens iron

1846
Elias Howe's sewing machine

1876
Alexander Graham Bell invents the telephone

1885
Gottlieb Daimler's gasoline engine

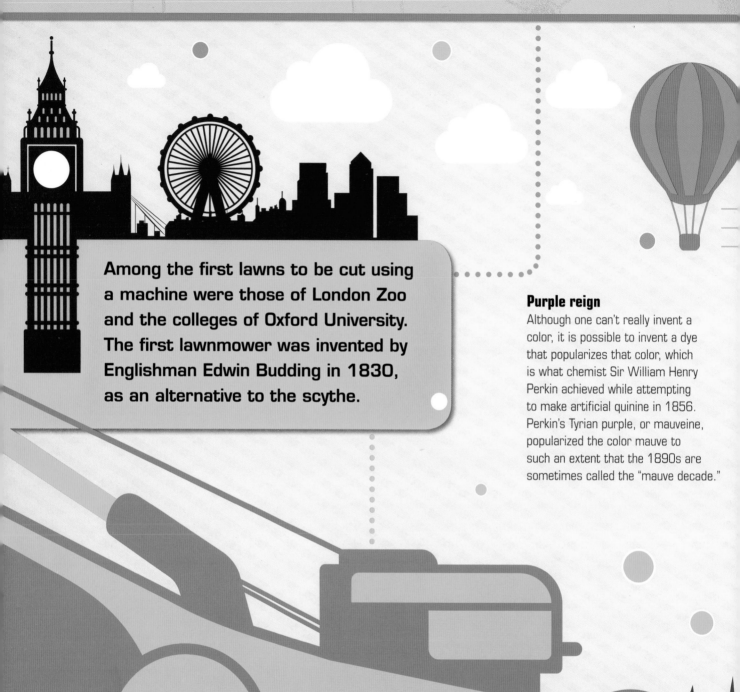

Among the first lawns to be cut using a machine were those of London Zoo and the colleges of Oxford University. The first lawnmower was invented by Englishman Edwin Budding in 1830, as an alternative to the scythe.

Purple reign

Although one can't really invent a color, it is possible to invent a dye that popularizes that color, which is what chemist Sir William Henry Perkin achieved while attempting to make artificial quinine in 1856. Perkin's Tyrian purple, or mauveine, popularized the color mauve to such an extent that the 1890s are sometimes called the "mauve decade."

24

The number of children Isaac Singer (1811–75) fathered by various wives and mistresses. The inventor of the easy-use home sewing machine was famously free with his affections.

Mac attack

The Mackintosh, or rubberized raincoat, was invented by Charles Macintosh—the extra "k" arrived some years later—and first sold in Britain in 1824. Early waterproof raincoats were prone to stiffness, bad smells, and melting in the heat.

Not butter

Margarine was invented after Emperor Napoleon III of France offered a prize to anyone who could make a satisfactory alternative to butter, to be used by the lower classes and the armed forces. French chemist Hippolyte Mège-Mouriès duly invented a substance he called oleomargarine, in 1869, although he didn't have much luck in selling it.

Plastic fantastic

The first manmade plastic was called Parkesine, and won its inventor Alexander Parkes a bronze medal at the 1862 International Exhibition in London. It was not, however, a commercial success as Parkesine was expensive to produce, prone to cracking, and highly flammable.

Fresh ideas

In 1767, Joseph Priestley invented soda water when he suspended a bowl of water above a beer vat at a local brewery. Priestley is also credited with the discovery of oxygen but felt soda water was his "happiest" discovery. He found this water had a pleasant taste, and offered it to friends as a cool, refreshing drink.

X-rated

The first picture taken using X-rays was of the hand of Anna Bertha, wife of X-ray machine inventor Wilhelm Conrad Röntgen, in 1895. When she saw her skeleton she exclaimed "I have seen my death!"

On the up

While escalators, or moving staircases, were patented by a number of inventors from the mid-19th century, the first one to be built was developed by American Jesse Reno and installed at Coney Island, New York, in 1896. The UK's first escalator was debuted in London department store Harrods in 1898—nervous customers were offered brandy and smelling salts at the top to revive them after their ordeal.

15%

The amount of the labor force made up of children during the English Industrial Revolution. Oxford professor Jane Humphries estimated that there were one million child workers, including 350,000 under the age of ten, by the early 19th century.

40

At one point Apple and Samsung had more than 40 patent lawsuits filed against each other. In 2014, they dropped all suits against each other, but only outside the United States.

PROLIFIC INVENTORS AND FEUDS

It's for you

Scottish inventor Alexander Graham Bell knew he had an American competitor as he worked to create the first telephone. Bell bribed a U.S. Patent Office clerk to show him his rival's patent so he could incorporate bits of it into his own design, then fudge the paperwork so it appeared Bell's patent had been submitted first.

Lightbulb moment

British scientist Joseph Swan demonstrated a working lightbulb in December 1878 but did not receive a patent until November 1880. U.S. inventor Thomas Edison meanwhile obtained a patent for a lightbulb in 1879: his advertising campaign claimed he was the inventor. In the end Swan and Edison joined together to market the lightbulb in the UK.

Safety first

George Stephenson, a mining engineer, and Humphry Davy, a gentleman scientist, were locked in a bitter dispute for years over the invention of the miners' safety lamp. Both came up with similar devices, but Davy claimed that only his design was the result of proper scientific process. The lamp is now called the Davy Lamp, but Stephenson did go on to invent the steam engine, so he has his own place in history.

Electrickery

In 1882, Thomas Edison was the first to supply people with electricity, using direct current. When his rival Nikola Tesla told the U.S. government alternating current was more efficient, Edison hit back by attempting to discredit AC—mainly through using it to electrocute animals, including an elephant. But AC triumphed regardless—probably because it is more efficient.

Most Inventions

1st

4,696

The world's most prolific inventor is 56-year-old Australian Kia Silverbrook, who holds 4,696 patents for inventions in fields such as digital paper, robotics, and DNA analysis.

2nd

3,865

Shunpei Yamazaki, a 72-year-old Japanese inventor with 3,865 patents in the fields of computer science and solid-state physics, is the world's second most prolific inventor.

Highly Commended

1,093

Known as the "Wizard of Menlo Park," American Thomas Edison, for many years the world's most prolific inventor, registered 1,093 U.S. patents before he died in 1931. His inventions included the phonograph and the motion-picture camera.

Code of honor

Samuel Morse went to great lengths to win a lawsuit for the right to be called sole "inventor of the telegraph," although a number of other men had patents for different methods. He called them "the most unprincipled set of pirates I have ever known."

Heated debate

Scottish chemist and physicist Sir James Dewar invented the vacuum flask in around 1892 as a way of preserving the gases he was studying. He later took the Thermos company, which commercialized the product, to court but failed to stop them from marketing it as he had never patented the flask. Scientists still call it a Dewar flask though.

80 pounds per square inch

(5.6 kg per square cm) was the pressure the first beer cans had to withstand—more than double that of canned food. Felinfoel Ale from Llanelli, Wales, was the first beer in Britain to be sold in a tin can. Its early cans had a beer-bottle top instead of the rings used today.

INVENTION OF EVERYDAY THINGS

Swell gel

Vaseline was invented when a young English chemist noticed that drillers and riggers in the Oil Rush of 1850s' America would cover their injuries with some of the thick gunk that came up on the drilling rods when they were extracted from the ground. The gunk-covered wounds seemed to heal faster, so Robert Chesebrough refined the gel in his lab and marketed it—first as Rod Oil and, when that didn't capture the popular imagination, as Vaseline, from the German for "water" and Greek for "oil."

Shady operators

Sunglasses made of smoky quartz were used in China in the 12th century to protect the eyes from glare, and may have been used even earlier—ancient Chinese documents tell of judges using such glasses to hide their expressions while questioning witnesses.

Cashback

Getting hold of your cash meant standing in line in a bank until the first ATM went into operation at Barclays Bank in Enfield, London, on June 27, 1967. Legend has it that engineer John Shepherd-Barron came up with the idea after failing to get to his bank before it shut.

Chocs away!

Solid milk chocolate was invented via collaboration between a candle maker and a baby-food manufacturer. When candle sales plummeted after the invention of oil lamps, Swiss Daniel Peter joined forces with Henri Nestlé to create the popular treat in the 1870s. The two went on to found the Nestlé company.

Zip it!

An early version of the zipper was patented in the US by Elias Howe in 1851. However the fastener we know today came from gradual improvements that led to the 1914 invention of the "Hookless Fastener No. 2," by Swede Gideon Sundback, which most resembles modern zippers.

1885
THE INVENTION OF THE CAN OPENER

Sticky business

Adhesive tape, often known by the brand names Scotch tape or Sellotape, was invented by Richard Gurley Drew, who worked for 3M, the company that later brought us Post-It Notes. In 1922, Drew invented masking tape to assist with two-tone paint jobs. Because at first it only had adhesive along its edges, aggrieved painters told him to take it back to his "Scotch" (meaning stingy) employers and get more stickiness on to it, which he did. Transparent sticky tape came along in 1925.

1772
THE INVENTION OF CANNED FOOD

130 BILLION
cans produced each year in the USA

Electric blanket

Electric blankets were first developed as a medical device to keep patients warm, particularly those with TB, who were urged to get plenty of fresh air. American doctor Sidney Russell devised the first electrically heated pad in 1912.

Alarm clock

User-settable alarm clocks date back to at least 15th-century Europe. Users had to put a pin in a hole to set the alarm to the right time.

Microwave

The microwave oven was invented by U.S. engineer Percy Spencer in 1945. The first food cooked was popcorn, and the second was an egg—which exploded in the face of one of his colleagues.

Dishwasher

The dishwasher was invented in 1886 by American society lady Josephine Garis Cochran, who was fed up with her servants chipping her plates and cups. Today's dishwashers still work in the same way as Cochran's design.

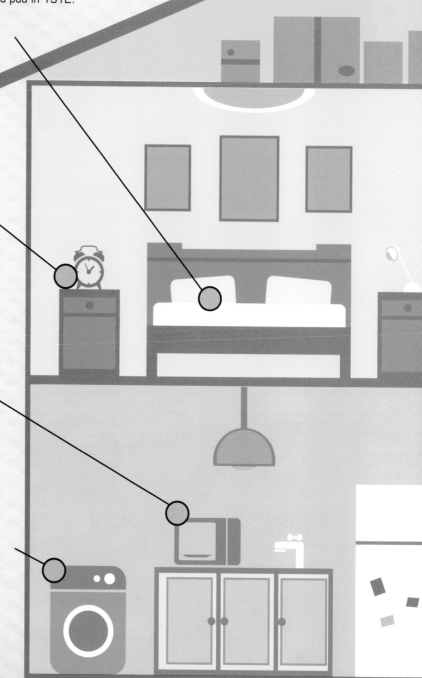

Toothbrush

The Chinese invented the bristle toothbrush in 1498. The first ones were made of pig bristles attached to a piece of bone or bamboo. Nylon bristle toothbrushes like the ones we use today were invented in 1938.

Toilet paper

The first toilet paper was invented in the U.S. in 1857 by Joseph C. Gayetty. It was softened with aloe gel and had Gayetty's name printed on every sheet. Toilet paper on a roll was invented by Walter Alcock in Britain in 1879.

Television

Scottish inventor John Logie Baird (1888–1946) created his first television in 1924—out of bits and pieces he had lying around—including a cardboard circle cut out of a hat box, an empty cookie box, a bicycle lamp, and sealing wax.

Vacuum cleaner

The first vacuum cleaners, invented by English engineer Hubert Cecil Booth in 1901, were so large they had to be pulled from house to house on a horse-drawn cart. Society ladies would invite their friends over for parties while they watched the machines at work.

The Ig Nobels

While the Nobel Prize is one of the pinnacles for scientists, the Ig Nobel Prize recognizes some of the more bizarre footnotes in research. Established in 1991 by the magazine *Annals of Improbable Research*, the awards claim to want to make people laugh and then think. Winning research includes ...

NOBEL PRIZES

Deathbed conversion

Alfred Nobel, the man behind the famous prizes, was inspired to fund this legacy after newspapers mistakenly published his own obituary after his brother was killed. Upset by headlines like "The Merchant of Death is dead," the inventor of dynamite changed his will to benefit those who create the greatest benefit to mankind.

Medallion men

Winners of a Nobel Prize receive a gold medallion featuring the image of Alfred Nobel, a diploma, and around eight million Swedish kronor (over $1 million). Although a tidy sum, this is only around a third of the relative value of the award in 1901 (32 percent to be precise).

Notable Nobels

Famous science laureates include Albert Einstein (for physics in 1921), Marie Curie (prizes in physics in 1903 and chemistry in 1911), James Watson, Francis Crick and Maurice Wilkins, who revealed the structure of DNA (1962), and Alexander Fleming, who discovered penicillin (1945).

Sold out

James Watson sold his Nobel medal for $4.1 million in 2014, the first time a living recipient had done so. Watson said he would donate part of the money to charity and scientific research. His colleague Crick died in 2004 and his medal was sold for $2.2 million in 2013.

Anonymity rules

Nobody can nominate themselves for a prize, and the list of nominees is kept secret for 50 years after the award.

Spending it

Winners have spent the prize fund in many different ways. American neuroscientist Paul Greengard used part of his to establish a prize for women in science to counteract discrimination. British biologist Richard Roberts spent some of his prize on a croquet lawn at his home. Albert Einstein signed over his prize to his wife Mileva Marić in 1919, strangely two years before he won his award.

Why people dislike the sound of fingernails on a chalkboard

PawSense software to determine when a cat is walking across a keyboard

Using slime mold to determine the optimal route for railroad tracks

A study of constipation among soldiers

The invention of a car alarm combined with a flame thrower

Andre Geim's levitation of a live frog using magnets. He is the first scientist to hold both Ig Nobel and Nobel Prizes

Nobel Prizes in numbers

1895

The year Alfred Nobel signed his last will and testament, giving over much of his wealth to a series of annually awarded prizes.

$215 million

The equivalent value of Nobel's estate today (1,702 million Swedish kronor).

6

The number of categories. Prizes are awarded in Physics, Chemistry, Physiology or Medicine, Literature, and Peace. In 1968, Sweden's central bank established a prize in Economic Sciences in memory of Nobel.

567

Nobel Prizes awarded.

889

Individual Nobel Laureates recognized.

3

Laureates who were under arrest at the time of their awards.

$100,000

is on offer for a computer that can pass the so-called Turing Test, by convincing judges that it is human. While some "chatterbots" have won smaller prizes, the Loebner Prize is still up for grabs.

EYES ON THE PRIZE

Sometimes it's all about the joy of creating, but sometimes scientists need to be spurred on by an incentive.

Can it!

In 1795, Napoleon offered 12,000 francs to anyone who could make it easier to preserve food for his conquering armies. Fifteen years later, sweet maker Nicolas François Appert devised a new canning process.

All at sea

The rulers of Spain, Britain, and the Netherlands all offered prizes for the first person to come up with a method to pinpoint the location of ships at sea. English clockmaker John Harrison's marine chronometer solved the longitude problem—but

the British Longitude Board reneged on the prize money.

Banging balls

In 1869, with elephants in short supply, the billiards industry offered a $10,000 prize for a replacement for ivory billiard balls. Inventor John Wesley Hyatt won but unfortunately his material would sometimes explode on impact—a Colorado saloon owner claimed every man in his bar would pull a gun at the sound.

To boldly go

The Ansari X Prize offered $10 million for the first nongovernment organization to launch a reusable manned spacecraft into space twice within two weeks. The prize was won in 2004 by the Tier One project with its experimental spaceplane *SpaceShipOne*.

$25m

can be won by the first person to come up with a way of removing greenhouse gases from the atmosphere. British entrepreneur Sir Richard Branson is fronting the cash.

100,000,000,000

Bic pens have been sold, but the inventor Lázló Biró didn't see much of the cash. The Hungarian journalist patented the ballpoint pen in 1938 after becoming fed up with leaky fountain pens. He then sold the invention to Marcel Bich in 1945.

But being an inventor is not always lucrative ...

Eastern blocks

Russian computer programmer Alexey Pajitnov developed the madly addictive game Tetris alongside colleagues at a Russian government-funded research center in 1984. He only started getting royalties 12 years later when he formed The Tetris Company.

Wireless operator

Italian Antonio Meucci discovered a way to transmit the human voice through wires when trying out a new electrotherapy device on a friend in 1849. But he didn't have enough money to patent his "telettrofono" and Great Western Union telegraph company lost his prototype. He died in poverty in 1889.

Dreams can come true, as popstar Gabrielle warbled in 1993. Here are some inventions and discoveries that were literally dreamed up by their creators.

Get the point

According to his mother, U.S. textile worker Elias Howe came up with the idea of putting the eye of the needle in his embryonic sewing machine at the bottom instead of at the top after dreaming a savage king ordered him to make the machine work or die. After realizing the savages' spears were pierced near the point, he woke up and got cracking with his new design, patenting it in 1846.

Rings true

Prominent German chemist August Kekulé said he discovered the ring shape of the benzene molecule after dreaming about a snake seizing its own tail in the 1860s.

5255452

The U.S. patent number held by King of Pop Michael Jackson as an inventor of a special shoe allowing dancers to lean forward beyond their center of gravity, Smooth Criminal-style.

OTHER INVENTORS OF NOTE

First lady
The first woman inventor to be granted a patent was widow Ayme Ball in Britain in 1637, for preserved saffron. The first woman to be granted a patent in the U.S. was Mary Dixon Kies in 1809. She invented a method of weaving straw with silk or thread, to be used in hat making, but died penniless in New York in 1837.

Wiped out
American real estate developer Mary Anderson invented the windscreen wiper in 1903. When she tried to sell the rights she was told it was not commercially viable, but her design was adopted by the automobile industry as standard when the patent ran out in the 1920s.

Patent discrimination
Sybilla Masters was the first person in America whose invention was given an English patent. She was not allowed to patent her new corn mill herself, but the document issued by King George I to her husband in 1715 acknowledged "a new Invention found out by Sybilla, his wife, for cleaning and curing the Indian corn."

Monkee business
Bette Nesmith Graham (1924–80) was not only the first person to invent liquid paper but also the mother of musician Mike Nesmith, one of The Monkees. She used her correction fluid to cover up mistakes at work in secret for five years, but when fellow secretaries started clamoring for it

she started marketing the product as Mistake Out in 1956.

Celebrity inventors

Weapons grade
Hollywood siren Hedy Lamarr was the unlikely coinventor of a device to stop enemies jamming torpedo guidance systems. She based the device on the workings of a roll piano, coming up with the idea after a conversation with the real-life Georg von Trapp, of *The Sound of Music* fame.

Big bang
American actor Marlon Brando held a U.S. patent for a device that makes it possible to tune a drum.

3

As well as penning classics like *The Adventures of Tom Sawyer*, Mark Twain found the time to come up with: a self-sticking scrapbook, detachable elastic straps for clothes, and a board game where players must match historical events to the year they occurred.

MODERN
TECHNOLOGY

1979

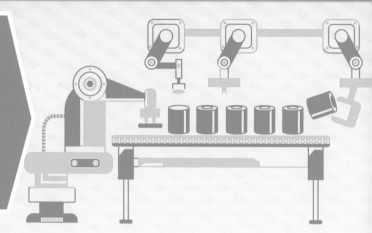

The Robotics Institute at Carnegie Mellon University in Pittsburgh was the first robotics department at a U.S. university when it was established in this year.

ROBOTICS

Sci-fi serf

The word "robot" was introduced to English by Czech playwright Karel Čapek in his 1920 science-fiction play, *Rossum's Universal Robots*. The word is derived from the Czech *robota*, meaning work performed by a serf. However, the characters in the play are more like clones than the machines commonly associated with automata.

Mechanical duck

Enlightenment inventor Jacques de Vaucanson was fascinated by the idea of artificial life. He created several mechanical figures that played music, but his most famous creation was the Canard Digérateur, or Digesting Duck, a robotic duck built in 1739. The duck, which had more than 400 parts, flapped its wings, appeared to eat grain, and then excreted afterward.

Let's work

The first industrial robot was designed by George Devol in 1954. However, it was 1961 before the first Unimate robot went to work on the General Motors production line, where it handled hot die castings and performed spot welding. The machine could handle parts weighing up to 500 pounds (227 kg).

Walkie talkie

Honda's ASIMO robot (that's Advanced Step in Innovative MObility) was developed in 2000. The humanoid robot is 51 inches (130 cm) tall and is designed to walk, climb stairs, recognize movement and faces, and interpret voice commands and human gestures. It has conducted the Detroit Symphony Orchestra, welcomed Prince Charles in Japan, and appeared on TV quiz *QI* in the UK, where it won with 32 points.

Dragon robot

The largest walking robot is a fire-breathing dragon 51 feet (15 m) long, called Tradinno. The dragon weighs 11 tons (10 tonnes) and was built for a German folk festival, where it regularly appears in a traditional play called *Drachenstich* (*Slaying the Dragon*), which has been performed for the past 500 years in the town of Furth im Wald, Bavaria.

10 jobs that robots could do in the future

- Locomotive drivers
- Driving other vehicles
- Hospital porters
- Pilots
- Astronauts
- Cleaners
- Teachers
- Pharmacists
- Security guards
- Soldiers

$11.3 billion

(¥1.2 trillion). The predicted value of Japan's robotics sector by 2020, when Japanese Prime Minister Shinzo Abe has announced that a Robot Olympics will coincide with Tokyo hosting the Olympic Games.

Mars explorers

NASA landed two robotic explorers on Mars in 2004. The explorers, *Spirit* and *Opportunity*, were supposed to last for about 90 Martian days. However, *Spirit* went on collecting data for six years, four of them driving backward owing to a damaged wheel. *Opportunity* is still in operation. They were joined by another explorer, *Curiosity*, in 2012.

K9

Sony's AIBO (Artificial Intelligence BOt) is the most sophisticated product offered in the consumer robot market. Launched in 1999, the robot dogs cost $1,500–2,500 and went on to sell around 130,000 units before production ended in 2006.

Buzz off

Scientists at Harvard created a flying robot that weighs 0.0003 ounces (80 mg) and can sit on a fingertip. Inspired by the biology of a fly, the RoboFly is able to perform the agile movements of an insect. Its carbon-fiber wings beat more than 120 times a second.

Mind control

Robots can now be controlled using your brain. The first person to operate a mind-controlled robotic hand was American Matthew Nagle, who was paralyzed from the neck down. In 2004, a computer interface was attached to the area of his brain that would control his left arm. It was able to translate his brain waves and allow Nagle to use a robotic hand.

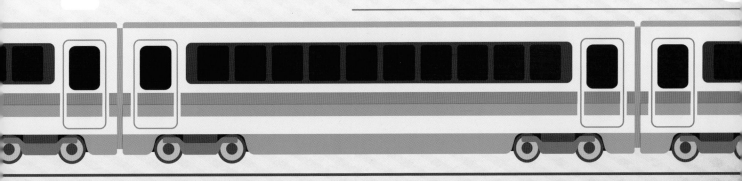

$16.5 million

The cost of the world's most expensive cell phone, which is owned by a Chinese businessman. His pimped-up iPhone has a solid gold chassis, sapphire glass screen, and more than 600 diamonds inlaid.

PHONES

Long distance
The first transatlantic telephone line was opened in 1956, after cables were laid between Scotland and Canada.

In hand
American inventor Martin Cooper was the first person to make a public phone call using a handheld cell phone, which he invented while working for Motorola in the 1970s. He called the landline of his chief competitor, Joel Engel at Bell Labs, and gloated.

Ringing Bell
The great-grandson of Alexander Graham Bell, inventor of the telephone, was the second person in the world to receive a commercial cell phone call, on October 13, 1983. The first call was made from insurance executive David Meilahn to Bob Barnett, former president of Ameritech Mobile Communications—Barnett then placed a call to Bell's great-grandson, who was in Germany.

Wise to it
The first cell phone call in the UK was purportedly made by comedian Ernie Wise, on January 1, 1985, while dressed in a top hat and standing in front of a mail coach. However, Michael Harrison, son of Vodafone chair Sir Ernest Harrison, had in fact made the first call some hours before, to wish his father Happy New Year from Trafalgar Square. He was wearing black tie.

First cell phone
The Motorola DynaTAC 8000X was the first cell phone to be commercially available, in 1984. It offered 30 minutes of talk time and eight hours of standby, and could store 30 numbers. It cost $3,995, weighed around 28 ounces (790 grams), and was 10 inches (25 cm) high, not including its antenna.

Waste-charging
Scientists have come up with a way of charging cell phones using urine. By passing urine through a cascade of microbial fuel cells they charged a Samsung phone with enough power to enable SMS messaging, web browsing, and to make a brief call.

250 million

The stubby little Nokia 1100, a basic GSM cell phone, is the world's bestselling handset—and the world's bestselling consumer electronics device. Nokia has sold more than a quarter of a billion 1100s since its launch in 2003.

Picture this
French engineer and entrepreneur Philippe Kahn created the first camera phone. The first photo he took with it, on June 11, 1997, was of his newborn daughter Sophie.

Not-so-simple Simon
The first smartphone—although it wasn't called that at the time—was the IBM Simon, launched in 1994. As well as making and receiving calls, users could send faxes and e-mails, and access functions including an electronic notepad and standard and predictive stylus input screen keyboards. Around 50,000 were sold in the six months the product was on the market.

16%
of all active U.S. patents relate to smartphones. There are about 250,000 patents in the smartphone sector.

17,468

The number of vacuum tubes contained in the first fully functioning, digital, programmable, general-purpose computer. The ENIAC was designed and built by two U.S. scientists, John Mauchly and J. Presper Eckert, between 1943 and 1946. It took up as much space as five school classrooms.

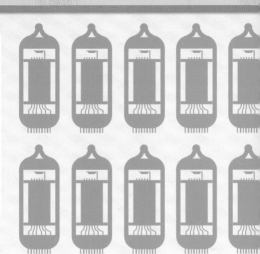

COMPUTERS

Need for speed
The fastest computer in the world is currently *Tianhe-2*, translated as *Milky Way 2*, located in Sun Yat-sen University, Guangzhou, China. It is nearly twice as fast as the previous title holder, the U.S. *Titan*, which it outpaced in June 2013. However, the *Tainhe-2* is likely to be eclipsed by two new computers being built in the United States by companies IBM and Nvidia—*Summit* and *Sierra* will be completed by 2018.

Game on
The first computer game was created in 1962 by Stephen Russell, a student at the Massachusetts Institute of Technology. Called *Spacewar*, the game had two simple spacecraft (triangles) which fired dots at each other as they orbited a planet (circle).

It's a dream
Studies have found that people who play video games regularly are better at controlling their dreams than others. Known as "lucid dreaming," gamers are more able to recognize they are dreaming and direct the events of the dream.

Byronic heroine
The first computer programmer was Ada Lovelace, daughter of Romantic poet Lord Byron. She created programs, made of cards with patterns of holes punched in them, for English mathematician Charles Babbage's analytical engine, a forerunner of modern computers designed in the 1840s.

Tune in
Tom's Diner by Suzanne Vega was the first song used by German audio engineer Karlheinz Brandenburg to develop MP3, the most common coding format for digital music. Brandenburg listened to the song over and over, each time refining the scheme, making sure it did not adversely affect the subtlety of Vega's voice.

Radio program
Before the advent of floppy disks, many home computers used cassette tapes to store data—when played on an ordinary cassette recorder,

$76.4 BILLION

In 2011, electronics company Apple had more money to spend than the U.S. government. The United States had an operating cash balance of $73.7 billion, while Apple's reserves were reported to be even higher.

$76.4 BILLION APPLE

$73.7 BILLION U.S. GOVERNMENT

30 MILLION GIGABYTES

The Large Hadron Collider at CERN, Switzerland, generates this amount of data a year—the equivalent of nearly nine million high-definition movies. Scientists set up the Worldwide LHC Computing Grid to tackle this data—the grid consists of more than 100,000 computers spread across 170 computer centers in 40 countries and was unveiled in October 2008.

they made a distinctive squeaking, groaning sound. In some countries, including the UK and Finland, cassette storage was so popular that radio stations would broadcast programs, which listeners could record on to blank tapes and run on their computers.

Smallest computer

A team of Israeli scientists have adapted molecules of DNA to act as tiny molecular computing devices. Experiments have shown that a microliter of salt solution, containing three trillion self-contained DNA computing devices, can perform 66 billion operations per second, with the necessary fuel for the computations provided by the DNA itself.

Quantum leap

While normal computers use a string of zeroes and ones to represent data, the newest quantum computers use qubits, which can be a zero, a one, or both at the same time, taking advantage of the ability of quantum particles to be in two places at once. This allows for problem-solving on a faster scale.

Game over

Between July and September 2002, it was illegal to play any computer game in public in Greece. The Greek government banned all electronic games as part of an attempt to crack down on online gambling, but repealed the law after two months.

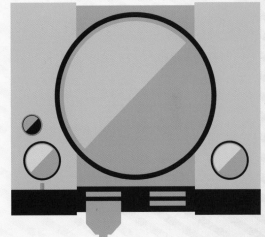

160 MEGAFLOPS

The speed of the world's first supercomputer, which was installed at Los Alamos National Laboratory, New Mexico, in 1976. The Cray-1 cost $8.8 million and was the fastest computer at the time.

Borrowed time

Computer users can help fight ebola, discover pulsars, tackle climate change, and take part in numerous other scientific projects from the comfort of their own home. Berkeley Open Infrastructure for Network Computing allows scientists to use the spare processing power of volunteers' computers to carry out immense research projects. First harnessed in the search for alien life, the network consists of around 1,148,029 active computers worldwide.

Computer mouse

The first computer mouse was invented by American Douglas Engelbart in 1964, and patented in 1970. It was rectangular, and made of wood. The patent ran out before the mouse became popular in home computing.

At home

The first home computers were sold as kits, which had to be put together by hobbyists. The earliest nonkit personal computer based on a microprocessor was the Micral N, produced by French company R2E in early 1973.

Sounds right

The alert sound made by Apple Inc's Macintosh 7 operating system in 1991 is called "Sosumi." The name is derived from "So sue me," thanks to a long-running court battle with music company Apple Corp over the use of music in Apple Inc's computer products. Meanwhile, over at Microsoft, pioneering musician Brian Eno was the musical brains behind Windows 95's start-up tune, "The Microsoft Sound."

Takes the cake

The first computer in commercial business use was set to work solving conundrums in cake production and delivery, in 1951. After successfully using the Lyons Electronic Office (LEO) to schedule deliveries to Lyons tea shops across England, J. Lyons & Co went into business manufacturing computers.

$365,000

Fewer than 50 of the original Apple 1 home computers were ever sold, which is why one sold at auction for this price in 2014.

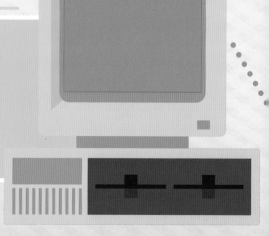

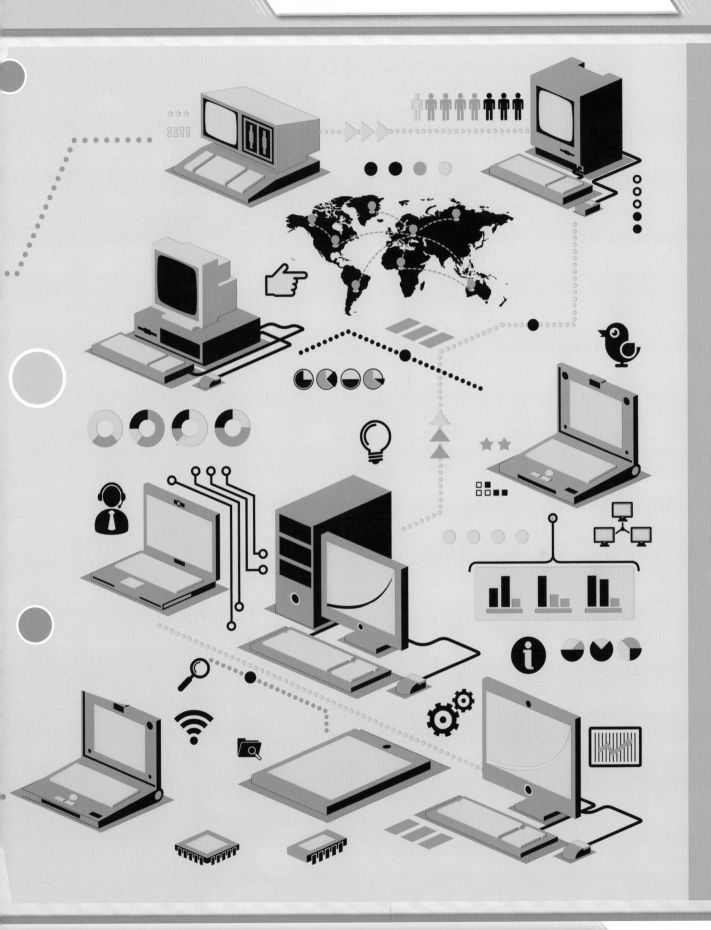

"JUST SETTING UP MY TWTTR"

The first Tweet, sent by Twitter founder Jack Dorsey on March 21, 2006.

THE INTERNET

First site
The first-ever website (info.cern.ch) was published on August 6, 1991, by British scientist Tim Berners-Lee, the inventor of the world wide web, while at research facility CERN, in Switzerland. Berners-Lee invented the web in 1989 as a way to link and navigate information on the Internet, which has been around since the 1960s.

You've got mail
The first e-mail ever sent was from U.S. computer engineer Ray Tomlinson, in 1971, just to see if he could send a message between two computers. It read: "QWERTYUIOP." It was Ray who decided to use the @ symbol to separate the recipient's name from their location.

Internet monitor
The largest communications surveillance network was set up by the intelligence organizations of the USA, UK, Australia, New Zealand, and Canada in 1947, and is still going. It is thought that Echelon can intercept 90 percent of Internet traffic as well as monitoring global telephone and satellite communications.

News from Atlantis
The first e-mail sent from space was beamed back from the NASA space shuttle *Atlantis* by U.S. astronauts Shannon Lucid and James C. Adamson in August 1991. It read: "Hello Earth! Greetings from the STS-43 Crew. This is the first AppleLink from space. Having a GREAT time, wish you were here ... send cryo and RCS! Hasta la vista baby ... we'll be back!"

Just browsing
The world's first Internet browser was NCSA Mosaic, released on April 22, 1993. It was created by researchers at the National Center for Supercomputing Applications, Illinois.

98%
of Bermudans used the Internet in 2014, the highest proportion of any country.

ONE BILLION

The number of websites on the Internet passed one billion in September 2014.

Early spam

The first-known spam e-mail, advertising a Digital Equipment Corporation product presentation, was sent in 1978 by Gary Thuerk to 393 addresses, which was all the users of proto-Internet ARPANET at the time. Today, 55.3 percent of e-mail is spam, and one out of every 329 e-mails contains a virus.

Link wars

In 2002, British Telecom tried to claim that it had patented the entire Internet—or at least the clicky bits. BT said it had patented hyperlinks back in the 1980s, and took a U.S. Internet service provider to court to try to force it to pay royalties every time someone clicked through a link.

BT lost the case—if it hadn't, using the Internet would be a lot more expensive.

Fastest connection

Singapore has the fastest average Internet connection speed, at 105.54 megabytes per second. Scientists in the UK recently created the fastest ever Internet connection at 1.4 terabits per second—that would allow users to download 44 high-definition movies in a single second, or the whole of English-speaking Wikipedia in 0.006 seconds.

Coffee cam

The world's first webcam was pointed at an ordinary coffeepot in the UK. Computer geeks working at the University of Cambridge's computer lab wanted to save themselves a trip to the coffeemaker and hooked it up to a camera to see if it was full or empty. The webcam was live from 1993 to 2001, and the coffeepot, auctioned on eBay, is now owned by the German magazine *Der Spiegel*.

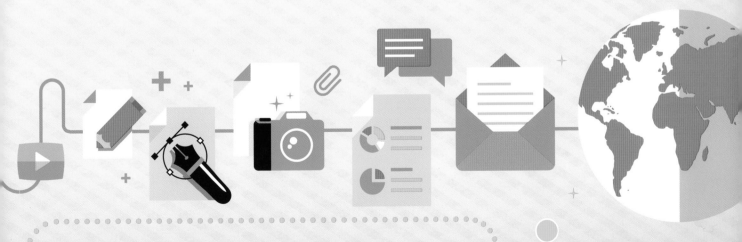

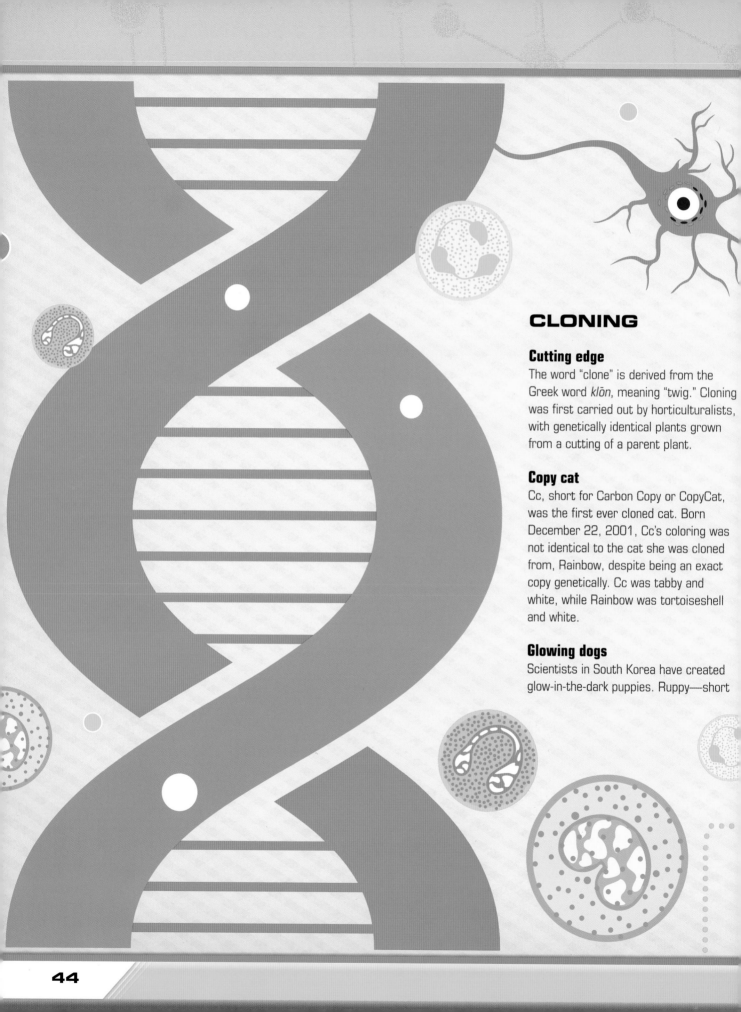

CLONING

Cutting edge

The word "clone" is derived from the Greek word *klōn*, meaning "twig." Cloning was first carried out by horticulturalists, with genetically identical plants grown from a cutting of a parent plant.

Copy cat

Cc, short for Carbon Copy or CopyCat, was the first ever cloned cat. Born December 22, 2001, Cc's coloring was not identical to the cat she was cloned from, Rainbow, despite being an exact copy genetically. Cc was tabby and white, while Rainbow was tortoiseshell and white.

Glowing dogs

Scientists in South Korea have created glow-in-the-dark puppies. Ruppy—short

11,000 PATENTS

have been issued that have involved HeLa cells, the first human cells to be successfully cloned. They were taken from Henrietta Lacks, an American who died of cancer in 1951, hence the name. Scientists have grown 20 tons (18 tonnes) of HeLa cells and her cells have also been used for research into cancer, AIDS, and countless other scientific areas.

for Ruby Puppy—and her children produce a fluorescent protein that glows red under ultraviolet light. Other glowing animals created by scientists include pigs, marmosets, and rabbits.

Hello Dolly

The first mammal to be cloned from an adult cell was Dolly the sheep, born in Scotland on July 5 ,1996. She was named Dolly after singer Dolly Parton, because she was cloned from a cell taken from a mammary gland.

No kidding

In the movie *Jurassic Park* scientists bring dinosaurs back to life through cloning, but in real life the first extinct animal to be cloned was a Spanish

ibex, called the "bucardo," in 2009. Sadly, the one kid that survived gestation died soon after birth because of a lung defect.

Animal magic

The list of animals that have been cloned to date includes frogs, carp, ferrets, water buffalo, pigs, rabbits, and wolves.

IDENTICAL TWINS

Although the process of human cloning sounds futuristic—and is banned in many countries across the world—it can happen naturally, when identical twins are born. Identical twins, the result of a single fertilized egg splitting into two embryos, are genetic copies of each other. Despite high-profile claims, no one has yet succeeded in cloning humans artificially.

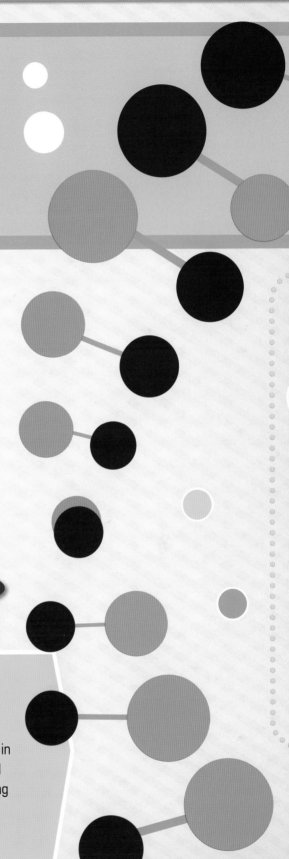

19,000

Russian nuclear bombs have been dismantled by the USA to fuel nuclear power stations. Under the Megatons to Megawatts project, nearly half of all commercial nuclear energy produced in the States came from nuclear fuel derived from Russian nuclear weapons.

POWER

Powerful battery

The world's most powerful battery is in Zhangbei, Hebei Province, China. It provides 36 megawatt hours of energy storage and is housed in a building larger than a soccer pitch. The battery regulates and stores energy produced by local 100-MW wind turbines and 40-MW solar photovoltaic panels, and can power 12,000 homes for up to an hour in the event of total grid failure.

National grid

The first-ever nuclear power station to supply electricity to a national grid was Calder Hall, England, in 1956. The first United States commercial plant opened four years later.

Palace of light

The world's first electrical power station was built in 1878 by Sigmund Schuckert in Ettal, Bavaria, Germany. It used 24 dynamos powered by a steam-driven engine and provided power to light up the gardens of the nearby Linderhof Palace.

Nuclear disaster

The two worst nuclear accidents in history are the Chernobyl Disaster in Russia, on April 26, 1986, and the Fukushima Daiichi nuclear disaster in Japan in 2011. Both are the only two accidents classed as a Level 7 event (the highest classification) on the International Nuclear Event Scale.

Public power

The first public power station was built at 57 Holborn Viaduct, London, England, by the Edison Electric Light Station company. It opened in January 1882 and supplied power to light the Holborn Viaduct and local businesses.

High voltage

The Ekibastuz-Kokshetau power line in Kazakhstan holds the record for having the highest operating transmission voltage in the world, at 1,150 kV. The overhead lines run for 268 miles (432 km), mounted on pylons with an average height of 197 feet (60 m).

438

The number of operational nuclear power plants in 31 different countries worldwide. The USA has the highest number of reactors followed by France and Japan. There are 71 plants under construction globally, the majority being in China (26) and Russia (10).

138 feet

(42 m) The deepest swimming pool in the world opened at the Hotel Terme Millepini in Padua in 2014. Called the Deep Joy, it contains 152,000 cubic feet (4,300 m³) of thermal water and is used by scuba and free divers.

ENGINEERING

Dam big

The Three Gorges Dam on the Yangtze River in China is the largest dam in the world. It is 7,660 feet (2,335 m) long, used 960 million cubic feet (27.2 million m³) of concrete in construction, and took 18 years to complete. The reservoir behind the dam contains 9.43 cubic miles (39.3 km³) of water and has a surface area of 403 square miles (1,045 km²). Its hydroelectric capacity is also the largest in the world at 22,500 MW.

Towering achievement

The Eiffel Tower in Paris was the tallest building in the world on completion in 1889. Intended as a centerpiece for the World Fair that year, the tower is 1,063 feet

211

The number of floors in Dubai's Burj Khalifa, the tallest building in the world at 2,722 feet (829.8 m). It has 3.3 million square feet (310,000m²) of space and cost $1.5 billion to build. Not suprisingly the building holds many other records, such as the world's highest observation deck (1,820 feet/555 m); the highest nightclub (144th floor), and the world's highest restaurant (1,450 feet/442 m).

(324 m) tall and remains the tallest structure in the French capital. Designed by engineer Gustave Eiffel, the tower is made of 18,038 wrought iron trusses held together with two and a half million rivets. Eiffel engraved the names of 72 eminent French scientists, engineers, and mathematicians on the Tower.

Light at the end
The Norwegian government has backed a plan to create the world's first ship tunnel. At 148 feet (45 m) highand 118 feet (36 m) wide, the Stad Ship Tunnel will let ships of up to 17,640 tons (16,000 tonnes) travel through 1 mile (1.7 km) of solid rock to avoid the treacherous seas around the Stad Peninsula. It will cost around 1.7 billion kroner ($216 million).

Protective shield
Marc Isambard Brunel developed the tunnelling shield in 1825 to protect workers excavating the Thames Tunnel in London. The shield allowed them to dig out the tunnel without fear of injury, and was gradually moved forward with the tunnel lining filled in behind them.

Shake it up
Researchers at the University of San Diego use the country's largest outdoor shake table to study the effect of earthquakes on buildings. It can handle loads of up to 2,200 tons (2,000 tonnes) and has hydraulic pistons that can shake buildings at up to 6 feet (2 m) per second.

Joined-up thinking
Builders had used improvised scaffolding for centuries but it was not until 1906 that Daniel Palmer-Jones started to standardize it. He invented the "Scaffixer" coupling device in 1913 and refined this to create the universal coupler that is still in use today.

$2,795

was the price of one of the earliest commercial touchscreen computers, the HP-150. Touchscreens were patented by E.A. Johnson in 1965, while engineers Bent Stumpe and Frank Beck developed a stylus-based touchscreen at CERN, Switzerland, in the 1970s.

GADGETS

Tiny TV
The world's first pocket television set was developed by UK inventor Sir Clive Sinclair. With a 2-inch (5-cm) cathode-ray tube screen, the Microvision TV was exhibited at the Radio and Television Show in London in 1966. When first marketed in 1977 it cost £200/$400.

Close shave
Colonel Jacob Schick patented the first electric razor in 1928, allowing men to dry shave when the device was launched in 1931. Schick also patented a boat for use in shallow water and an improved form of pencil sharpener.

Pocket sized?
In 1891, the Swiss Army issued its troops with a new multifunction knife, which had a blade, a reamer, a screwdriver, and a can opener. The 2.6-pound (1.2-kg) Giant model, released in 2007, features 87 different tools, including:
- cigar cutter
- compass
- bike chain rivet setter
- laser pointer
- tire tread gauge
- toothpick

Heath Robinson
William Heath Robinson is often invoked in relation to gadgets. The British Victorian cartoonist found fame drawing imaginary contraptions of ridiculous complexity to fulfill straightforward tasks. The 1943 Ideal Homes exhibition in London even had a full-size model of a Heath Robinson house, which included pulley systems to deliver people from their beds to the breakfast table.

What is it?
American company Ronco became a byword for bizarre and pointless gadgets in the 1970s, with such nonessential products as the Inside the Egg Shell Scrambler, the Record Vacuum, and the Buttoneer. It filed for bankruptcy in 2007.

Road sense
Although we think of GPS as a modern driving aid, incar navigation assistance

60 SECONDS

is the time it took instant Polaroid pictures to develop. Founder Edwin Land came up with the idea after his daughter asked why she had to wait to see pictures. His first Polaroid Land Camera was launched in 1948.

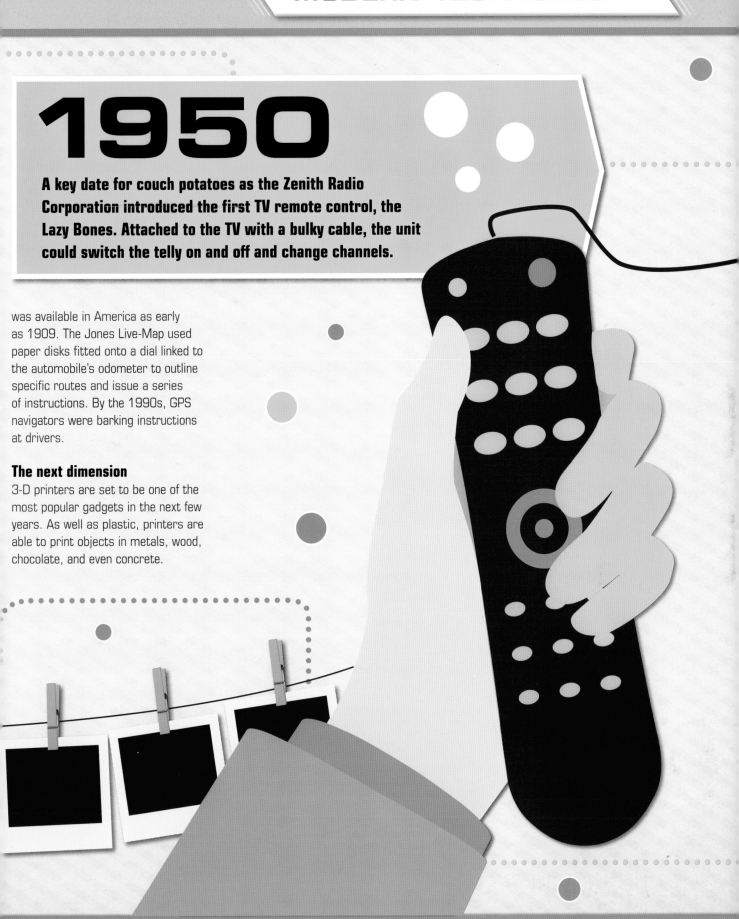

1950

A key date for couch potatoes as the Zenith Radio Corporation introduced the first TV remote control, the Lazy Bones. Attached to the TV with a bulky cable, the unit could switch the telly on and off and change channels.

was available in America as early as 1909. The Jones Live-Map used paper disks fitted onto a dial linked to the automobile's odometer to outline specific routes and issue a series of instructions. By the 1990s, GPS navigators were barking instructions at drivers.

The next dimension

3-D printers are set to be one of the most popular gadgets in the next few years. As well as plastic, printers are able to print objects in metals, wood, chocolate, and even concrete.

26 BILLION

The estimated number of devices connected to the Internet of Things by 2020, according to research company Gartner.

SMART HOMES

Future homes

The term "smart house" was invented by the American Association of Housebuilders in 1984. However, the idea of automating homes has been around for a lot longer. Home-automation systems were envisaged at World Fairs as early as the 1930s.

Racing certainty

Former British racing driver Sir Stirling Moss built his own smart house in London's Mayfair in the 1960s. The gadget obsessive spent £25,000 ($70,000) building the town house and packing it with state of the art technology, including an automated bath, a hydraulic dining table that can move between floors, and an electric letter tray.

Sliding doors

The first automatic door was developed by Lee Hewitt and Dee Horton and installed in 1960 at the City of Corpus Christi utilities department. Standing on a mat actuator triggered the door to open.

Open invitation

Smart locks are doing away with keys, allowing homeowners to control access to their homes via cell phone. Systems such as Goji and August let users unlock their homes remotely.

Uplifting experience

New York's Equitable Life Building, completed in 1870, was the first office building to have electric passenger elevators. The seven-story building was the tallest building in the world at the time, at 130 feet (40 m) high, and is considered by some to be the world's first skyscraper.

Home help

The Netatmo system uses facial-recognition software to identify individual members of a household and inform the householder who is home at any particular time.

$3.2 BILLION

What Google spent buying smart thermostat company Nest in 2014.

SPACE

SPACE RACE TIMELINE

1926 First liquid-fueled rocket launched by American Robert Goddard. It reached 41 feet (12.5 m) and the flight lasted 2.5 seconds.

October 4, 1957
The first artificial satellite, *Sputnik 1*, was launched by the Soviets.

THE SPACE RACE

Knight time
The first men on the Moon wore spacesuits modeled on a suit of armor made for Henry VIII, after the NASA design team visited the armory at the Tower of London. Visitors to the Royal Armouries Museum in Leeds, England, can now see the moonsuit, standing beside its historical inspiration.

Mirror mirror
During the Moon landing, a mirror was left on the Moon's surface to reflect a laser beam that measured the Moon's distance from the Earth with amazing accuracy. It is still in use today.

Lunar dozen
The Moon has only been walked on by 12 people, all male Americans. Neil Armstrong was the first in 1969, on the *Apollo 11* mission, while the last man to walk on the Moon was Gene Cernan in 1972, on the *Apollo 17* mission. NASA plans to return astronauts to the Moon to set up a permanent space station by 2019, if all goes well.

Moon bomb
During the Cold War the United States Air Force planned to detonate a nuclear bomb on the Moon. The project, known as Project A119, or "A Study of Lunar Flight," aimed to answer some of the mysteries of planetary astronomy and astrogeology, as well as creating a great big flash that people could see from Earth. The Russians were working on a similar project, E-4. Neither project ever came to fruition.

Leftovers
The surface of the Moon is littered with man-made objects left from manned and unmanned lunar missions. As well as the remains of some 76 orbiters, rovers, and other spacecraft, items left behind include five American flags, two golf balls, a feather, a small disk bearing messages from 73 world leaders, and 96 bags of urine, feces, and vomit.

9 countries have the ability to launch something—or someone—into orbit. These are Russia, the United States, France, Japan, China, India, Israel, Iran, and North Korea. A few other countries have inherited technology allowing them to make orbital flights. These include Ukraine and South Korea, and nine European countries, which have access through the combined effort of the European Space Agency and Arianespace.

April 12, 1961 Russian Yuri Gagarin became the first person in space after launching in *Vostok 1* for a 108-minute flight.

June 16, 1963 Soviet Valentina Tereshkova became the first woman in space on *Vostok 6*—the flight lasted 70 hours 50 minutes.

March 18, 1965
The first spacewalk was undertaken by Soviet Alexei Leonov.

July 20 1969 American Neil Armstrong became the first person to walk on the Moon.

1977 NASA launched probes *Voyager 1* and *2* to explore the solar system—they are still sending back information.

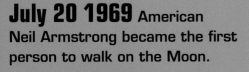

1986 The Russians launched the first part of spacestation *Mir*, the first permanent residence in space. It was almost continually occupied until 1999; it burned up in 2001.

1998 The first part of the International Space Station was launched. The station has been continuously occupied since November 2, 2000, by more than 200 different individuals.

Products of the space race

The Dustbuster
NASA asked Black & Decker to come up with a battery-powered drill to help collect rock samples in 1961. In 1979, the technology was used to help keep homes clean.

Smoke detectors
NASA improved existing technology to allow detectors on the *Skylab* to distinguish between toxic fumes and water vapor.

One-handed joystick
It was originally developed to steer the *Apollo* Lunar Rover.

Swimsuits
Speedo's superfast LZR suit was developed using NASA wind tunnels and fluid-flow-analysis software.

Memory foam
First used to provide seats for a softer landing.

BUT Velcro was invented by a Swiss scientist in 1948, although it was used in astronauts' suits.

Mineral discovery
Three minerals were first discovered on the Moon—armalcolite, tranquillityite, and pyroxferroite. Armalcolite was named after the three *Apollo 11* astronauts: Neil Armstrong, Buzz Aldrin, and Michael Collins. All three minerals have since been discovered on Earth as well.

Toilet training
Today's astronauts receive space toilet training on Earth to make sure they will be able to wee and poo in zero gravity. They use a training toilet with a camera at the bottom to make sure they are getting it right when it comes to solid waste. Urine goes into a funnel which attaches to a hose, with different shapes for men and women.

1992

The year of the first "space burial." Gene Roddenberry, creator of the *Star Trek* TV series, was the first person to have their ashes taken into space. Since then hundreds of people have had their cremated remains launched into space, including U.S. astronaut Gordon Cooper and actor James Doohan, who played Scotty in *Star Trek*.

Space creatures

The first living creatures sent into space were fruit flies, aboard a United States-launched V2 rocket in 1947, as part of an experiment to explore the effects of radiation at high altitudes. The fruit flies were recovered alive. Albert II, the first monkey in space in 1949, and the dog Laika, the first animal in orbit in 1957, were not so lucky. Albert died on impact after a parachute failure, and Laika died from overheating on her fourth circuit of the Earth in Soviet-launched *Sputnik 2*.

Gravity growth

Astronauts grow taller in space because there is almost no gravity pushing the disks in their spines together. But they shrink again when they return to Earth.

Space survival

Nobody knows how long a human being could survive in space without a spacesuit, but it is thought you could survive for one or two minutes. You would not instantly freeze, boil, or explode, but you would pass out and eventually die from lack of oxygen as well as suffering from bubbles in your blood ("the bends"), severe sunburn, and damage from cosmic rays.

Elevator pitch

The next generation might be able to take an elevator into space, as a number of organizations are working on the development of a space elevator—one Japanese company has claimed it could be ready by 2050. The idea is that a cable fixed to the equator reaches into space beyond geostationary orbit. Climbers will carry people and cargo up and down.

437.7

The number of days that Russian Valeri Polyakov spent in space during one trip—the longest time by any astronaut. He spent the time on the *Mir* space station between January 1994 and March 1995. Russian Sergei Krikalev holds the record for most time spent cumulatively in space—803 days, nine hours, and 39 minutes over the span of six spaceflights on *Soyuz*, the Space Shuttle, *Mir*, and the International Space Station.

22,236 miles

(35,786 km). The distance above the Earth that a satellite must reach in order to become "geosynchronous" and appear to "hover" over the same part of the planet, because its orbit speed has matched the Earth's rotation speed.

SATELLITES

Technical necessity

Many aspects of modern technology depend on satellites. They are important in television broadcasting, communications including cell phones and GPS navigation, instant credit-card authorization, weather forecasting, map making, space exploration, and defense, among other things.

Fiction meets fact

English science-fiction writer Arthur C. Clarke, author of *2001: A Space Odyssey*, came up with the concept of geostationary satellites, which orbit the Earth at the same speed at which it rotates, in 1945. The first such satellite was launched in 1963 and broadcast TV to half the world.

Space station

The International Space Station is the largest artificial satellite orbiting the Earth, and is about the same size as an American football pitch. In its first ten years it traveled almost 1,550 million miles (2,500 million km) in 57,361 orbits around the Earth—the same as eight return trips to the Sun.

Small things

Nanosatellites can be as small as 4 inches (10 cm) long and are usually released in "flocks" or swarms. Flocks of nanosatellites called "Doves" were released from the International Space Station in 2014 and aim to capture images of Earth to be used in humanitarian, environmental, and commercial applications.

Lightsaber

In 2007, the lightsaber prop used by *Star Wars*' Luke Skywalker (Mark Hamill) was taken on a mission to the International Space Station. The lightsaber spent two weeks in orbit, and was later returned to George Lucas's movie company.

Orbital collision

On February 10, 2009, Russian military communications satellite *Kosmos-2251* and U.S. commercial telecommunications satellite *Iridium 33* were destroyed when they crashed into each other in orbit. *Kosmos-2251* was not in service at the time of the accident, but *Iridium 33* was operational.

23 inches

(58 cm). *Sputnik 1*, the first artificial satellite to orbit the Earth, was about the size of a beach ball—and weighed 184 pounds (83.6 kg). It was launched by the Russians in 1957 and spent three months in orbit before it burned up.

1,235

The number of operational satellites orbiting the Earth.
The USA has 512, Russia 135, and China 116.

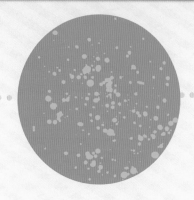

4.5 BILLION YEARS OLD

The approximate age of the Sun, which is currently around halfway through its life. It has enough hydrogen left to last around another five billion years.

SOLAR SYSTEM

Dwarf planets

As well as the eight planets of the solar system there are five officially recognized dwarf planets—too small to be planets but too large to be asteroids. These are Eris, Pluto, Makemake, Haumea, and Ceres. Pluto was reclassified from a planet to a dwarf planet in 2006. There are thought to be at least another six objects in the solar system that are almost certainly dwarf planets, and potentially up to 10,000.

License to orbit

There is an asteroid called James Bond—designation number 9007. There are also asteroids called Monty Python, Sherlock, Doctorwatson, and Mr. Spock. If you find an asteroid you

can suggest a name for it yourself, under certain rules. Commercial names are banned, names must be nonoffensive, and names of pets are strongly discouraged.

Mine now

A number of companies have plans in train for the mining of asteroids, which are rich in resources such as iron, nickel, and titanium.

Shooting stars

There are 21 established meteor showers throughout the year, mostly between April and December. One of the most spectacular is the Perseid shower, which peaks around August 12 each year when Earth encounters the debris of the comet Swift-Tuttle.

Another busy shower is the Leonid, which occurs in mid-November and rains debris from Comet 55P/Tempel-Tuttle.

Name game

Pluto was named by an 11-year-old girl from Oxford. Venetia Phair, then Venetia Burney, suggested the name over breakfast with her grandfather in March 1930. Granddad passed it on to former British Astronomer Royal, Herbert Hall Turner, who cabled the idea to American astronomers at the Lowell Observatory in Arizona.

Astronomical unit

The distance between the Earth and the Sun (91–94 million miles/147–152 million km depending on where the Earth is in its orbit) is known as an Astronomical Unit, or AU, and is used for measuring distances in space.

Dark side

The dark side of the Moon gets just as much sunlight as the other side. It's just that we can't ever see it from Earth because the Moon takes the same time to rotate on its axis as it does to orbit the Earth, so the same side is always facing us. The Moon has no atmosphere, which means no sound can be heard there and the sky always appears black.

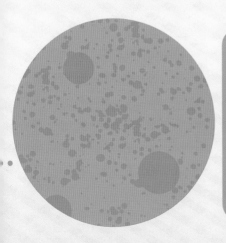

243

On Venus, a year is shorter than a day. The planet takes longer to rotate on its axis (243 Earth days) than it does to orbit the Sun (224.65 Earth days). Jupiter has the shortest day of all the planets, turning on its axis once every nine hours and 55 minutes.

Mercury

Average distance from Sun 36m miles (58m km) **Length of year** 88 Earth days
Moons none **Circumference at the equator** 9,525 miles (15,329 km)
Length of day 58.6 Earth days **How many probes** Two—*Mariner 10* (1974–75)
Messenger (2011) **Temperature** -279°F to 801°F (-173°C to 427°C)
Atmosphere composed mostly of oxygen, sodium, hydrogen, helium, and potassium

Venus

Average distance from Sun 67m miles (107.5m km)
Length of year 225 Earth days **Moons** none
Circumference at the equator 23,627 miles (38,024.6 km)
Length of day 243 Earth days
How many probes More than 40, from countries including
Russia, Japan, and the USA
Temperature 864°F (462°C)
Atmosphere carbon dioxide and nitrogen, with clouds of
sulfuric acid droplets

Earth

Average distance from Sun 93m miles (150m km)
Length of year 365 Earth days **Moons** one
Circumference at the equator 24,873 miles
(40,030 km) **Length of day** 24 hours
How many probes n/a
Temperature -128°F to 135°F (-89°C to 57°C)
Atmosphere nitrogen and oxygen

Mars

Average distance from Sun 142m miles (227.8m km) **Length of year** 687 Earth days
Moons two **Circumference at the equator** 13,233 miles (21,297 km)
Length of day 24.6 hours **How many probes** more than 40 from countries including India,
China, Russia, and the USA **Temperature** -243°F to 68°F (-153°C to 20°C)
Atmosphere carbon dioxide, nitrogen, and argon

Jupiter

Average distance from Sun 485m miles (780.42m km)

Length of year 11.9 Earth years

Moons 50 known moons (plus 17 awaiting official confirmation)

Circumference at the equator 272,945 miles (439,264 km)

Length of day: 10 hours **How many probes:** more than ten

Temperature -234°F (-148°C) **Atmosphere** hydrogen and helium

Saturn

Average distance from Sun 889m miles (1,431m km) **Length of year** 29.1 Earth years

Moons 53 known moons (plus nine awaiting official confirmation)

Circumference at the equator 227,348 miles (365,882 km)

Length of day 10.656 hours

How many probes five, from USA and Europe

Temperature -288°F (-178°C)

Atmosphere hydrogen and helium

Uranus

Average distance from Sun 1,788m miles (2,877m km) **Length of year** 84 Earth years **Moons** 27

Circumference at the equator 99,018 miles (159,354 km) **Length of day** 17.2 hours

How many probes one—*Voyager 2* in 1986

Temperature -357°F (-216°C)

Atmosphere hydrogen, helium, and methane

Neptune

Average distance from Sun 2,787m miles (4,486m km)

Length of year 164.8 Earth years

Moons 13 known moons (plus one awaiting official confirmation)

Circumference at the equator 96,130 miles (154,705 km)

Length of day: 16 hours **How many probes** one—*Voyager 2* in 1989

Temperature -353°F (-214°C) **Atmosphere** hydrogen, helium, and methane

100+

tons (91+ tonnes) of material from asteroids and comets falls toward Earth every day. Most of it burns up in the atmosphere, but if material does hit the ground it is called a "meteorite." An object the size of a soccer pitch hits Earth approximately once every 2,000 years. A car-sized meteoroid falls into Earth's atmosphere about once a year.

No eclipses
The Moon is gradually moving away from the Earth. In about 600 million years, there will be no more total eclipses of the Sun on Earth, as the Moon will be too far away to cover the disk of the Sun entirely.

Spin drift
Venus and Uranus are the only planets in the solar system that rotate clockwise. This could have been caused by a collision with an asteroid or other object in the past.

Two tails
A comet has two tails. The first is made of dust and ice crystals, which blows away from the comet nucleus in the solar wind. The second, plasma

tail forms when molecules of gas are excited by interaction with the solar wind. It cannot be seen with the naked eye, but can be photographed.

Alien moon
Europa, one of Jupiter's 63-odd moons, is the most likely place for extraterrestial life in our solar system. Scientists believe its icy surface may cover a liquid salty ocean, with a possibility of aquatic life.

Saturn's rings
Saturn's rings are not solid. They are made up of particles of ice, dust, and rock, some as tiny as grains of sand, some much larger than skyscrapers. Although other planets have rings, too, Saturn's rings are the only ones that are visible from Earth: they can be seen with a small telescope.

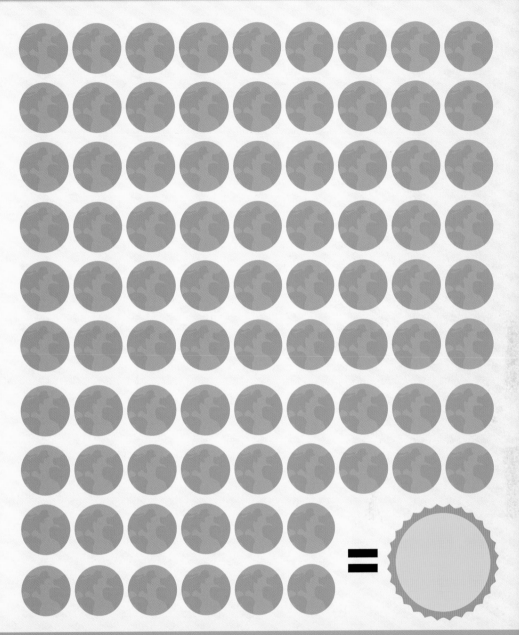

Lunar view

The Moon looks different depending on where you are on Earth, but will always be in the same phase. So on the same night in Canada an observer might see a crescent shaped like a C, on the equator a smiley face, and in Australia a reversed crescent like the curve of a D.

Moon illusion

When the Moon is low in the sky it appears larger because of something called the "Ponzo" illusion—your brain inflates its size because clues in the landscape tell you it is a distant object. If you block out everything else with your hands and look just at the Moon, it will shrink.

960,000

The number of spherical Earths that would fit inside a hollow Sun. If these Earths were squashed inside with no wasted space, then around 1,300,000 would fit. The Sun contains 99.86 percent of the mass in the solar system.

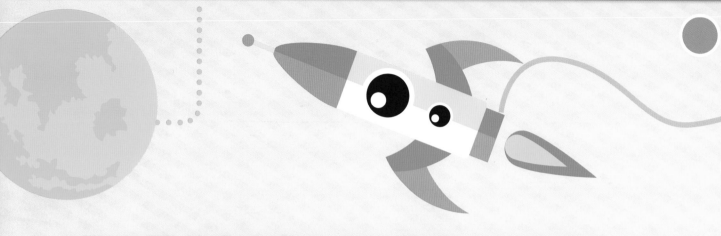

EXPLORATION AND THE WIDER UNIVERSE

Voyage of discovery

Voyager 1 is the farthest man-made object from Earth, as well as the first man-made object to leave the solar system. As of December 2014, it lies about 12 billion miles (19.6 billion km) from Earth. Like its sister, *Voyager 2*, the probe carries a gold-plated copper disk containing information about life and culture on Earth, and will continue to send information back to Earth until at least 2020. Although both probes were launched in 1977, *Voyager 2* was actually dispatched before *Voyager 1*.

Just right

A "Goldilocks planet" is one that falls within a star's habitable zone, having the right conditions for life by being neither too cold nor too hot, too large nor too small, but "just right." Goldilocks planets are of key interest to researchers looking for life in the universe or for future homes for humanity.

Crash course

Our Milky Way is set to collide with neighboring galaxy Andromeda, currently 2.5 million light years away. No worries though, because it won't happen for another 4.5 billion years—around the same time as our Sun is set to run out of hydrogen to burn.

Nearest neighbor

The closest star to our Sun is Proxima Centauri, part of the triple star system Alpha Centauri, 4.37 light years from the Sun. Astronomers think they have discovered a planet orbiting Alpha Centauri B, and have given it the catchy name of Alpha Centauri Bb—it is roughly the same size as Earth but much hotter.

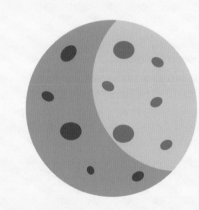

20

The number of active probes exploring the solar system and beyond. These include NASA's *New Horizons*, set to reach Pluto in 2015; *Dawn*, which is heading for dwarf planet Ceres; and *Juno*, which will arrive at Jupiter in 2016. The first Indian interplanetary probe, *Mangalyaan*, is currently orbiting Mars, while the first Chinese moon lander, *Chang'e*, is studying the Moon.

UNIVERSE TIMELINE

JANUARY 1
BIG BANG

MARCH 31
MILKY WAY GALAXY FORMS

AUGUST 31
SUN AND PLANETS ARE CREATED

DECEMBER 25
DINOSAURS APPEAR

DECEMBER 30
DINOSAURS DISAPPEAR

DECEMBER 31
LAST TEN SECONDS BEFORE MIDNIGHT
THE ENTIRETY OF HUMAN HISTORY

Singing Sun
Stars make a noise. We can't hear them directly though—partly because sound doesn't travel through the vacuum of space, and also because the sound waves the Sun is putting out are at too low a frequency for the human ear. However, scientists can capture the sound waves using a special orbiting instrument and speed them up enough for humans to hear the Sun singing.

Space sugar
Scientists have discovered sugar in a giant cloud of dust and gas near the center of the Milky Way. A simple sugar molecule, glycolaldehyde, was discovered in the Sagittarius B2 cloud, some 26,000 light years away.

5%

All the stars, galaxies, and black holes in the universe compose only about five percent of its mass. The other 95 percent is unaccounted for. Scientists decided to label this mystery material "dark matter" and "dark energy" and to this day they are still not sure where or what it is.

Empty space

Interstellar space is pretty empty, with an average of one atom every cubic centimeter, although there are regions with higher densities. Nebulae, for example, have millions of atoms per cubic centimeter. Some 99 percent of the material in interstellar space is gas (the other one percent is dust), with around 90 percent of the atoms in the gas being hydrogen, nine percent helium, and one percent heavier elements.

Diamond star

In 2004, astronomers discovered a star made of crystallized carbon, which they named "Lucy" after The Beatles song "Lucy in the Sky with Diamonds"—since a diamond is also formed of crystallized carbon. The white dwarf measures 2,485 miles (4,000 km) across and is 50 light years from Earth.

Big star

The most massive star that we know of is named R136a1 and is located in the Tarantula Nebula in the Large Magellanic Cloud, a small satellite galaxy that orbits the Milky Way. It is a whopping 265 times the mass of the Sun.

Huge hole

Scientists believe there is a supermassive black hole in the center of our galaxy, with four million times more mass than the Sun. The nearby Andromeda galaxy is thought to have an even bigger black hole at its center—100 million times more massive than the Sun.

Gasoline ban

Diesel-powered automobiles are used near radio observatories, as the spark plugs in gasoline-powered engines can create radio waves that cover up the ones from space.

Flat universe

No one knows what shape the universe is. Scientists have suggested it is ball-shaped, tube-shaped, or even shaped like a doughnut, but the latest evidence suggests it is flat—and infinite.

13 BILLION

Nobody knows the size of the universe, but we can see to a distance of around 13 billion light years in all directions. It is time, not space, that limits our view, as beyond a certain distance light has not had a chance to reach us yet. The image we see of the most distant known galaxy, UDFj-39546284, shows what it looked like 13 billion years ago—480 million years after the Big Bang.

HOW THE
UNIVERSE WORKS

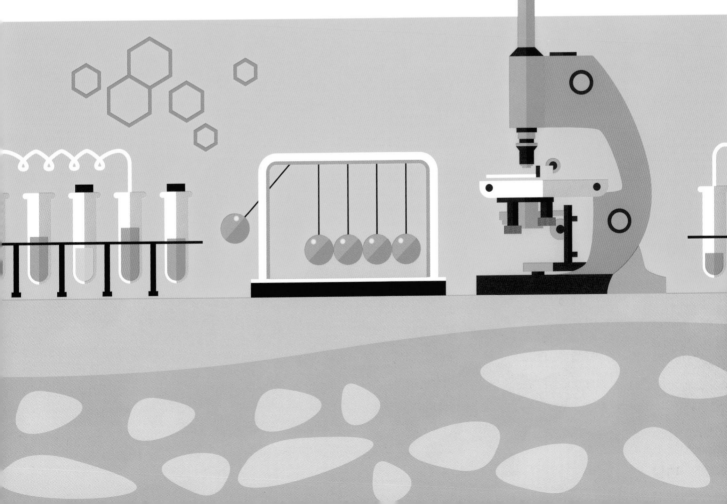

ELEMENTS

Star born

Elements are forged in stars. At the beginning of the universe there was only one element—hydrogen—but when the first stars were born the hydrogen atoms got squished together to create all the other elements, which were sent out into the universe when the stars eventually exploded.

Smell of success

Ozone was first detected when Swiss-German chemist Christian Friedrich Schönbein noticed a strange smell while walking through a lab at the University of Basel in 1840, where experiments were being carried out on the electrolysis of water. Schönbein called the new gas "ozone" after the Greek *ozien* (to smell).

Empty spaces

There are some gaps on the official periodic table. Elements 113, 115, 117, and 118, known as ununtrium, ununpentium, ununseptium, and ununoctium, have yet to be officially accepted as elements and given permanent names, although scientists have synthesized atoms of each in the laboratory.

Precious thing

Although aluminum is the most common metal on Earth, in the 19th century it was more valuable than gold, because it was so difficult to extract. Napoleon III reportedly served his most important guests with aluminum cutlery while others had to make do with gold or silver.

Gas shortage

Helium is the second most abundant element in the universe—but on Earth we are facing a potential helium shortage. The helium molecule is very light, so once it is released into the Earth's atmosphere it will eventually go up into outer space.

Two thirds

The proportion of all aluminum that has ever been purified that is still in use today. Recycling aluminum makes sense because it takes only 5 percent of the total energy required to extract it in the first place.

Dinosaur killer

Iridium, atomic number 77, is often found in meteorites but is rarely found

in the Earth's crust. However, it is relatively abundant in one particular layer of clay, formed 66 million years ago, which backs up the theory that a massive meteorite hit the Earth at that time and played a part in the extinction of the dinosaurs.

Noisy metal

Tin will cry when it is bent. Known as the "tin cry," the effect is caused by the rupture of the crystal structure and is actually more like a crackle than a scream, despite the name. A similar effect occurs in other metals, such as niobium, indium, zinc, and gallium.

8

of the Earth's 88 naturally occurring chemical elements can trace their origin to the same mine in Sweden in the 19th century. The mine at Ytterby was the first source of the rare earth mineral yttria, which was found to contain the four elements—yttrium, erbium, terbium, and ytterbium. Four other elements—holmium, thulium, gadolinium, and scandium—were also derived from samples from the mine.

WHAT IS THE...

Rarest naturally occurring element?

Berkelium, a soft radioactive metal that is pale silver in appearance, atomic number 97. It's named after the city of Berkeley, the home of the University of California campus where it was first synthesized in December 1949. There are only 10 to 50 atoms of berkelium in the Earth's crust at any given time.

Most explosive element?

Probably francium, atomic number 87, named after the home country of French physicist Marguerite Perey who first discovered the radioactive alkaline metal. We say probably, because no one has ever seen enough of it to test it out—it is estimated that less than 1 ounce (28 g) of francium are present throughout the Earth's crust.

Most abundant element?

The most abundant element in the universe is hydrogen, atomic number 1. Hydrogen is estimated to make up more than 90 percent of all the atoms in the universe, and three quarters of its mass.

Most common element on Earth?

Oxygen, making up about 47 percent of the Earth's crust. Silicon is second, at 28 percent, followed by aluminum (8 percent) and iron (5 percent). In terms of the whole planet, the most common element is iron, which makes up 32.1 percent of the Earth's mass.

Lightest metal?

The lightest usable metal is magnesium, atomic number 12. Magnesium is the ninth-most abundant element in the universe and the eighth-most abundant in the Earth's crust.

Highest melting point?

Tungsten is the element with the highest melting point. It changes from solid to liquid at 6,192°F (3,422°C), making it an excellent choice for use as the filament in a lightbulb. Carbon is sometimes said to have the highest melting point at 6,422°F (3,550°C) but rather than turn from solid to liquid, it changes directly into a gas.

Most conductive element?

Silver is the element that best conducts electricity, and is also the best conductor of heat. However, copper, the element with the second highest electrical conductivity, is more commonly used because it is less expensive.

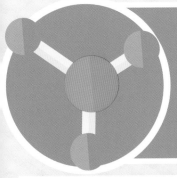

Densest element?

Osmium, atomic number 76, is the densest naturally occurring element, around twice as dense as lead, although it only just wins out over iridium. Osmium is a hard, brittle, bluish-white metal that is used as a platinum alloy in applications such as fountain pen nibs and electrical contacts.

Lowest melting point

Helium, atomic number 2, is the only element that will not become solid however cold it gets (at normal atmospheric pressure)—it remains a liquid even at Absolute Zero (-460°F/-273.15°C).

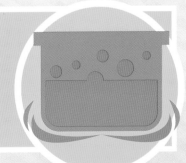

983,571,056
FEET PER SECOND
(299,792,458 meters per second)
Speed of light in a vacuum

56
FEET PER SECOND
(17 meters per second)
Speed of light through supercooled material—the slowest speed light has been recorded traveling. The same researchers also made the light stop traveling and then start up again.

1,126
FEET PER SECOND
(343.2 meters per second)
Speed of sound through air

39,400
FEET PER SECOND
(12,000 meters per second)
Speed of sound through diamond

4,911
FEET PER SECOND
(1,497 meters per second)
Speed of sound through water

PHYSICS

Time travel
The passage of time is affected by both speed and gravity. Going faster makes time slow down, while a decrease in gravity causes time to speed up. Astronauts on the International Space Station are affected by both, but the lack of gravity trumps the speed they are traveling at, and clocks on the ISS run slightly slower than on Earth.

Mighty mites
Billions of neutrinos pass through your body every second and you don't notice. The tiny particles are generated in the Sun and can pass through matter unimpeded. Neutrinos are 100,000 times smaller than electrons, but there are so many of

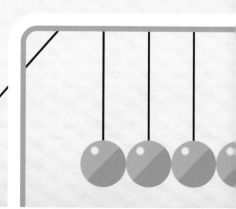

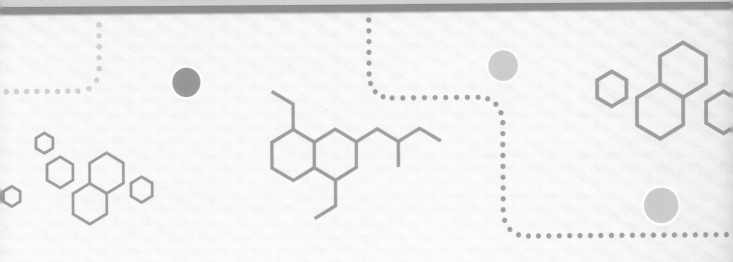

them they may outweigh all the visible matter in the universe.

Radioactive papers

The possessions and papers of pioneering chemist and physicist Marie Curie are so radioactive they are stored in lead-lined boxes and anyone wishing to see them has to put on a special suit. Polish-born Curie studied radioactivity but did not know the dangers, carrying radium samples in her pockets and eventually succumbing to radiation exposure in 1934.

Strange flavors

Quarks are elementary particles that come together to form hadrons, such as the protons and neutrons

that make up the nucleus of an atom. They come in six "flavors": up, down, strange, charm, bottom, and top. Up and down quarks are generally stable and common, while strange, charm, bottom, and top quarks can only be produced in high-energy collisions, such as in those found in particle accelerators.

Political particle

The science behind the Higgs Boson, the so-called "God particle," is so complicated that in 1993 British science minister William Waldegrave offered champagne to the scientist who could explain it to him on one page. The winning professor came up with a comparison involving former Prime Minister Margaret Thatcher

moving through a room of evenly spaced political party workers and attracting them to form a cluster around her as she walked.

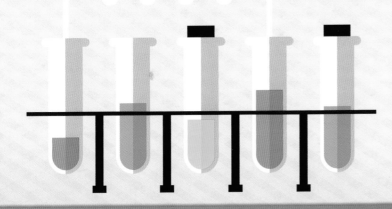

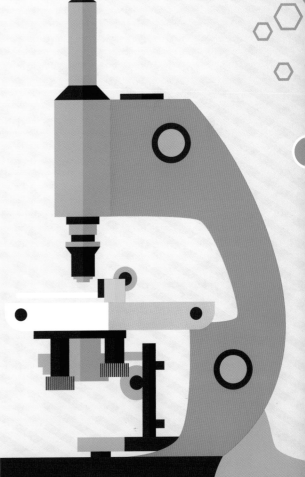

FALLING OBJECTS

Heavier objects do not fall faster than lighter things. If you drop an elephant and a mouse out of a plane they will land at the same time. Scientists have known this for centuries—Galileo Galilei was supposed to have dropped balls of different weights off the leaning Tower of Pisa to prove it—but people still get confused. Some objects do fall less quickly on Earth because of their shape—a feather will fall less quickly than a hammer for example, because of air resistance. On the Moon, where there is no air resistance, the two will fall at the same rate.

Pole swap

Compasses do not always point north. The magnetic field of the Earth can and does reverse direction, with North and South poles flipping over. This used to happen every five million years or so, but scientists think the process is speeding up and now occurs every 200,000 years. We may be due another flip relatively soon—in 2,000 years or less.

Quantum weirdness

When two photons are created at the same time, they spin in both directions at once, until one is observed. Once observed, it will either spin clockwise or counterclockwise and its twin will spin the other way—even if it is on the other side of the galaxy.

Energy conservation

The total amount of energy in the universe will always be the same—energy can't be created or destroyed; it can only change from one form to another.

Atomic structure

Most of an atom is actually empty space. If an atom was the size of a soccer pitch, its nucleus would be a raspberry in the center of the field and its electrons would be flies buzzing around the edge.

Fastest thing

The fastest things that exist are waves in the electromagnetic spectrum, including light, X-rays, gamma rays, ultraviolet rays, microwaves, and radio waves.

Wonderland phenomenon

A boojum is a phenomenon associated with superfluids—liquids that can flow uphill. It was named by David Mermin of Cornell University, after a creature imagined by *Alice in Wonderland* author Lewis Carroll. Mermin had to struggle to get his name accepted but it is now the term used.

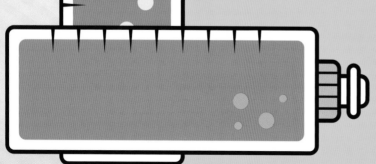

CENTER OF GRAVITY

It is easier to push over a bottle that is full of liquid than one that is half full. The center of gravity in the half-full bottle is low, making the bottle more stable.

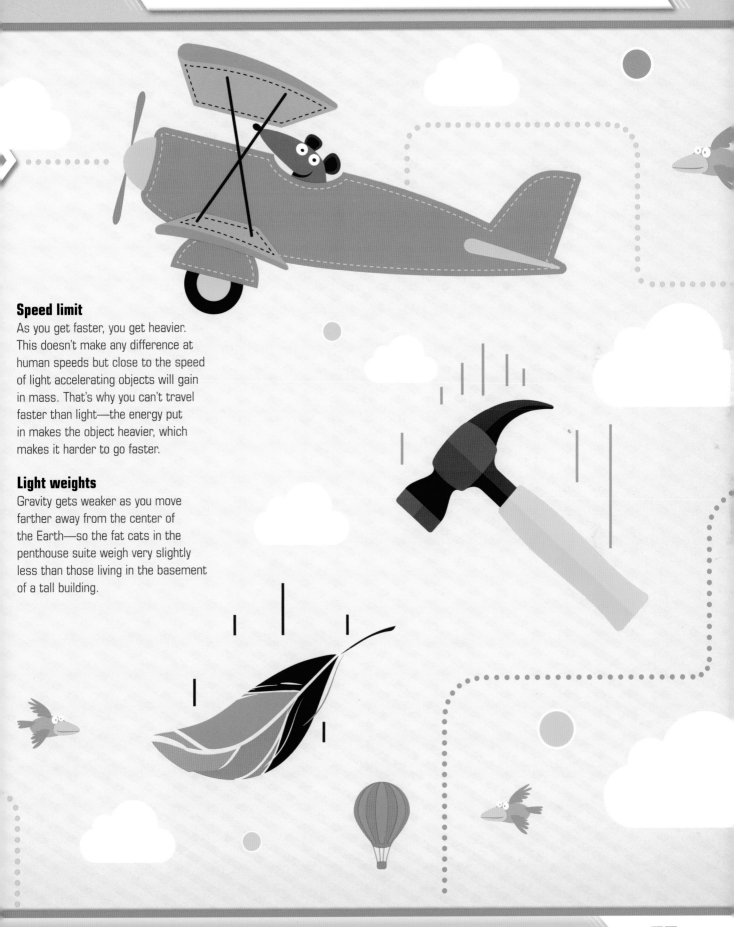

Speed limit

As you get faster, you get heavier. This doesn't make any difference at human speeds but close to the speed of light accelerating objects will gain in mass. That's why you can't travel faster than light—the energy put in makes the object heavier, which makes it harder to go faster.

Light weights

Gravity gets weaker as you move farther away from the center of the Earth—so the fat cats in the penthouse suite weigh very slightly less than those living in the basement of a tall building.

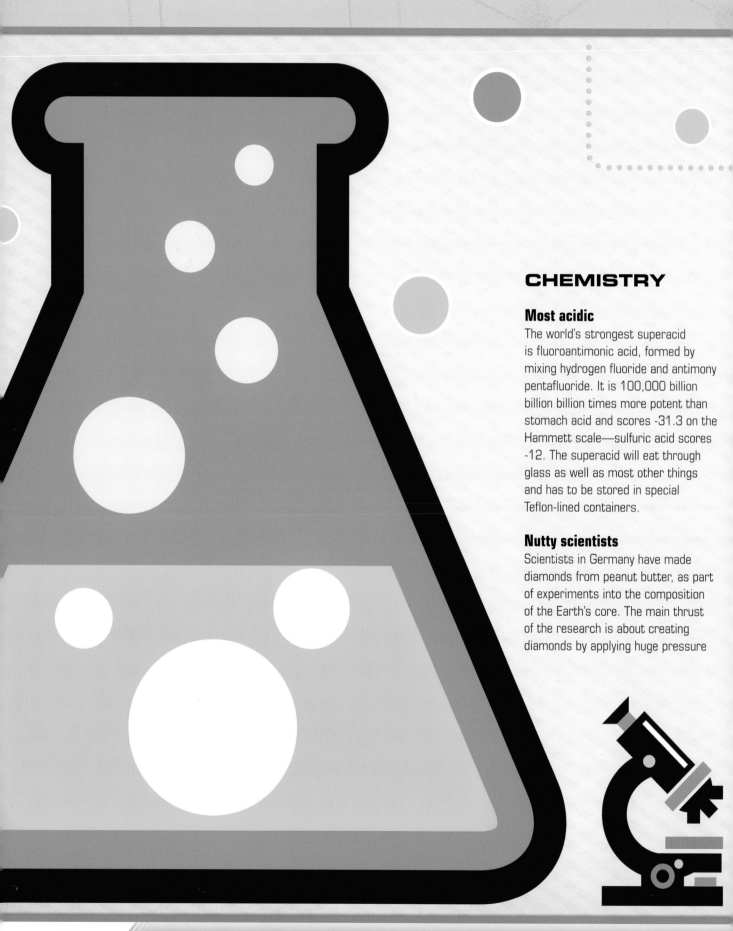

CHEMISTRY

Most acidic

The world's strongest superacid is fluoroantimonic acid, formed by mixing hydrogen fluoride and antimony pentafluoride. It is 100,000 billion billion billion times more potent than stomach acid and scores -31.3 on the Hammett scale—sulfuric acid scores -12. The superacid will eat through glass as well as most other things and has to be stored in special Teflon-lined containers.

Nutty scientists

Scientists in Germany have made diamonds from peanut butter, as part of experiments into the composition of the Earth's core. The main thrust of the research is about creating diamonds by applying huge pressure

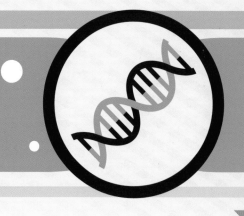

189,819

The number of letters in the chemical name for titin, the world's largest known protein.

to carbon dioxide, but they tried it with peanut butter and it worked—although apparently it was messy.

Mirror molecules
Mint and caraway are opposites. They contain chemically identical molecules that are mirror images of each other. The same is true of oranges and lemons.

Explosive invention
Experimenting in his makeshift kitchen laboratory while his wife was out, chemist Christian Friedrich Schönbein mopped up a mixture of nitric and sulfuric acids with his wife's apron. After letting it dry he gave the apron a jaunty flick to smarten it up. The resulting explosion knocked him

unconscious and led to the invention of gun cotton, a smokeless powder used in warfare.

Material success
Supermaterial nylon was developed in 1934 by chemist Wallace Hume Carothers, working for the massive U.S. company, Du Pont. It was first used commercially in toothbrushes in 1938, but by then Carothers had committed suicide.

Cannonball chemistry
When graphite was first discovered in the 14th century it was immensely valuable, because it could be used to line the molds for cannonballs. Graphite mines in England were taken over by the Crown and

guarded. When enough graphite was extracted, the mines were flooded to prevent theft until more was required. Early pencil makers had to smuggle the graphite they needed out of the mines.

Same elements
Caffeine is made from carbon, hydrogen, oxygen, and nitrogen—heroin, thalidomide, cocaine, nylon, and TNT are also made from the same elements.

Molecular martyrs
Flourine is such a reactive chemical that a group of scientists are known as the "fluorine martyrs" after becoming injured or dying during fluorine-related experiments.

213 MINUTES

The length of time it takes to pronounce the chemical name for titin in full, as demonstrated by the editor of Russian *Esquire*, Dmitry Golubovskiy, in 2012.

1 The world's strongest material is said to be carbyne, a form of carbon only a single atom thick, but scientists have not been able to synthesize enough to use. Graphene, also only an atom thick, is much easier to make and is 200 times stronger than steel and a million times thinner than paper.

Cartoon chemicals

Some chemicals are named after fictional characters. Ranasmurfin, a blue protein found in the nests of tropical tree frogs, is named after the blue Smurfs, while the Pikachurin protein was named after a Pokémon character. There is another protein called Sonic hedgehog, while a number of antibiotic agents including Musettamycin and Mimimycin are named after characters from the opera, *La Bohéme*.

In shape

Some molecules are named after their shape. Hence, we have ladderane, basketane, penguinone, and churchane.

Lowered voice

It is commonly known that inhaling helium makes your voice higher. Breathing in sulfur hexafluoride, a colorless, odorless, nontoxic, and nonflammable gas, does the opposite, making your voice very deep. The weight of the gas slows the sound waves produced in your vocal tracts to just under half their usual speed.

First chemist

The first known chemist was a woman. A Mesopotamian tablet from the second millennium BCE describes

Tapputi, a perfumer and palace overseer who distilled the essences of flowers and other aromatic materials, filtered them, added water, and returned them to the still several times until she got just what she wanted.

Eye burn

Onions make you cry because they release a sulfur compound that reacts with the water in your tears to form sulfuric acid. This causes more tears to form to wash the acid away. Refrigerating an onion before cutting it or cutting it underwater changes the chemical reactions and makes you less likely to cry.

OCTOBER 23
FROM 6.02 A.M. TO 6.02 P.M.

The duration of Mole Day, an unofficial holiday celebrated by chemists, which commemorates Avogadro's Number (6.02×10^{23}), a basic measuring unit in chemistry.

THE
HUMAN BODY

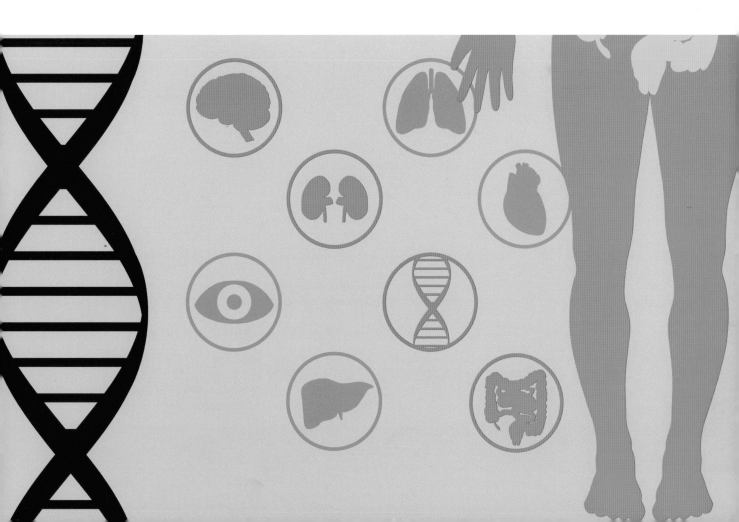

10 pounds

(4.5 kg). The weight of the hairball taken from the stomach of an 18-year-old woman at Rush University Medical Center in Chicago, in November 2007. It was one of the heaviest things ever removed from a human body.

MEDICINE/HEALTH

Cough syrup
From 1898 through to 1910, heroin was marketed as a cough medicine and nonaddictive substitute for morphine by the Aktiengesellschaft Farbenfabriken (today the Bayer pharmaceutical company). The drug's name came from the German word for "hero" or "strong."

Fighting cancer
During World War II several hundred people were accidentally exposed to mustard gas, and the survivors were found to have very low white blood cell counts. Researchers were inspired to uncover other substances that might have a similar effect, leading to the development of chemotherapy.

Viral infection
Viruses can catch viruses. A giant virus called "mamavirus," first detected in amoebae in a watercooling tower in Paris, has been shown to have a much smaller virus, dubbed Sputnik, attached to it. Sputnik causes the host virus to grow abnormally and damages its ability to replicate.

Guinea pigs
The two scientists most involved in developing penicillin as an antibiotic, Australian Howard Florey and German Ernst Boris Chain, used mice for their experiments as they had run out of guinea pigs. Had they gone with their first option the creatures would have died, as penicillin is fatally toxic to guinea pigs.

Antibiotic irony
Irish doctor James Twomey routinely grew and administered his own penicillin in the 1920s, well before the antibiotic was widely known. In 1938, he collapsed in a London street and was taken to St. Mary's Hospital, where Alexander Fleming was working on the development of penicillin. Twomey died on May 17 in the building that would have housed his cure had he been able to ask for it.

Face off
The first successful full face transplant was performed by a team of doctors in Barcelona, Spain, on March 20, 2010. The 31-year-old patient, known as "Oscar," was the victim of a shooting accident. The operation took 24 hours.

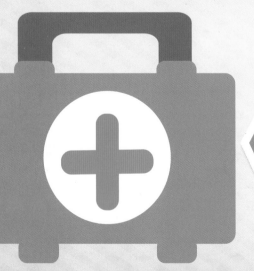

3,800 YEARS OLD
The oldest known medical writing. The papyrus covers women's health and contains 35 separate paragraphs relating to issues such as fertility, pregnancy, and contraception.

99.5 mph

(160 km/h). The speed at which a sneeze blows CO_2, mucus, and germs from your mouth.

Space operation

On September 27, 2006, a team of five doctors led by Dominique Martin from France successfully removed a benign tumor from the arm of volunteer Philippe Sanchot while on board a modified Airbus A300 flying in parabolas in order to mimic the microgravity of space. The operation was an experiment to test the feasibility of performing operations in space.

Death watch

People over age 60 are more likely to die on their birthday than any other day (14 percent more likely). Older people are also more likely to die at 11 a.m. than any other time.

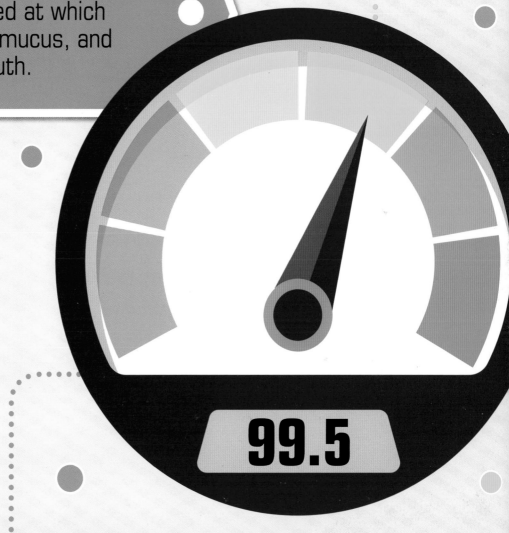

99.5

33 PERCENT

Proportion of Americans diagnosed with leprosy each year who caught it from an armadillo. In some places more than 20 percent of armadillos are infected with leprosy. Scientists think their low body temperature provides a good environment for the leprosy bacteria.

6 YEARS

The global increase in life expectancy at birth since 1990. A baby born in 2012 could expect to live to 70 years on average—62 years in low-income countries and 79 years in high-income countries.

79 years

70 years

62 years

Hair loss
Chemotherapy can lead to hair loss because the hair follicle cells—like cancer cells—divide rapidly. Many anticancer drugs target rapidly dividing cells, so destroy the follicle cells as well as the cancer cells. The follicle cells quickly recover when treatment stops.

Gender divide
Research suggests that aspirin protects men against heart attack but not strokes, while it protects women against strokes but not heart attack.

Different stings
A wasp's sting is an irritant alkaline while a bee's sting is acidic. To counteract a wasp's sting you should apply vinegar, an acid, while to ease the sting of a bee try the alkaline sodium bicarbonate.

Canadian cure
After insulin was first discovered by a group of scientists in Canada in the 1920s, it was obtained from the pancreases of slaughtered pigs and sheep. The lifesaving hormone was first tested on a 14-year-old diabetic boy—near death, he rapidly regained his strength. Scientists can now manufacture insulin by inserting a copy of a human gene into the DNA of a bacterium and harvesting the resulting hormone. One in ten adults worldwide now suffers from diabetes, according to the World Health Organization.

Milking medicines
Rather than manufacturing medicines in laboratories, scientists can now milk them from a cow or goat. In a process known as "pharming," genetically engineered farm animals can produce useful medicine in their milk. Sheep have been modified to produce a blood-clotting agent and cows to produce a protein used to treat traumatic injuries.

1979

was the year that the disease smallpox was declared to have been wiped out, following a global immunization campaign. The last known natural case was in Somalia in 1977. Since then, the only known cases have been caused by a laboratory accident in 1978 in Birmingham, England, which killed one person and caused a limited outbreak. The only places the smallpox virus now exists are two laboratories—one in the USA and one in the Russian Federation.

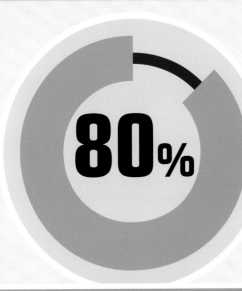

80%

of deaths caused by cardiovascular diseases could be prevented through a healthy diet, regular physical activity, and avoiding the use of tobacco. These diseases are the leading causes of death in the world, with around three in ten deaths caused by diseases of the heart and blood vessels.

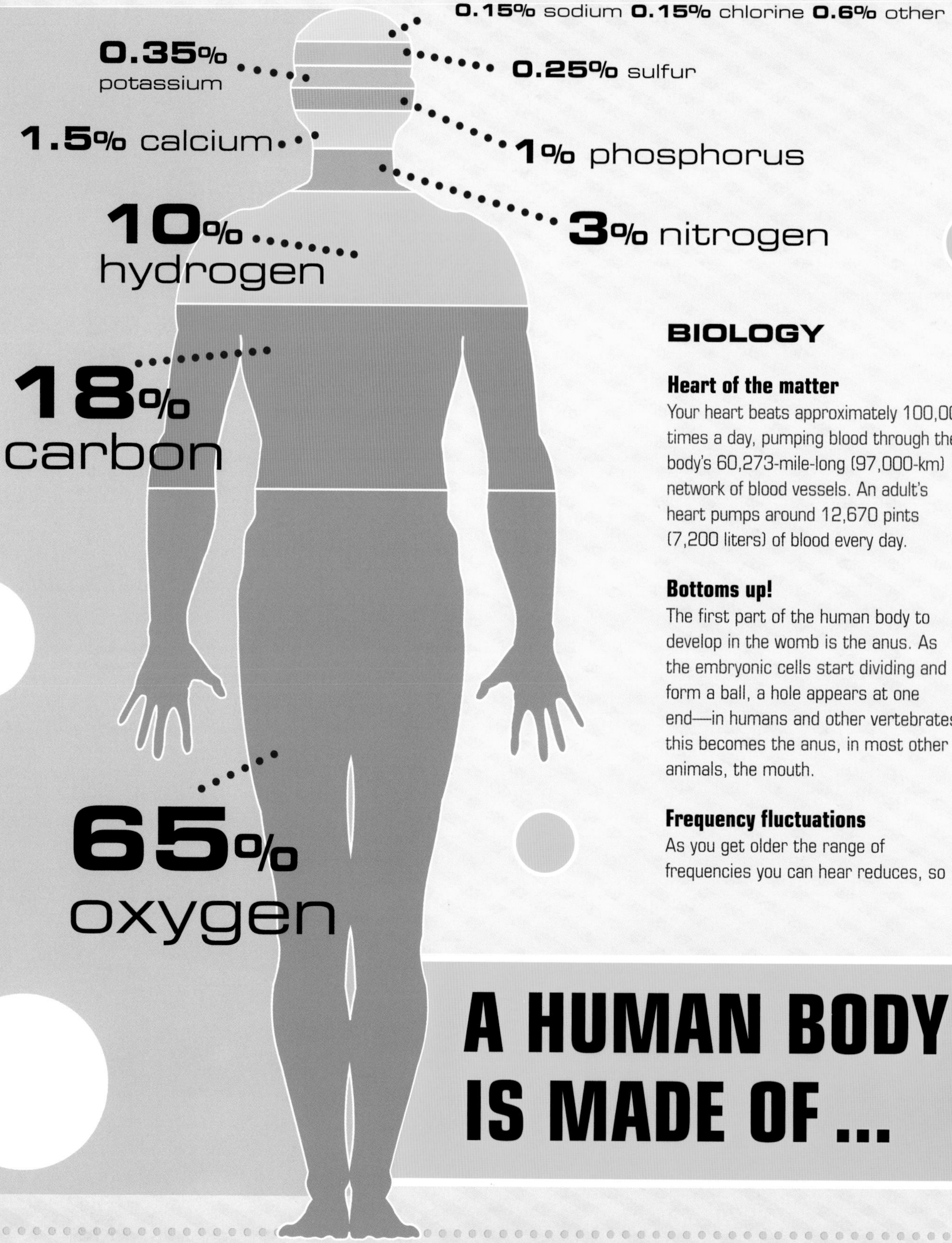

0.15% sodium 0.15% chlorine 0.6% other

0.35% potassium

0.25% sulfur

1.5% calcium

1% phosphorus

10% hydrogen

3% nitrogen

18% carbon

65% oxygen

BIOLOGY

Heart of the matter
Your heart beats approximately 100,000 times a day, pumping blood through the body's 60,273-mile-long (97,000-km) network of blood vessels. An adult's heart pumps around 12,670 pints (7,200 liters) of blood every day.

Bottoms up!
The first part of the human body to develop in the womb is the anus. As the embryonic cells start dividing and form a ball, a hole appears at one end—in humans and other vertebrates this becomes the anus, in most other animals, the mouth.

Frequency fluctuations
As you get older the range of frequencies you can hear reduces, so

A HUMAN BODY IS MADE OF ...

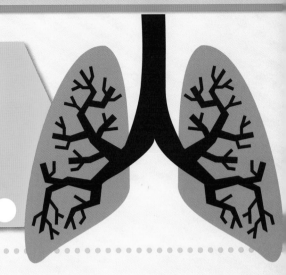

1,500 MILES

(2,400 km) of airways and more than 300 million alveoli make up your lungs. Spread out flat, the alveoli would cover an area almost the size of a tennis court.

children can hear higher frequencies than adults. As a result there are some cell phone ringtones that are so high only children can hear them—useful for secretive pupils at school. On the other hand the idea is also used in Mosquito devices that aim to stop gangs of kids hanging around in the street by emitting annoying sounds only children can hear.

Pregnancy test
Before modern pregnancy tests were introduced, scientists injected a woman's urine into mice, rabbits, or frogs. If the woman was pregnant the animal would ovulate. The first two tests involved killing the animal but the frog test allowed the animal to remain alive.

Mutant eyes
Humans originally all had brown eyes. People with blue eyes have a genetic mutation that limits the production of melanin in the iris. Estonia has the highest concentration of blue-eyed people—99 percent of Estonians have blue eyes. People with blue eyes do not have a blue iris. The coloring in their iris is actually brownish black. It just looks blue because of the way it reflects the light.

Billions of bacteria
There are more bacteria in your body than there are cells. One scientific study showed that microbes that live in and on our bodies outnumber our own cells by ten to one. There are 100 million bacteria in each milliliter

of the saliva of human beings and more than 600 different species in the mouth alone.

Mighty muscles
The largest muscle in your body is the gluteus maximus in the buttocks. The smallest muscle is the stapedius in your middle ear. The strongest muscle in the body is the masseter, on each side of the mouth, which is responsible for the action of biting.

Snoring heads
According to a United States study, people with round heads are more likely to snore. Researchers were able to predict whether someone was a snorer or not just by looking at their heads 75 percent of the time.

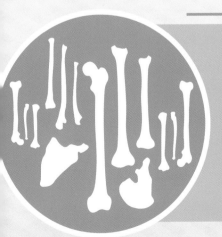

300+

Babies are born with more than 300 bones but some of them join together—adults have 206 bones. The longest bone in the body is the femur and the smallest is the stirrup bone in the ear, which is only 0.1 inch (2.5 mm) long.

20 PERCENT

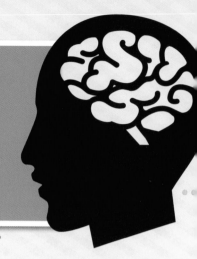

The brain uses more energy than any other organ, burning up one fifth of the food that you eat. Your brain has more than 100 billion neurons. Information travels at different speeds within different types of neuron—it can be as slow as 18 inches per second (0.5 m per second) or as fast as 394 feet per second (120 m per second).

Smell power
Until recently it was thought the human nose can sniff out 10,000 different odors, but recent research suggests the number is actually one trillion. U.S. scientists say we only use a tiny part of our olfactory powers.

Sunlight sneeze
Between one in five and a third of humans have the photic sneeze reflex—they sneeze in bright sunlight. It seems to be hereditary, but no one knows exactly how it works.

Tongue twister
Tongue movements can distract the brain. That's why some people stick out their tongues when they are concentrating, to hold them still. The longest tongue in the world is 4 inches (10 cm) and belongs to California's Nick Stoeberl.

No kidding
In the womb we develop three pairs of kidneys. The first two represent kidneys from way back in our evolution—the first is used in lampreys and the second in amphibians. These are absorbed before we end up with the pair that will develop into our adult kidneys.

Hot air
Most people break wind eight to 20 times a day and produce enough gas to blow up a balloon.

Mirror image
The heart is usually situated on the left-hand side of the body—except in one in 10,000 people, when it is on the right. The phenomenon is sometimes seen in mirror-image twins, where the fertilized egg splits later than is typical. Mirror-image twins can also be opposites of each

122 YEARS

Jeanne-Louise Calment was the oldest person ever, living to the age of 122 years and 164 days when she died at a nursing home in Arles, France, in 1997. She was also the oldest actress, portraying herself in a movie at the age of 114, and the oldest person to undergo surgery, in the same year.

There is enough fat in the average person's body to make about seven bars of soap.

other in terms of whether they are left or right handed.

Human genes

Before the completion of the human genome project it was thought we had around 100,000 genes, but in fact we only have around 24,000, not many more than a mouse or a chimpanzee, and far fewer than some species of rice. Our genome contains about 3.2 billion A, C, G, and T bases—the molecules that go to make up the DNA code.

Colossal chromosome

The biggest molecule in nature is part of the human body. Chromosome 1 is the biggest of 23 pairs of chromosomes in a normal human cell,

each a single, very long molecule of DNA. It contains around 10 billion atoms.

Eyelash mites

Around half the population have eyelash mites living at the base of their eyelashes. These tiny transparent creatures live on old skin cells and the natural oil (sebum) produced by human hair follicles.

There is enough carbon to make 900 pencils.

Enough phosphorus to make 2,200 match heads.

$332,000

Cost of the world's most expensive burger, made from meat that had been grown in a lab at Maastricht University, the Netherlands, using cattle stem cells.

FOOD

Good taste

The human tongue does not have distinct zones for discerning different tastes as was once thought. Taste buds actually all have 50 to 100 receptors for all five tastes—sweet, sour, bitter, salty, and umami (savory).

Food music

Research has found that people tend to associate sweet and sour tastes with high-pitched sounds and umami (savory) and bitter tastes with low-pitched ones, and that people enjoy food more when "matching" music is played while they are eating.

Nerve tonic

Nineteenth-century pharmacist John Pemberton, who was addicted to morphine, invented Coca-Cola while searching for a cure for his addiction. His first variant was alcoholic and known as Pemberton's French Wine Coca. The nonalcoholic sister product was marketed as a valuable brain tonic that would cure headaches, relieve exhaustion, and calm nerves.

Healthy hips

Most living things can make Vitamin C, but some that can't—including humans, guinea pigs, and bats—rely on their diet to get it. One of the best sources of Vitamin C is rose hips, which yield more than 400 mg per 100 g. Oranges are much less vitamin-packed, with only 50 mg per 100 g. You can eat rose hips raw, as long as you remove the seeds.

Factory farms

Electronics companies are starting to grow lettuce, strawberries, and other crops in their factories. Panasonic started experimenting with indoor farming at its Singapore factory in 2014, while Toshiba, Fujitsu, and Sharp Corporation have also branched out into hi-tech agriculture.

Cuboid fruit

It sounds like a hoax, but is actually true—Japanese melon growers have created cube-shaped melons, which stack more easily in supermarkets. The melons are grown in glass boxes.

On the run

Commercial tomato ketchup is a non-Newtonian fluid—it changes how

10 DAYS
Average life expectancy of a taste bud.

it flows when under stress. Giving a bottle of ketchup a bang will make the liquid less thick and cause it to flow better. It's best to thump the bottle near the top, as hitting it on the base only makes the liquid at the bottom runnier.

ZERO
(BELL PEPPER)

2,500–10,000
(JALAPEÑO)

100,000–350,000
(SCOTCH BONNETS)

2,200,000

The heat rating of the world's hottest chilli, the Carolina Reaper, on the Scoville scale, which is used to measure the pungency of chillies.

1888

The first deodorant to be sold commercially was the Mum brand, in 1888. The first antiperspirant—which aims to reduce sweating rather than just covering up the smell—was called Everdry.

COSMETICS

Bad beads

Modern cosmetics often use plastic microbeads as exfoliating agents in creams and toothpastes. The tiny nonbiodegradable beads are washed into the ocean after being flushed away, where they can be consumed by marine creatures, so environmentalists are campaigning for an end to the practice. One study found around 35 percent of 670 fish examined had microplastics in their stomach; the highest number in one fish was 83.

Smooth face

The first person to be injected with Botox for cosmetic reasons was Cathy Bickerton Swann, a surgery receptionist. Her bosses asked Cathy to test it out after a patient who was receiving injections for medical reasons demanded they continue even after her symptoms had abated, as she liked her nice smooth forehead.

Tiny bits

Some cosmetics contain nanoparticles, which can be 1,000 times smaller than the width of a human hair. Sunscreen can contain minuscule particles of titanium dioxide and zinc oxide, which absorb damaging ultraviolet light while remaining transparent on the skin.

Hot stuff

Nail polish contains nitrocellulose, a flammable and explosive ingredient also used in making dynamite.

Fizzy water

A bath bomb is a hard-packed bundle of chemicals that fizzes when wet. The main ingredients are a weak acid and a bicarbonate base, which are unreactive when dry but react vigorously when soaked in water.

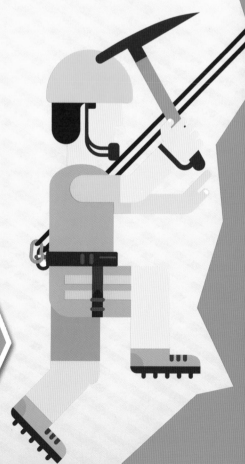

1946

Gletscher Crème (Glacier Cream), one of the first sunscreens, was launched. Chemist Franz Greiter developed it after being burned by the sun while climbing mount Piz Buin on the Austrian-Swiss border. The peak gave his company its name.

OUR
PLANET

3,000 BCE

Early philosophical writings from India discuss weather concepts such as cloud formation, rain, and the seasons. Our ancestors were obsessed with the weather—hardly surprising given its importance for agriculture.

WEATHER

Weather report

English Admiral Robert FitzRoy popularized the term "weather forecast." On retiring from the navy he collected data on weather at sea, which eventually led to the establishment of the British Meteorological Office. Looking for patterns, Fitzroy started to issue storm warnings to the general public in 1861—the first weather forecasts.

Wind scale

In 1805, British Admiral Sir Francis Beaufort gave his name to the scale indicating the strength of wind at sea. The 13-point scale was adapted for use on land and ranges from 0 (calm), through 6 (strong breeze), up to Force 12 (hurricane).

The long run

The Central England Temperature series, which covers the temperature from the south Midlands to Lancashire in England, is the longest-running meteorological record in the world, dating from 1659.

Strike one!

Lightning can and does strike twice and more times in any one spot. Tall buildings and aerials are often hit several times during violent storms.

Big bang

A typical lightning bolt contains about 15 million volts of electricity and heats up the air around to more than 50,000 °F (27,760 °C). A big storm releases more energy than a nuclear explosion. Several people have tried to capture and store lightning energy, but without much success so far.

Stone me!

The largest hailstone ever recorded fell in the town of Vivian, South Dakota, in 2010. It was 8 inches (20 cm) in diameter and weighed around 2 pounds (900 g).

Hurricane names

The system of naming hurricanes was started in 1890 by Englishman Clement Wragge, who named them after politicians he disagreed with. Today, hurricanes are named from a precompiled list of alphabetical names from the World Meterological Organization. For years this consisted

5 INCHES

(127 mm) of precipitation a year falls on the world's biggest desert—Antarctica.

1,800

The number of thunderstorms happening somewhere on Earth at any given moment—16 million storms each year. We know the cloud conditions that produce lightning, but we cannot forecast the location or time of a lightning strike.

of only women's names, but in 1979 men's names were added. The names of particularly violent storms are "retired" and not used again.

First weathermen

Clinton Youle is thought to be one of the first-ever TV weathermen for Chicago's WNBQ station, and the first to broadcast nationally in the United States in 1949. He also invented a gate to keep cows in fields. Britain's George Cowling became the first TV weatherman for the BBC when he gave the forecast at 7.55 p.m. on January 11, 1954.

In the clouds

Clouds are identified using a ten-category system devised by English pharmacist and amateur meteorologist, Luke Howard. Devised in 1803, the system is based on versions of the three basic cloud forms: puffy cumulus clouds, layered stratus clouds, and feathery cirrus clouds.

TEMPERATURE SCALES

BOILING POINT OF WATER

Kelvin	373.15
Celsius	100
Fahrenheit	212

FREEZING POINT OF WATER

Kelvin	273.15
Celsius	0
Fahrenheit	32

ABSOLUTE ZERO

Kelvin	0
Celsius	-273.15
Fahrenheit	-459.67

TEMPERATURE

Which scale?

In the early 18th century, as people grappled with the challenge of measuring temperature, there were around 35 different temperature scales that they could choose from.

Enter Fahrenheit

Galileo Galilei is often credited with developing the first thermometer, although earlier scientists had studied ways of measuring the temperature. His thermoscope was not very reliable and was gradually improved by his assistant Torricelli. Daniel Fahrenheit created the first successful thermometer, which used alcohol, in 1709, later refining it as a mercury version in 1714.

FOUR TRILLION °C

Scientists created the hottest temperature ever by smashing together gold ions at Brookhaven National University in New York in 2010. The temperature only lasted for less than one billionth of a second and was an experiment to help explain how the universe developed after the Big Bang.

... then Celsius

In 1742, Swedish astronomer Anders Celsius created a temperature scale divided into 100 points—and hence sometimes known as centigrade. He originally placed the boiling point of water at zero, and its freezing point at 100, although this was later reversed after his death. Celsius was adopted by most of the world, outside of the USA, as the scientific scale in 1948.

Back to zero

William Thomson (later Lord Kelvin) introduced the absolute temperature scale, now known as Kelvin, which uses the Celsius scale but starts at absolute zero. The scale is commonly used in science because it has no negative numbers.

Feeling hot

The highest atmospheric temperature ever recorded was 134°F (56.7°C) on July 10, 1913, at the aptly named Furnace Creek Ranch, California.

... and cold!

On July 21, 1983, a record low temperature of -128.6°F (-89.2°C) was recorded in Antarctica at the Russian research station, Vostok.

Wonderful Wunderlich

German Dr. Carl Wunderlich established that "normal" body temperature was 98.6°F (37°C) while working as medical director at Leipzig University from 1850. He introduced taking a patient's temperature as standard practice in diagnosis.

The thermometer he used was apparently 12 inches (30 cm) long and took 20 minutes to work.

Ouch!

Yakutsk in Russia is the coldest city in the world, with temperatures dipping below -58°F (-50°C). It's so cold that it's not advisable to wear spectacles outside as the metal frames can stick to, and rip, your skin.

Warm center

The center of the Earth is as hot as the surface of the Sun at 10,832°F (6,000°C), scientists have discovered.

IT VARIES

Today, we understand that body temperature varies depending on things such as where in the body the reading is taken, the time of the day, and the activity level of the subject.

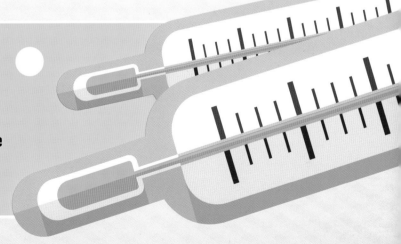

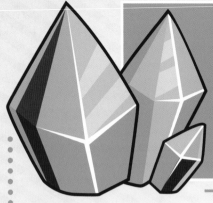

THERE ARE THREE BASIC ROCK TYPES:

- Igneous rocks are formed from the magma that extrudes from the Earth's core, for example, granite.
- Sedimentary rocks, such as limestone, are created from layers of material settling and compacting together.
- Metamorphic rocks form when rocks undergo change after being put under pressure or subjected to heat. Examples include slate and marble.

GEOLOGY

Thin skin
The Earth's outer rock layer is called the crust and is up to 37 miles (60 km) thick. This might seem a lot, but the crust only makes up one percent of the earth's volume.

Moho working
The boundary between the Earth's crust and the softer mantle that it floats on is called the Moho, after Croatian seismologist Andrija Mohorovicic who discovered it in 1909. Scientists are trying to drill into the Moho to find out more about the Earth's composition.

The drifter
German geologist Alfred Wegener proposed the theory of continental drift in 1912. Wegener's idea was that the continents were slowly moving on the Earth's surface, but it was not accepted until the 1950s.

Ancient rocks
The Jack Hills in Western Australia are composed of the oldest rocks in the world. The iron-rich rocks are 4.4 billion years old and were formed about 160 million years after the formation of the solar system.

Maori boulders
The Moeraki Boulders in New Zealand are weird, spherical rocks on the Otago coast that can be up to 10 feet (3 m) in diameter. According to Maori legend, they were the petrified remains of eel baskets from a giant mythical canoe, but they are actually caused by erosion of sedimentary rocks.

Sweet name
There are more than 1,200 Chocolate Hills in the Philippines. The rounded hillocks are a geological formation covered in grass that turns brown in the dry season, giving them their name.

Crazy crystals
Miners working in Mexico's Naica silver mine in 2000 discovered some of the biggest crystals ever seen when they accidentally smashed through into a new cave. The selenite crystals in the "Cave of Crystals" are up to 33 feet (10 m) long.

75 PERCENT
of the Earth's crust is made up of oxygen and silicon.

Float on

Pumice stone is formed when hot lava is rapidly cooled by air or water. This results in bubbles being trapped in the stone, making it less dense than other rocks, and able to float in water.

3106.75 CARATS

The Cullinan Diamond is the largest gem-quality diamond ever found. The stone was mined in South Africa and yielded what was, until 1985, the largest cut diamond in the world—the Great Star of Africa, which is part of the British Crown Jewels.

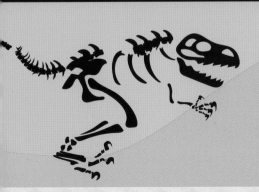

€5 BILLION

($5.38 billion) in lost revenue and damages was the cost of European aircraft flights being suspended for seven days because of the ash cloud from the 2010 eruption of Iceland's Eyjafjallajökull.

VOLCANOES AND EARTHQUAKES

Active Etna

Sicily's Mount Etna is one of the most active volcanoes in the world and exists in a state of almost continuous eruption from its five craters and 300 vents. The first written record of an Etna eruption dates from 425 BCE.

Crater of death

Japan's Mount Mihara volcano became a gruesomely popular place to commit suicide, with more than 600 people jumping into the crater in 1936 alone. The volcano also featured as the place where Godzilla is imprisoned in the 1984 movie, *The Return of Godzilla*.

Summer's cancelled

The explosion of Mount Tambora on the island of Sumbawa in Indonesia is considered the largest ever recorded by humans, ranking a 7 (or "super-colossal") on the Volcanic Explosivity Index (VEI), the second-highest rating. Reaching its peak in April 1815, the explosion was heard on Sumatra Island, more than 1,200 miles (1,930 km) away. An estimated 71,000 people died, and the amount of material blasted into the air effectively held off summer in 1816.

Around the world

The eruption of Krakatoa is more widely known that that of Tambora, although it was only about a third as powerful. However, the 1883 eruption occurred in the age of the telegraph, making it a worldwide story.

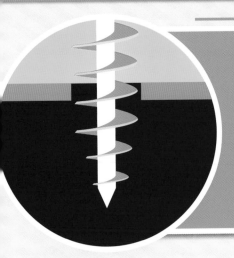

240

Oklahoma had this many earthquakes of magnitude 3.0 and over in the first half of 2014. Scientists have linked this to fracking for natural gas, as prior to fracking the state had an average of one a year.

The big freeze

Between 10,000–25,000 inhabitants of the towns of Pompeii and Herculaneum were killed by the eruption of Vesuvius in 79 CE. Volcanic rock and dust were dumped so quickly on the towns that many victims were killed on the spot and their cadavers remain frozen in time.

On the scale

Seismologists Charles Francis Richter and Beno Gutenberg developed the Richter scale in 1935 to measure the energy release of earthquakes.

Biggest quake

At 9.5 on the Richter scale, the 1960 Valdivia earthquake in Chile is the most powerful quake ever recorded.

Lasting for ten minutes, the event led to a death toll of between 3,000 and 6,000, and the devastation cost Chile the equivalent of $3–6 billion.

Mix up

Italian geophysicists studying the baffling occurrence of hundreds of microearthquakes in the country concluded that they were actually caused by heavy machinery used in the production of cement.

Hot stuff

Scientists in Iceland are studying how the power of volcanoes and magma could be used to heat water and drive energy-producing turbines.

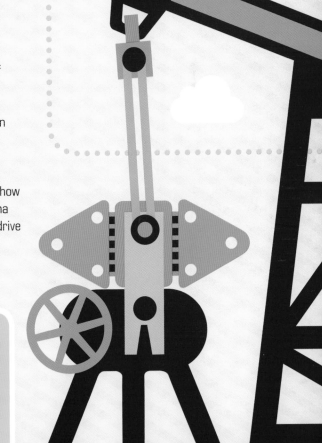

230,000

Nearly a quarter of a million lives were lost following the 2004 Boxing Day tsunami off the coast of northern Sumatra—170,000 were lost in Indonesia alone.

WINGS, WHEELS, & RAILS

INTRODUCTION

People have always been obsessed by travel. From the earliest days of trudging after hairy mammoths in search of his next meal, man has been concerned with getting from A to B.

The numerous ways that we have found to achieve this over the centuries are ingenious and fascinating. When we first started to devise new ways of traveling, a few miles an hour was the most that could be expected, but today we think nothing of zooming from one side of the planet to the next at speeds of hundreds of miles an hour. And the future could see us going even faster.

This book provides hundreds of fascinating facts about all the major modes of transportation, and a few unexpected ones, too. From the legend of Icarus, man has yearned to take to the air, although early attempts were not always very successful. However, once balloons came on the scene with the Montgolfier Brothers in the 18th century, flight became a possibility rather than just a mere dream. After the Wright Brothers made their inaugural powered flight in 1903, there was no turning back for the possibility of flight. In actual fact, there was an even earlier claim to powered flight than the Wrights, although it only managed a flying altitude of 8 inches (20 cm). Read about it here in this book.

This section explores the development of flight since then, marking the fastest, highest, biggest, and strangest flying machines. It also looks at the future and ponders how we may cross the skies in years to come—get ready for hypersonic travel, 3-D printed airplanes, and even planes that fly in flocks, like birds.

Meanwhile, back on planet Earth the wheel has been the mainstay of movement for thousands of years, but did you know that its original use was nothing to do with transportation—find out what it was in these pages. From the chariots of the ancients and the original horsepower, to cars, bikes, and electric vehicles, we've got it covered. If you've ever wondered about the fastest car in the world, or the most expensive, wonder no more. We've even rounded up the best of James Bond's gadget-filled automobiles.

Of course, before cars became mainstream, railroads were one of the first mass forms of transportation that allowed everyman to travel across countries and eventually around the world. We take you on a journey from the earliest railroads, including the primitive "Clapham Junction" of Malta, through the golden age of steam to the superfast modern trains of today.

There's also the possibility that we'll end up going back to steam—did you know that scientists are working out how this dirtiest of technologies can be made greener and more efficient? There are also some detours along subways, up and down funiculars, and via some weird and wacky wheeled modes such as the car built entirely of cake.

If that isn't enough, we'll then set sail on and below the seas and oceans. Whether you want to know about sail, steamships, modern tankers, or submersibles, we have the facts and statistics to amaze and astound.

Finally, we'll take a look at the infrastructure that makes it all happen, by touring the most impressive airports, stations, and docks of the world, and taking in the roads, bridges, and tunnels that are the world's travel arteries.

WINGS

1890

Before the Wright brothers flew into the history books, Frenchman Clément Ader built a steam-powered bat-winged plane called the *Éole*. It flew for 164 feet (50 m) at just 8 inches (20 cm) above the ground.

1903

The first sustained powered flight was on December 17, when Orville Wright flew *The Wright Flyer* for 12 seconds, covering 121 feet (37 m). By sunset they had notched up three more flights, with a longest time of 59 seconds.

1910

The first pilots' licenses were issued by the Aéro-Club de France. The first eight were awarded retrospectively to pioneering aviators and dated January 7, 1909. The first 16 were awarded in alphabetical order, with number 1 going to French aviator Louis Blériot and number 15 to Wilbur Wright. The first woman to receive a pilot's license was French aviator Raymonde de Laroche—the same year—number 36.

1912

The first parachute jump from an aircraft took place on March 1, from a height of 1,500 feet (457 m). The U.S. Army's Captain Albert Berry jumped from a Benoist biplane over Jefferson Barracks in St. Louis, Missouri.

1947

Charles "Chuck" Yeager, the pilot of the first plane to fly faster than the speed of sound, broke two ribs before his record-breaking flight. He pretended to be fit and succeeded in reaching 768 mph (1,236 km/h) in the Bell X-1—even though pain stopped him from reaching the cockpit door handle. His friend cut him a broomstick long enough to reach the latch.

1939

The first jet plane, the Heinkel He 178, took to the air. The first jet airliner, the de Havilland DH 106 Comet, followed ten years later. It could carry around 36 passengers.

1969

First flight of the Boeing 747 jumbo jet.

1967

The X-15A-2 rocket plane flew at 4,520 mph (7,274 km/h), or Mach 6.72, still the record speed for a crewed rocket-plane flight.

1914

The first commercial airline using a plane started operations on New Year's Day, using a two-seat Benoist flying boat. The plane flew 22 miles (35 km) from St. Petersburg, Florida, to neighboring Tampa. The ticket for the 23-minute journey cost $5, with an extra charge if you weighed more than 200 pounds (91 kg). In all, 1,025 passengers used the airline.

1919

The first nonstop transatlantic flight was made by British aviators John Alcock and Arthur Whitten Brown. The plane was a modified Vickers Vimy IV twin-engined bomber, with the bomb carriers replaced by extra fuel tanks. The flight covered 1,890 miles (3,040 km) in 15 hours 57 minutes, at an average speed of 115 mph (185 km/h).

1927

The first nonstop solo flight across the Atlantic Ocean from New York to Paris. Charles Lindbergh flew alone on the 3,610-mile (5,810-km) trip. The plane didn't have a windshield as the fuel tank was right in front of the cabin—Lindbergh used a periscope on the side window to see forward.

The first U.S. Federal pilots' license was issued to William P. MacCracken, Jr., the Assistant Secretary of Commerce for Aeronautics. Before accepting the license, MacCracken offered the honor to Orville Wright, promising to waive the fee and examination. Wright declined because he did not think he needed a Federal license to show that he had been the first man to fly.

1986

The first round-the-world flight without refueling, by Jeana Yeager and Dick Rutan in *Voyager*, designed by Dick's brother Burt, who also designed spaceplane *SpaceShipOne*. The plane covered 24,987 miles (40,212 km) nonstop.

2005

First flight of the giant double-deck Airbus A380, the biggest jetliner in the world.

1981

The flight of the first stealth aircraft, the F-117 Nighthawk. The plane was made of special materials that soaked up some radar waves and sharp angles to deflect others.

2004

The first flight to the edge of space— 62 miles (100 km)—by the *SpaceShipOne* private rocketplane.

111 HOURS

The time taken to cross the Atlantic by the *Graf Zeppelin* airship on its first flight from Friedrichshafen, Germany, to Lakehurst, New Jersey. The first nonstop commercial transatlantic flight started on October 11, 1928, and arrived on October 15.

BALLOONS AND AIRSHIPS

Balloon animals

The first human flight took place on November 21, 1783. Two volunteers, a science teacher and a soldier, flew for about 5.5 miles (9 km) above the streets of Paris in a balloon built by Joseph and Jacques Montgolfier. Before this the brothers had sent a duck, a rooster, and a sheep (called Montauciel, or Climb-to-the-sky) on a test flight.

Bad smell

The Montgolfiers' early balloons were very stinky. The brothers burned old shoes and rotten meat to create the hot air needed to lift the balloon. They didn't realize that hot air by itself would rise and thought they needed a special smoke.

Air monster

The first hydrogen-filled balloon was launched on August 27, 1783, from what is now the site of the Eiffel Tower in Paris. Excited viewers followed it on horseback, but when it drifted to earth 13 miles (21 km) away, terrified French villagers thought it was a monster and attacked it with pitchforks.

Commercial break

Count Ferdinand von Zeppelin, inventor of the eponymous airship, was sniffy at first about plans to use them commercially, seeing this as a vulgar tradesman's enterprise. He wanted use to be limited to the German army, which wasn't that keen at the time.

First fatality

The first fatal aviation accident was the crash of a Rozière balloon, which used a combination of hot air and hydrogen, on June 15, 1785. The accident, which took place near Wimereux in France, killed the balloon's inventor, Jean-François Pilâtre de Rozier, as well as the other occupant, Pierre Romain.

Mooring mast

The Art Deco spire of the Empire State Building in New York was originally designed to serve as a mooring mast for Zeppelins and other airships, though it was found that high winds made this impossible, and the plan was abandoned.

Earliest airline

The world's first commercial airline was DELAG, or Deutsche Luftschiffahrts-Aktiengesellschaft (German Airship Travel Corporation). The company operated Zeppelins from 1909 until 1935.

Cabin crew

The first flight attendant was German Heinrich Kubis, who started work on the DELAG Zeppelin LZ-10 *Schwaben* in March 1912. Kubis was on board the *Hindenburg* airship when it burst into flames in New Jersey on May 6, 1937—he escaped by jumping out of a window.

127,851 feet

(38,969.4 m). The distance Austrian Felix Baumgartner skydived after he was lifted up 24 miles (39 km) by a 550-foot (167.6-m) helium balloon. Baumgartner became the first skydiver to break the sound barrier on October 14, 2012, 34 seconds into his fall, and continued accelerating to 843.6 mph (1,357.64 km/h).

1,350 GALLONS

(6,137 liters). The amount of water the Bombardier 415 Superscooper can carry at one time. The firefighting plane can operate from land or water and skims the surface of a lake, scooping up a full load of water in 12 seconds.

PLANES

Feature presentation

In 1925, passengers on an Imperial Airways flight traveling over Germany were treated to one of the first in-flight movies—silent classic, *The Lost World*—with accompanying orchestral music courtesy of the radio. The pilot helpfully flew the plane through banks of dense cloud to darken the cabin for the movie.

Wrap up warm

Planes in the 1930s were so cold and noisy passengers had to wear heavy coats and earplugs. But at least the food was served on china plates.

Safety first

The safest airline in the world is generally held to be the Australian airline Qantas, which has seen no fatalities in the jet era. One of the worst safety records historically belongs to Cubana de Aviación, the national carrier of Cuba, which has been involved in 45 incidents and accidents between 1950 and 2008, with more than 500 fatalities.

Still going

The oldest airline that is still operating is KLM, the Netherlands' national carrier, which launched in 1919. It merged with Air France in 2004 but both airlines continue to fly under their own brand.

Feeling queasy

Gilmore Tilmen Schjeldahl (1912–2002) was an American businessman and inventor in plastics, adhesives, and circuitry. He was awarded 16 U.S. patents but may be best known for inventing the lined airsickness bag.

Flying boat

The fastest and largest plane that can land and take off on land or water is the Beriev A-40 submarine hunter plane from Russia, which first flew in 1986. It has two jet engines mounted above its wings to keep the air intakes away from the water spray. It has a wingspan of 140 feet (42.5 m) and is 150 feet (45.7 m) long.

Nice moves

One of the most agile planes ever flown was the X-31, a single-seater jet with a triangular delta-wing shape.

525

The number of passengers carried by the double-decker Airbus A380, the biggest passenger plane ever built. The air giant has space for onboard bars, restaurants, and stores, is 239 feet (72.72 m) long, and can fly up to 9,755 miles (15,700 km) without refueling. But the airships that ferried passengers across the Atlantic in the 1930s were more than three times as long.

At its back three ultratough metal paddles dipped in and out of the jet engine's powerful exhaust gases. As the paddles angled the jet thrust from side to side the plane, which could reach speeds over Mach 1.28, twisted and turned through the air.

Penguin power

A 13-year-old was the first person to fly using solar power. Marshall MacCready, son of the inventor, flew in *Gossamer Penguin* on May 18, 1980, at Shafter Airport near Bakersfield, California. The first unmanned aircraft to use solar power was the AstroFlight *Sunrise*, on November 4, 1974, in California.

472 million cubic feet

(13,385,378 m³). The volume of Boeing's largest aircraft assembly facility, which is also the largest building in the world. The factory has a floor space of 4.3 million square feet (399,480 m²), large enough to house most of Vatican City and voluminous enough to contain five copies of the Great Pyramid of Giza.

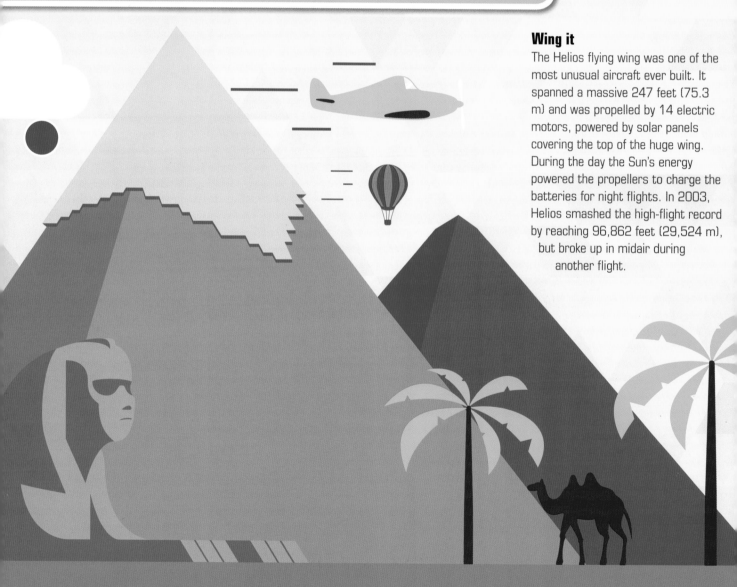

Wing it

The Helios flying wing was one of the most unusual aircraft ever built. It spanned a massive 247 feet (75.3 m) and was propelled by 14 electric motors, powered by solar panels covering the top of the huge wing. During the day the Sun's energy powered the propellers to charge the batteries for night flights. In 2003, Helios smashed the high-flight record by reaching 96,862 feet (29,524 m), but broke up in midair during another flight.

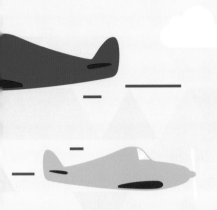

2,000

The number of Boeing 737 planes that are in the air at any given time. The most popular plane in the world, the 737 has been continually manufactured since 1967, and was the first commercial plane to sell more than 10,000 units. One 737 takes off or lands every two seconds.

Boxing clever

The so-called "black boxes" that record flight information in the case of an accident are actually orange. They are not allowed to be black, as this would make them too difficult to find after an accident.

Invisible jet

Although the F-117 Nighthawk has a wingspan of 43 feet (13.2 m), on radar it shows up as only as big as a marble. The F-117 was the first combat plane to be designed from the outset as a stealth jet—its strangely angled shape and special materials deflect and absorb enemy radar beams.

Mind your language

All air traffic controllers and international pilots worldwide must be able to speak English, since new rules were introduced in 2006. The regulations were brought in, in a bid to reduce the number of accidents, by ensuring everyone could talk to each other.

Free fall

Yugoslavian air hostess Vesna Vulović survived falling 33,333 feet (10,160 m) without a parachute when the plane she was working on blew up in January 1972. It is the highest fall survived without a parachute.

Ashtray required

Commercial airplanes must incorporate public ashtrays—even though smoking is now banned on practically all flights. A British Airways flight to Mexico was delayed by 25 minutes while crew searched for a replacement ashtray in 2009, after noticing the existing one had been removed from the toilet door.

DOWN TO EARTH

The space shuttle is a glider when it returns to Earth. Its rocket engines are only used during liftoff. The shuttle flew 135 missions before retiring in 2011.

GLIDERS

One minute 40 seconds
The time taken for members of Kouvola's Glider Association in Finland to assemble a glider from its component parts and launch it to an altitude of 1,300 feet (400 m).

Glory story
The Morning Glory is a tube-shaped cloud, sometimes up to 620 miles (1,000 km) long, and often only 330–660 feet (100–200 m) above the ground. It appears regularly in the Gulf of Carpentaria in northern Australia, and attracts glider pilots keen to ride it, much as particular wave formations attract surfers.

Military attack
Gliding was popular in Germany after World War I because the Treaty of Versailles banned any other form of pilot training in the country. Hitler used gliders in several important attacks during World War II, including a successful assault on a seemingly impregnable Belgian fort, a key step in the invasion of France.

Space race
The development of hang gliding was one of the by-products of the space race. Space agency NASA tested new materials and designs as part of its research into recovering the *Gemini* space capsules in the 1950s and 1960s.

Mountain museum
The birthplace of gliding is said to be an airfield on a mountain called Wasserkuppe in Germany's Rhön Mountains range. The site of the first glider pilot school, the mountain is now home to the world's largest gliding museum.

High flyers
Americans Steve Fossett and Einar Enevoldson reached the altitude of 50,720 feet (15,460 m) in a glider in 2006. Since the glider cockpit was unpressurized, the pilots wore full pressure suits. They could have gone higher but their suits expanded so much inside the cabin that they couldn't move the flight controls.

474.7 miles

(764 km). The farthest flown in a hangglider. This record was achieved in Texas by Dustin Martin in 2012, flying a Moyes Delta Litespeed RX 3.5. The trip took 11 hours and Martin was fueled by energy bars and drinks.

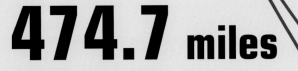

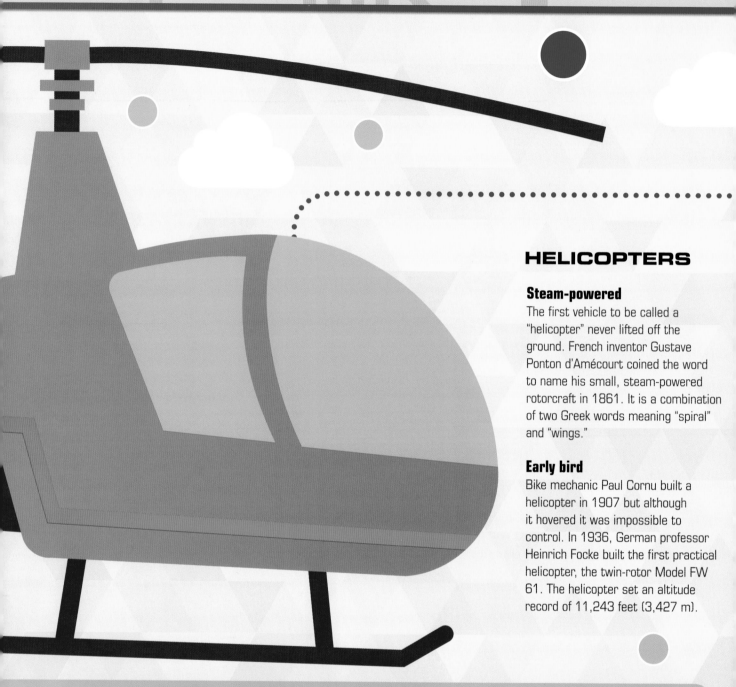

HELICOPTERS

Steam-powered
The first vehicle to be called a "helicopter" never lifted off the ground. French inventor Gustave Ponton d'Amécourt coined the word to name his small, steam-powered rotorcraft in 1861. It is a combination of two Greek words meaning "spiral" and "wings."

Early bird
Bike mechanic Paul Cornu built a helicopter in 1907 but although it hovered it was impossible to control. In 1936, German professor Heinrich Focke built the first practical helicopter, the twin-rotor Model FW 61. The helicopter set an altitude record of 11,243 feet (3,427 m).

$470 MILLION

The potential cost of the most expensive helicopter ever made. The cost for a proposed fleet of 28 VH-71 Kestrel helicopters for the U.S. Marine Corps was estimated at a record $13.2 billion in total. The program was cancelled in February 2009.

220 feet

(67 m). The length of the rotor blades on the world's largest helicopter, the Russian Mil Mi-12. The vehicle, 121 feet (37 m) long with a takeoff weight of 114 tons (103.3 tonnes), first flew in 1968 but never went into mass production.

Speedy Sikorsky

The world's fastest helicopter was the experimental Sikorsky X2, which set a new unofficial world record for a helicopter, reaching 250 knots (287 mph/461.9 km/h) during flight testing in Florida in 2010. The official world record is still held by a Westland Lynx helicopter, which reached 216 knots (249 mph/400.7 km/h) in 1986.

They've got bottle

Helicopters can open bottles of beer. Skilled pilots use the skid of the helicopter to take the cap off a bottle, as part of tournaments and competitions. The record for the number of caps removed in three minutes is four, by German pilot Jan Veen, on January 26, 2008.

Electric dreams

The first manned flight in an electric-powered helicopter took place in 2011 in France. French pilot Pascal Chrétien hovered about 20 inches (50 cm) above the ground for two minutes ten seconds while tethered. The aircraft later flew for a total of 99.5 minutes during 29 flights.

Essential part

The nut that holds the main rotor to the mast of some helicopters is called the Jesus nut or Jesus pin. It must be checked before each flight. The name is thought to have been coined by U.S. soldiers in Vietnam, who knew that if the nut failed in flight, the helicopter would detach from the rotors and the only thing to do would be to pray.

Peak performance

The only pilot to land a helicopter on the summit of Mount Everest is Frenchman Didier Delsalle. His Eurocopter AS350 Squirrel touched down on the 29,030-foot (8,848-m) peak—the world's highest point of land—in May 2005.

25,000 pounds

(11,340 kg) The amount of freight a Chinook transport helicopter can carry, either inside, or slung underneath on up to three hooks. The twin-engined helicopter can carry 54 troops and has room inside for two Land Rovers.

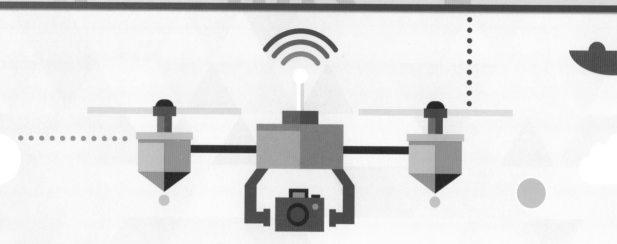

DRONES

On the up
Economists predict spending on drones worldwide in the next decade will reach $98 billion, with 12 percent of that going on drones used for commercial purposes.

Special delivery
Delivery company DHL is already using a "parcelcopter" to make regular flights to an island in the North Sea, while Internet retailer Amazon wants to use small drones to deliver packages up to 5 pounds (2.3 kg) in weight. Amazon now has a drone R&D lab in Cambridge, England.

Doing good
Drones have their own World Cup. The UAE Drones for Good Award was held in Dubai in 2015 and aimed to find the best ways in which drones can improve people's lives. There were more than 800 entries, with $1 million in prizes.

Plume raiders
NASA has flown drones into an active volcano to study its toxic plume. The unmanned aircraft can carry a 1-pound (450-g) payload for up to an hour.

Martian maps
The next mission to Mars hopes to include a helicopter drone, which could help land-based probes cover three times the distance. Rovers like *Curiosity*, currently investigating the Martian surface, have to travel slowly in case they hit an obstacle—the flying drone could map out the terrain in advance to allow the robot to travel more quickly.

Robot insects
Engineers at Harvard University have developed RoboBees, which measure about half the size of a paper clip and weigh less than one tenth of a gram. The minuscule flying robots could be used for important tasks including crop pollination, traffic monitoring, and surveillance.

Sky giant
Among the largest drones is Israel Aerospace Industries' Heron TP UAV, named the *Eitan*. It has a maximum takeoff weight of 10,230 pounds (4,650 kg), a wingspan of 85 feet

(26 m), and a length of 43 feet (13 m), and can carry high-resolution cameras, electronic systems, and possibly weapons. It is capable of staying airborne for well over 20 hours at an operational altitude of around 45,000 feet (13,700 m).

Breaking in

Prisoners and their accomplices have tried to use drones to smuggle contraband into jail. In Ireland, a quadcopter carrying drugs got caught on antihelicopter wires and crash landed inside a Dublin jail. In the State of Georgia four people were arrested after trying to deliver tobacco to a prison using a drone.

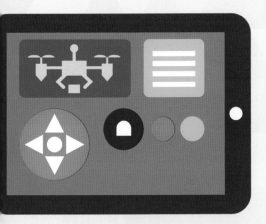

DRONES ARE ALSO KNOWN AS UNMANNED AERIAL VEHICLES (UAVs). HERE ARE SOME JOBS THAT UAVs HAVE BEEN DEVELOPED TO DO:

1. WINDOW CLEANING

Drones can safely clean high windows that no one else can get to.

2. CLEAR FOG AWAY FROM AIRPORT RUNWAYS AND OTHER AREAS

3. PLANT TREES ON AN INDUSTRIAL SCALE

One drone maps out the area to be planted and another fires biodegradable nutrient-rich seed pods into the ground.

4. SEARCH-AND-RESCUE MISSIONS

5. SOME POLICE FORCES USE DRONES TO IDENTIFY AND FOLLOW SUSPECTS

6. MONITOR LONG PIPELINES OR OFFSHORE ENERGY PLATFORMS

Many countries have their own official aerobatic squadron, often part of the air force or navy. Some of them are:

1. Red Arrows (UK) Officially called the Royal Air Force Aerobatic Team, the squadron was named after a previous team, the Black Arrows, with the red coming from the color of training airplanes in the 1960s.

2. Blue Angels (U.S.) The U.S. Navy's flight demonstration squadron was formed in 1946, making it the second oldest formal flying team in the world, after France's Patrouille de France. The U.S. Air Force also has a display team, the Thunderbirds.

3. Smokey Bandits (Malaysia) The name comes from the characteristic smoke that comes out of the Royal Malaysian Air Force team's five MiG-29N/NUB fighters.

4. Blue Impulse (Japan) The team was given its name after the original, Tenryu, proved too difficult to pronounce in Western languages. The team has been immortalized in its own video game, Aero Dancing.

5. Scorpion (Poland) The Scorpion team is one of the few helicopter aerobatic teams in the world.

SPORT

First race
The first airplane race was held on May 23, 1909, at the Port-Aviation airport south of Paris, France. Four pilots entered the race, two started, and nobody completed the distance. The winner was declared to be Léon Delagrange, who covered slightly more than half of the course. He died in a plane crash the following year.

Slalom run
Pilots have to slalom though inflatable pylons at the annual Red Bull Air Race. The so-called Air Gates stand 82 feet (25 m) high and must be delicate enough to burst as soon as they are touched by a plane but sturdy enough to remain stationary in stormy weather.

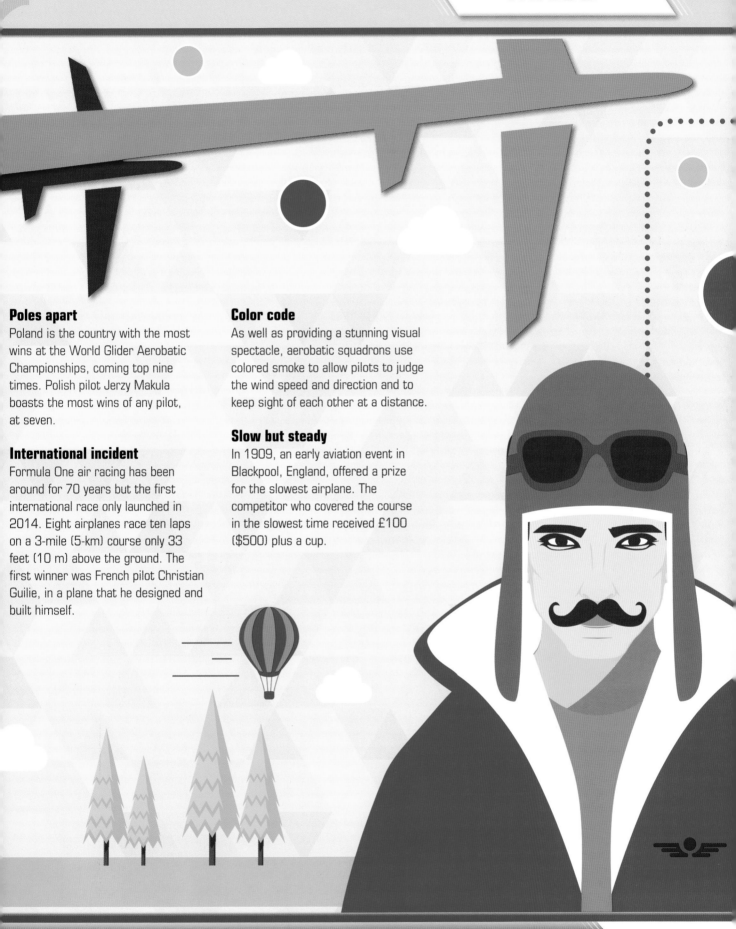

Poles apart
Poland is the country with the most wins at the World Glider Aerobatic Championships, coming top nine times. Polish pilot Jerzy Makula boasts the most wins of any pilot, at seven.

International incident
Formula One air racing has been around for 70 years but the first international race only launched in 2014. Eight airplanes race ten laps on a 3-mile (5-km) course only 33 feet (10 m) above the ground. The first winner was French pilot Christian Guilie, in a plane that he designed and built himself.

Color code
As well as providing a stunning visual spectacle, aerobatic squadrons use colored smoke to allow pilots to judge the wind speed and direction and to keep sight of each other at a distance.

Slow but steady
In 1909, an early aviation event in Blackpool, England, offered a prize for the slowest airplane. The competitor who covered the course in the slowest time received £100 ($500) plus a cup.

2014

saw the lowest number of fatal plane crashes (21) since 1945. However, the number of fatalities—990—was higher than average, with four of the crashes accounting for 815 deaths.

DISASTERS

First fatality
The first person to die in an airplane accident was U.S. Army lieutenant Thomas E. Selfridge, who was a passenger in a plane crashed by aviation pioneer Orville Wright on September 17, 1908. Selfridge would probably have survived if his head had been protected—as a result the U.S. Army's first pilots wore large, heavy helmets.

Pilot death
The first pilot to die in a powered aircraft crash was Eugène Lefebvre, who crashed the plane he was testing for the Wright Company on September 7, 1909, in Juvisy-sur-Orge, France.

Accident prone
Africa is the least safe continent when it comes to air travel, accounting for 43 percent of all fatal airliner accidents in 2014 but only three percent of all world air traffic. The airlines of 15 African nations are not allowed to fly into the EU, and three are banned in the U.S.

Crocodile crash
A crocodile was the cause of an airplane crash that killed 20 people in 2010 in the Democratic Republic of Congo. The reptile was smuggled on board the vessel but escaped midflight. The resulting stampede unbalanced the plane, which crashed into a house. The crocodile survived but was later killed with a machete.

Celebrity victims
Famous singers who have died in air crashes include John Denver (1997), Patsy Cline (1963), and Buddy Holly, Ritchie Valens, and J. P. Richardson (The Big Bopper) who all died in the same plane crash in 1959. Country music star Waylon Jennings was supposed to be traveling on that plane but gave up his seat for Richardson. More recently, in 1999, golfer Payne Stewart died when his jet depressurized.

1972

The worst year for plane fatalities, when 2,429 people died in 55 crashes. These included 174 deaths when Aeroflot Flight 217 crashed in Russia and 155 fatalities following the crash of the Spanish Convair 990 Coronado.

583

The number of passengers and crew who died in the airline disaster with the greatest loss of passenger life. A KLM Boeing 747, attempting to take off without clearance, collided with a taxiing Pan Am 747 at Los Rodeos airport, Tenerife, in 1977.

RECORD BREAKERS

SMALLEST

The smallest aircraft ever capable of carrying a passenger was the biplane *Bumble Bee II*, designed and built by Robert H. Starr in Arizona. It was 9 feet (2.69 m) long and was capable of carrying one person. However, it was destroyed after crashing in 1988.

LONGEST AND HEAVIEST

The Russian-built Antonov An-225 is the longest and heaviest plane ever built, with a wingspan of 290 feet (88.4 m) and a maximum takeoff weight of 705 tons (640 tonnes). Known as *Mriya* (Dream), it was constructed in 1988 to carry Russia's space shuttle, the Buran. It is powered by six turbo-fan engines and can reach a speed of 528 mph (850 km/h).

FASTEST

The greatest speed reached by an unmanned aircraft is 7,000 mph (11,270 km/h), or Mach 9.6, achieved by U.S. research plane X-43 in 2004. The X-43's experimental engine fired for just 10 seconds but in that time the tiny craft hurtled more than 13 miles (21 km) through the air. The record speed for a crewed flight was 4,520 mph (7,274 km/h) achieved by the U.S. X-15A-2 rocket-plane in 1967.

LONGEST SCHEDULED FLIGHT

The longest nonstop scheduled commercial flight is currently a Qantas route from Dallas/Fort Worth, Texas, to Sydney, Australia, using an Airbus A380-800. The flight takes around 16 hours and 55 minutes and covers 8,577 miles (13,804 km).

WHEELS

5,500 YEARS AGO

The first wheeled vehicles were probably created by fixing wheels to a sled at least 5,500 years ago. However, the most important transport discovery in history was not actually invented for use in vehicles. The wheel was first used by potters making clay bowls in ancient Sumer (now Iraq).

HISTORY OF THE WHEEL

Slide rule
Before the invention of the wheel, people transported heavy loads by dragging them on sleds. Archaeologists have found 9,000-year-old sled runners in Finland.

Land sailors
Early Chinese engineers used single wheels to create wheelbarrows fitted with sails. This allowed the heavily loaded vehicles to be more easily pushed across China's windy plains. They may also have created sailed passenger vehicles.

Toy story
The Aztecs knew about wheels—they put them on children's pull toys—but they never built them on to vehicles. This is probably because they had no draft animals until European invaders conquered Mexico in the 16th century. Heavy loads were carried on people's backs.

Driving terror
Pulled by onagers (Asiatic asses) and later horses, light chariots with spoked wheels unleashed terror on the ancient world, enabling warriors to sweep down on their enemies. Chariots enabled the Hyksos people to conquer Egypt around 1630 BCE.

Crash course
The first working, self-propelled mechanical vehicle was built by French inventor Nicolas-Joseph Cugnot in 1769. Steam-powered, it was slow and hard to drive and crashed into a brick wall in 1771—possibly the very first auto accident.

On the road
The first long-distance road trip was taken by Bertha Benz, wife of Karl Benz, the inventor of the first motor car. She took her teenage sons in one of the prototype vehicles and traveled 121 miles (194 km) to her mother's house and back in August 1888. Bertha acted as mechanic on the trip, cleaning a fuel pipe with a hatpin, insulating a wire with a garter, and inventing brake lining on the way.

60 YARDS

Until 1896, cars in Britain were only allowed to travel at walking pace. They had to have three people with them, one of whom walked 60 yards (55 m) in front waving a red flag. In 1896, a law was brought in to increase the speed limit—to 12 mph (19.3 km/h).

1 SHILLING

The fine (around 25 cents) given to the first motorist caught speeding in the UK. In 1896, speed demon Walter Arnold was summonsed for driving at 8 mph (12.9 km/h) in a 2-mph (3.2-km/h) zone.

OCTOBER 20, 1816

The Quicksilver mail coach was traveling from Exeter to London when one of its horses—Pomegranate—was attacked by a lioness. The passengers rushed into an inn for safety but shut out the guard, who was persuaded not to kill the lioness by its owner—she had escaped from a nearby menagerie.

HORSEPOWER

Regency race

The light and speedy curricle was the racing car of the Regency period. Drawn by two horses, the vehicle could reach 16 mph (25.7 km/h) when driven by a skilled driver on a good road. They were notorious for accidents.

Sunday drivers

In the 18th century, it was more expensive to travel on a Sunday in Britain. The cost of hiring horses was doubled and tollgates charged two or three times over the normal rate. But on the upside, highwaymen tended to take Sunday off.

Cold comfort

In the early 19th century, the Royal Mail stage coach was the fastest

2.43 MILLION POUNDS (1.1 MILLION KG)

The amount of manure produced every day by horses transporting New Yorkers in the 1890s. The horses also produced 40,000 gallons (181,844 liters) of urine a day.

way of transporting goods and people around the United Kingdom—they were able to reach speeds of 9–10 mph (14–16 km/h). They weren't very comfortable though—guards and passengers sometimes froze to death on the journey.

Public transport

The word "bus" is a shortening of the Latin word *omnibus*, meaning "for all." The earliest horse-drawn omnibus service started in Nantes, France, in 1826. It transported passengers from the town center to a nearby bathhouse. The baths failed but the bus was very popular, even though it was hardly quicker than walking.

Short lives

Horses often dropped dead on the job, blocking streets which were already overcrowded. The average streetcar horse had a life expectancy of about three years. Street cleaners often waited several days for the corpses to decay so they could be sawn into pieces more easily.

Rail users

Some of the first public buses ran on rails even though they were pulled by horses, as this made the carriages roll more easily. New York's first horse cars could hold 50 people in 1852, but were pulled by only two horses.

Shire power

Powerful draft horses were bred for tough jobs such as pulling agricultural machinery, brewery drays, and canal boats. The largest-ever horse was probably Sampson, a Shire horse born in Bedfordshire, England, in 1846. He was 21.2½ hands high (7 feet 2½ inches/220 cm at the shoulder) and weighed around 3,350 pounds (1,520 kg).

12 MPH (19 KM/H)

Average speed of horses and carts moving through London 100 years ago. 12 mph (19 km/h): Average speed of cars moving through London today.

AUTOMOBILES

Global statistics

- There are more than a billion automobiles in the world.
- The United States has the most (239.8 million), followed by China (just over 78 million).
- There are 1.3 people for every car in the United States, while in China there are 6.75 people per vehicle.

Beyond sound

The Thrust SSC is the world's first supersonic car. On October 15, 1997, it became the first to go faster than the speed of sound, and two days later set a new land speed record of 763 mph (1,228 km/h). It has the racing power of 145 Formula One cars. Its engines were developed for jet-fighter planes.

Speeding bullet

The team behind Thrust SSC is developing another supersonic car, Bloodhound SSC, which it hopes will reach a record-breaking 1,050 mph (1,690 km/h)—that's faster than a bullet fired from a Magnum 357. The pencil-shaped vehicle is powered by a jet engine and a rocket engine.

Miles away

American Irv Gordon's 1966 Volvo P-1800S has more than 3 million miles (4.8 million km) on the clock—that's a distance of more than 120 times around the world. Gordon bought the coupé in 1966, and it has needed 857 oil changes, 30 drive belts, 150 points and spark plugs—and got through 120 bottles of transmission fluid.

Record producer

China is the world's largest automobile manufacturer. In 2013, the country produced more than 20 million vehicles out of a world total of 86 million—the biggest year on record. North America was second, with 11 million vehicles, and Japan came third, with a total of 9.5 million.

Old timer

The Morgan 4/4 is the oldest automobile that is still being manufactured. The 4/4 was the first four-wheeled car built by Morgan, in 1936, and new cars are still being made at the original factory in the heart of the British countryside. In 1936 it cost £194 ($768) but today it costs around £27,500 ($41,500).

SOME CARS WITH SILLY NAMES

The Mitsubishi Lettuce

Introduced in January 1989, this sixth-generation Mitsubishi Minica model did come in colors other than green.

The Honda That's

That's what? The Honda That's was a small car made only for sale in Japan.

The Isuzu GIGA 20 Light Dump

A dump truck, clearly.

The Isuzu Mysterious Utility Wizard

Another 1980s' example, in this case an SUV, which perhaps sounded less odd in Japanese.

The Bongo Friendee

Mazda's eight-seater MPV (MultiPurpose Vehicle).

EXPENSIVE CARS

1. A 1962 Ferrari 250 GTO was sold by auctioneers Bonhams in 2014 for a record-breaking $38.1 million. Ferrari made only 39 GTOs and they rarely come up for sale. This one had a checkered history—its driver was killed in a crash in 1962 during a race at Montlhéry, near Paris.

2. The Lamborghini Aventador J was the only one of its kind. It was built in 2012 and has no roof or windshield. It sold in 2012 for $2.8 million.

3. The Pagani Zonda Tricolore sold for £1,340,000 ($2,144,000) in 2010. The Tricolore was built as a tribute to Italy's aerobatic team, and includes a small wing placed behind the cockpit imitating the tail wing of a stunt plane.

Two wheels good?

In Saudi Arabia, young men have invented a new way of driving called "sidewalk skiing." The dangerous pastime involves driving on two wheels while passengers climb outside the car—or even change tires while the vehicle is in motion. The official record for the longest distance traveled by a car driving on its side on two wheels is 230.57 miles (371.06 km).

Pretty in pink

In 1955, the Chrysler Corporation brought out a car especially for women. Dodge La Femme came in three shades of pink, and was upholstered in pink fabric featuring pink rosebuds. Standard equipment included a pink purse containing a compact, lipstick case, cigarette case, comb, and cigarette lighter; and a raincoat, rain bonnet, and umbrella matching the car's interior.

Fashion police

Rome's police cars have style— the police force fleet includes a Lamborghini Huracan supercar. It is fitted with a camera transmitting real-time video footage to the control room. An aerodynamically optimized light has been designed to cope with high speeds. The luggage compartment to the front of the car is equipped with a refrigerator to transport lifesaving organs.

4. The Bugatti "Royale" Type 41 was designed and built to transport royalty—although founder Ettore Bugatti is said to have refused to sell one to King Zog of Albania, blaming his poor table manners. Only six of these huge 21-foot (6.4-m) automobiles were ever built. In 1930 they sold for $30,000; in 1999 Volkswagen, current owner of Bugatti, reportedly bought one for $20 million.

1,647 FEET

(502 m). The length of the biggest mobile industrial machine, the F60 conveyor bridge, which is used to move rock and earth from mines. Five were built in Germany in the 1980s and four are still in use.

HEAVY MACHINERY

Monster machines

The world's largest industrial machines tend to be used in mining. The Komatsu D575A Super Dozer weighs 168 tons (152.6 tonnes) and can shift 2,437 cubic feet (69 m³) of material in one scoop. It is mainly used in mining in the USA, Australia, and Canada.

Road trains

Australia has the largest and heaviest road-legal vehicles in the world. Its road trains consist of a tractor towing two, three, or four trailers, and can be up to 164 feet (50 m) long. In some areas they are even longer. Lack of filling stations means road trains carry enough fuel for 1,000 miles (1,600 km).

Trash talk

In some parts of the world garbage trucks are powered by garbage. In California, for example, the methane given off by decomposing trash is used to run a fleet of 350 trucks.

Giant dump

The biggest dump truck in the world was created in Belarus by manufacturer Belaz. The Belaz 75710 is as long as two double-decker buses parked end-to-end, is six times as powerful as today's Formula 1 racing cars, and weighs more than a fully loaded Airbus A380 passenger plane. It is designed to work in temperatures from -58°F–122°F (-50°C to 50°C) and in altitudes up to 16,000 feet (4,877 m).

Top model

Every vehicle used by British trucking firm Eddie Stobart has a girl's name emblazoned on the front. The first Eddie Stobart truck was named "Twiggy," after the 1960s' supermodel. Members of fan group the Stobart Club are allowed to put forward new name suggestions.

Fast times

The fastest speed reached by a monster truck is 99.1 mph (159.49 km/h). The driver was American Mark Hall, in monster truck *Raminator*, in Austin, Texas, on December 15, 2014.

113

The highest number of trailers towed by a single prime mover. Australian John Atkinson towed a road train 4,836 feet (1,474 m) long for around 492 feet (150 m) on February 18, 2006. The length was the equivalent of 156 double-decker buses.

99 TONS

(90 tonnes). The weight that the world's biggest forklift trucks are capable of lifting. Three of them were made by Swedish firm Kalmar LMV to lay water pipelines in Libya, and each is 54 feet (16.6 m) long and 16 feet (4.85 m) wide.

1885

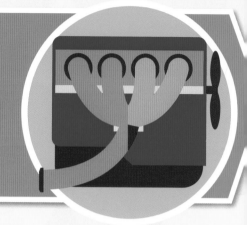

The first motorcycle with an internal combustion engine was designed and built by Gottlieb Daimler and Wilhelm Maybach in Germany. It had a wooden frame and a top speed of 7 mph (11 km/h).

MOTORBIKES

Rapid racer

The record for fastest speed on a conventional motorbike is held by New Zealand's Richard Assen, who reached 261.315 mph (420.546 km/h) in September 2011 at the Bonneville Salt Flats, Utah.

Fast lady

The UK's Becci Ellis became the fastest female motorcycle rider on Earth in October 2014, at an airfield in Yorkshire, clocking up 264 mph (424.8 km/h) on her Suzuki Hayabusa.

It says potato

Motorbike company Harley-Davidson tried to patent the noise its bikes make (described as the sound of someone saying "potato potato potato") in 1994. After some years of legal wrangling, the application was withdrawn in 2000.

Production history

The first mass-production motorbike was produced by German company Hildebrand & Wolfmüller in 1894. The company produced more than 1,000 bikes in its first two years, each with a water-cooled 1,488cc twin cylinder four stroke engine.

Funny peculiar

"Funny bikes" are a class of motorbike in drag racing. They developed from the "funny cars" built by drag racers in the 1970s, so-called because they looked like normal family cars with comically distorted bodies. In some countries funny bikes can be fueled by laughing gas (nitrous oxide) as well as nitromethane, methanol, and other fuels.

Hog heaven

In the 1920s, the Harley-Davidson motorcycle racing team had a pig as a mascot, which they used to take on a victory lap after winning a race—and they won a lot of races. Since then Harley-Davidson motorbikes have been known as "hogs."

376.363 mph
(605.697 km/h)

The average speed attained by American Rocky Robinson, riding his streamlined bike Top Oil-Ack Attack, over 0.6 mile (1 km) at Bonneville Salt Flats, Utah, in 2010.

15,494,000

Honda is the world's biggest selling brand of bike, with almost 15.5 million sales in 2013—more than 13 million of them in Asia.

83.13 mph
(133.78 km/h)

is the speed record for conventional cycling, achieved by Dutch cyclist Sebastiaan Bowier in September 2013. Bowier was riding a recumbent bicycle, the VeloX3, designed by students in the Human Power Team at Delft University of Technology and the VU University Amsterdam.

BICYCLES

Cycle lessons

Learning to ride an early bicycle was so difficult that cycle manufacturers gave lessons in special riding halls. Velocipedagogues (or "bike teachers") taught cycling skills within a week. Although it was safer than on the roads, students still emerged with cuts and bruises.

Wind power

The Dutch-produced Whike is a bike with a sail. The recumbent tricycle has 18 gears and allows the cyclist to cruise along if the wind is blowing in the right direction. In 2014, three cyclists traveled 1,009 miles (1,623 km) across Chile on Whikes, including traversing mountain ranges.

Giving a lift

The city of Trondheim in Norway has the world's first—and currently the world's only—cycling elevator. Looking a bit like a tram rail, the elevator, known as Trampe, has carried more than 200,000 cyclists up a 426-foot (130-m) hill since it was installed in 1993. Cyclists simply rest one foot on a moving footplate, towed by a cable, which drags them and their bike up the hill.

Marathon men

Six-day racing was popular in New York in the 1890s. At first riders slept every night and joined the race again when they woke up. But cyclists began to compete 24 hours a day, leading to hallucinations and delusions. The *New York Times* said the races were not a sport but brutality, and described the riders' faces as "hideous with the tortures that rack them."

Gone dotty

The leading cyclist in the mountain stages of iconic bicycle race Le Tour de France wears a white jersey with red polka dots. The design is down to the race sponsor in 1975, when the jersey was introduced. Chocolat Poulain's chocolate bars had red and white wrappers.

167.043 mph
(268.831 km/h)

is the highest speed ever reached on a bicycle, achieved by Fred Rompelberg of the Netherlands in 1995. Rompelberg was traveling in the slipstream of a dragster in a process known as "motor-pacing."

11 feet

(3.3 m). The wheel diameter of the world's largest rideable bicycle. The bike is 25.6 feet (7.8 m) long and 12 feet (3.7 m) high. It was built by German Didi Senft, also known as El Diablo because of his habit of turning up at bike race, Le Tour de France, dressed as a devil. Senft has also created bikes in the shape of a guitar, a fish, and the Eiffel Tower.

712

The number of cities worldwide that operate bicycle share schemes. Between them they provide more than 800,000 bikes.

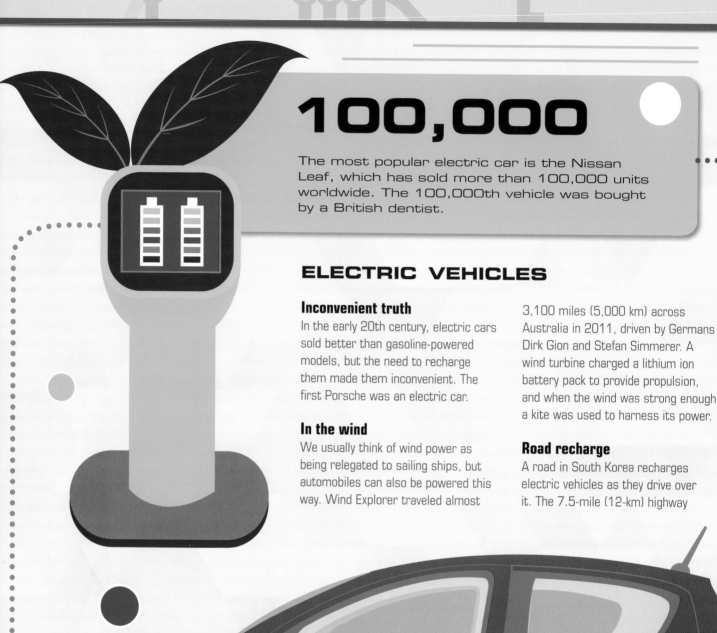

100,000

The most popular electric car is the Nissan Leaf, which has sold more than 100,000 units worldwide. The 100,000th vehicle was bought by a British dentist.

ELECTRIC VEHICLES

Inconvenient truth

In the early 20th century, electric cars sold better than gasoline-powered models, but the need to recharge them made them inconvenient. The first Porsche was an electric car.

In the wind

We usually think of wind power as being relegated to sailing ships, but automobiles can also be powered this way. Wind Explorer traveled almost

3,100 miles (5,000 km) across Australia in 2011, driven by Germans Dirk Gion and Stefan Simmerer. A wind turbine charged a lithium ion battery pack to provide propulsion, and when the wind was strong enough a kite was used to harness its power.

Road recharge

A road in South Korea recharges electric vehicles as they drive over it. The 7.5-mile (12-km) highway

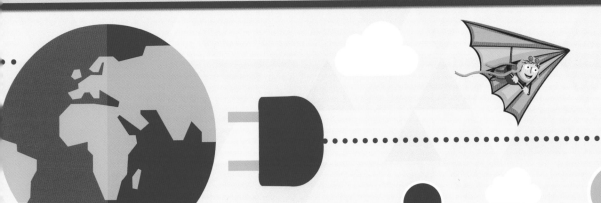

means vehicles fitted with compatible equipment don't need to stop to recharge and can also be fitted with smaller than normal batteries. A number of buses are already using the service.

Winning formula
Formula E is the world's first fully electric racing series. Launched in 2014, the first season kicked off in Beijing, China, and featured ten teams with two drivers each. The first race was won by Brazilian Lucas di Grassi from team Audi Sport ABT.

Wired up
Iconic motorcycle company Harley-Davidson is working on an electric motorbike. The Project LiveWire

prototype bikes are not for sale, but have been touring the United States. The bike can go 130 miles (210 km) before it needs charging and will offer riders a top speed of 92 mph (148 km/h). Recharges will take between 30 minutes to one hour.

Need for noise
The quietness of electric automobiles is sometimes used as a selling point, but research has shown the lack of noise can pose a danger to pedestrians and cyclists. A number of countries worldwide are working on legislation that will compel e-cars to make warning noises, including the United States and the countries of the European Union.

Solar power
The Nuna series is a set of solar-powered automobiles that are among the fastest in the world, having won the World Solar Challenge more than four times. Nuna 7, which won the 2013 World Challenge, is powered by 391 solar cells and has an average speed of 56.36 mph (90.71 km/h).

307.666 mph
(495.140 km/h)

The speed achieved by the Venturi Buckeye Bullet 2, designed and built by engineering students at the Ohio State University. The e-car was driven by American Roger Schroer at the Bonneville Salt Flats, Utah, on August 24, 2010.

RECORD BREAKERS

FASTEST

The Bugatti Veyron is a four-wheel-drive sports car with an engine more powerful than most Formula One racing cars. The Super Sport version of the Veyron is the fastest production automobile in the world, with a top speed of 268 mph (431 km/h).

SMALLEST

The Peel P50 is the world's smallest production automobile and was built in the 1960s on the Isle of Man. The P50 has no reverse gear—to turn it around, the driver has to get out and lift it up using a handle on the back. Its top speed is 38 mph (61 km/h).

LONGEST

The world's longest automobile is a 100-foot (30.5-m) long 26-wheeled limousine, designed by Jay Ohrberg of California. The limo contains a swimming pool with a diving board and a king-size waterbed. Other cars designed by Ohrberg include the DeLorean from *Back to the Future*, the Batmobile, and KITT, driven by Michael Knight in TV's *Knight Rider*.

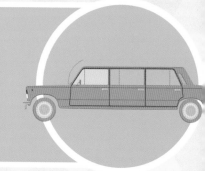

FASTEST ACCELERATION

The Hennessey Venom GT supercar holds the record for the fastest 0–300 km/h by a production automobile, hitting an amazing 186 mph in only 13.63 seconds. The car is powered by a 7-liter V8 engine.

BEST-SELLING

The world's best-selling automobile is the Toyota Corolla—more than 40 million have been sold since it launched in 1966, although the vehicle has been through a number of redesigns.

FARTHEST TRAVELED

Swiss couple Emil and Liliana Schmid have traveled 430,130 miles (692,227 km) and counting in their Toyota Land Cruiser. Their voyage, which has taken them to 180 countries so far, began on October 18, 1984, and is still ongoing.

FIRST CIRCUMNAVIGATION

The first car to drive around the world was driven by German racing driver Clara Eleonore Stinnes, accompanied by Swedish moviemaker Carl-Axel Söderström. They set off from Frankfurt on May 25, 1927, in an Adler Standard 6. The two met only two days before the trip but married shortly after they returned, two years and one month later.

FIRST CIRCUMNAVIGATION BY AMPHIBIOUS VEHICLE

Australian adventurer Ben Carlin had the opposite experience during his journey around the world, which was the first and only circumnavigation in an amphibious vehicle, traveling by sea and land. The trip, which started out as a honeymoon, took ten years, and Carlin's wife left halfway through.

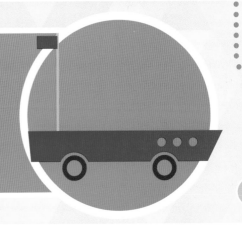

FASTEST STEAM-POWERED CAR

The record for the world's fastest steam-powered car was held by the American Stanley Steamer for more than 100 years, until it was beaten in 2009 by British-made vehicle *Inspiration*. It set a new world record of 151 mph (243 km/h).

FARTHEST TRAVELED ON A SINGLE TANK OF FUEL

Couple Helen and John Taylor managed to travel 1,626.1 miles (2,616.95 km) on a single tank of fuel in 2012. Their Volkswagen Passat averaged 84.1 miles per gallon (100 km for every 2.79 liters) of fuel.

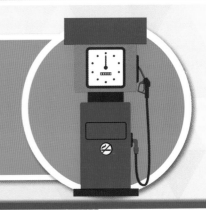

6 feet 2 inches

(1.88 m). Toyota chopped the roof off its 2000GT, turning it into a convertible as Sean Connery was too tall for the hardtop version in *You Only Live Twice* (1967).

JAMES BOND CARS

One careful owner

The first of 007's many vehicles was the humble Sunbeam Alpine he drove in *Dr. No* (1962). It was curiously gadget free and had a 0–60 mph (0–96.6 km/h) time of 13.6 seconds.

Gadgets aplenty

The Aston Martin DB5 from *Goldfinger* (1964) is many fans' favorite Bond vehicle. Its stylish chassis bristled with gadgets, including a revolving license plate, GPS dashboard, tire slashers, a smokescreen, machine guns, and, of course, the passenger ejector seat.

Yellow peril

Bond drove a yellow Citroen 2CV in *For Your Eyes Only* (1981) in one of his more memorable chase scenes. After being given a bump start, it drives backward down a mountain road, and leaps over the car of the pursuing baddies.

Vanishing trick

As well as machine guns and missile launchers, the Aston Martin Vanquish from *Die Another Day* (2002) had a cloaking device to hide from enemies.

Ford's gamble

The Ford Mondeo in *Casino Royale* (2006) had to be handmade as the movie was made so far ahead of the car's launch.

BURIED TREASURE

The Lotus Esprit, featured in *The Spy Who Loved Me* (1977), turned up in 1989 in a cargo container that was bought at a blind auction for $100. The submarine car went on to sell for £550,000 ($685,000) at auction in 2013.

RAILS

1768

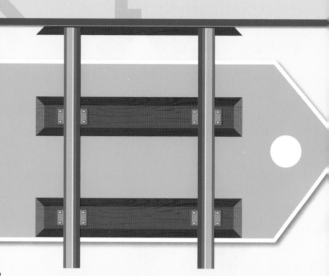

The Coalbrookdale Company of Shropshire, England, began producing the first iron rails, replacing the wooden ones on its wagonways.

THE EARLY DAYS OF RAIL

In a rut
The first railroads were made by the ancient civilizations, including the Assyrians, Babylonians, Persians, and Greeks, who cut ruts into tracks so that their carts would run more smoothly.

Cart tracks
One of the greatest concentrations of cart ruts is in Malta at the prehistoric site of Misrah Ghar il-Kbir. The multiple rutted tracks were nicknamed "Clapham Junction" by the English, after the busy London railroad station.

Over land to sea
The ancient Greeks used a rudimentary form of railroad to transport their ships across land at the Isthmus of Corinth. Named the Diolkos, the 3.7-mile (6-km) route saved captains a perilous trip around the Peloponnese and operated from about 600 BCE.

On track
Prior to steam power, wagonways allowed greater weights to be pulled by horses, or pushed by men. Early examples in 16th-century coal mines in Keswick, England, used slots between boarded tracks, to keep wagon wheels on track.

Trevithick's triumph
The first railroad locomotive journey was to win a bet of 500 guineas (£525). On February 21, 1804, a locomotive designed by mining engineer Richard Trevithick pulled a load of 10 tons (9 tonnes) of iron from the Penydarren ironworks in South Wales to a canal 9.75 miles (16 km) away. The journey took more than four hours at a speed of around 2.4 mph (3.9 km/h).

American engine
The first American steam locomotive is thought to have been John Stevens' steam waggon of 1825. The inventor ran the locomotive on a circular track on his Hoboken estate.

Enter the Rocket
In 1829, a competition was held to find a faster and more reliable locomotive for the new Liverpool & Manchester Railway in northern

1604

The Wollaton Wagonway is often credited as the first overground wagonway. It ran for 2 miles (3.2 km), transporting coal on the land of Sir Percival Willoughby in Nottinghamshire, England.

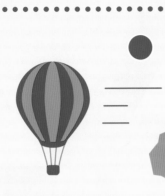

England. The winner was George Stephenson's *Rocket*, which was the only one of five locomotives to complete the 1-mile (1.6-km) trial at Rainhill in Lancashire. It achieved a record speed of 29 mph (47 km/h). Stephenson won the £500 prize and the contract to produce locomotives.

Coal train

The Stockton and Darlington line in England was the first public railroad and opened on September 27, 1825, to move coal to the nearby port. The initial journey of 9 miles (14.5 km) took around two hours.

4x

Four times as much coal could be pulled by a horse-drawn wagon on a railroad, compared to a standard wagon on a road.

THE LAST OF STEAM

As well as many heritage railroads, there are still a few places around the world where steam locomotives remain in service:

- **China**—steam locomotives are still used by industry.
- **Germany**—in East Germany and on the Baltic Coast there are several lines that operate a year-round service.
- **Poland**—daily steam locomotives run in the Wolsztyn area.
- **Zimbabwe**—working Beyer-Garratt locomotives are to be found in Bulawayo.

AGE OF STEAM

Speed kills
In 1830, London Professor Dionysius Lardner issued a warning that train passengers traveling at high speeds would be unable to breathe and would die of asphyxia.

Manic building
Between 1830 and 1850, some 6,000 miles (9,650 km) of public railroads were built in Britain in what became known as "Railway Mania."

High five
There were at least five different gauges (the distance between railroad tracks) in Victorian Britain, meaning that trains could not run on all lines. A standard gauge was not agreed on until the 1890s, when most

100 mph

(160 km/h). The first steam locomotive to travel at this speed was the Flying Scotsman on November 30, 1934.

companies adopted the so-called Stephenson Gauge of 4 feet 8½ inches (1,435 mm). About 60 percent of world railroads still use this gauge.

Safety whistle
George Stephenson also designed the world's first locomotive whistle to improve safety, after the engine *Samson* collided with a horse and cart on the Leicester to Swannington line in England.

On your marks
The first American steam locomotive lost a race to a horse-drawn wagon. Engineer Peter Cooper was testing his *Tom Thumb* locomotive on the Baltimore & Ohio railroad on August 28, 1830, when he was challenged.

He lost because of a mechanical problem, but railroad executives were impressed enough to convert from horse-drawn trains to steam.

Continental travel
On May 10, 1866, the east and west coasts of North America were linked by railroad as the Union Pacific and Central Pacific Railroads were joined. This 2,983-mile (4,800-km) long railroad enabled people to travel from New York to California in days.

Big engines
The largest steam locomotives ever were the "Big Boys," which operated on the Union Pacific Railroad. Built by the American Locomotive Co., the

engines could generate 6,300 horse-power to pull freight over mountains.

Moving pictures
Cinematic pioneers, the Lumière brothers, made a steam locomotive arriving at a station in the French seaside town of La Ciotat the subject of their first movie screening in 1895.

125.88 mph

(202.58 km/h). *Mallard* remains the fastest steam locomotive ever, reaching this speed on July 3, 1938, on track near Grantham in England.

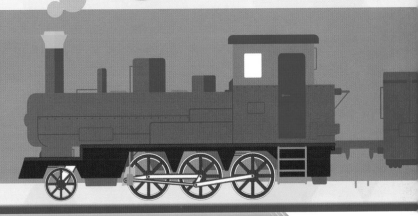

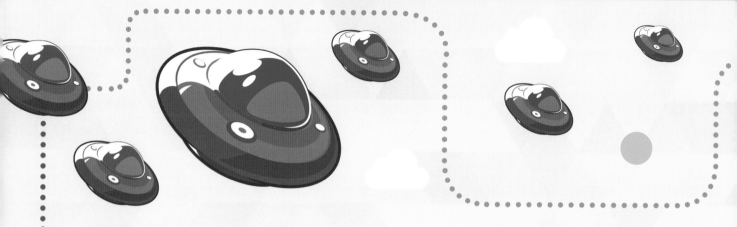

MODERN TRAINS

Clean options

By the 1940s, railroad companies were beginning to explore alternative methods of powering their locomotives as steam power was dirty and inefficient. Diesel and electric power were the preferred options.

Doubling up

Double decker trains first ran in France in the second half of the 19th century. Today they are widely used as a way of increasing passenger capacity.

Tram competition

Britain's first electrified suburban railroad line was opened between Newcastle and Benton in 1904, after the North Eastern Railway company introduced wholesale electrification to try and win back the two million passengers it had lost to trams.

Going nuclear

In the 1950s, British Rail considered nuclear-powered locomotives. In 1970 the organization also filed a patent for a nuclear-powered flying saucer.

Wind powered locos

Dutch trains will be completely windpowered by 2018. The country's train system is being supplied by wind energy from domestic wind farms and those in Belgium and Scandinavia.

Busiest station

Shinjuku rail station in Tokyo is the busiest in the world, with more than three million people using it every day. It has 36 platforms, more than 200 exits, and caters for 25,000 trains a day—one every three seconds. In fact, Japan accounts for all five of the world's busiest stations.

The big network

The United States has the world's largest rail network with 139,200 miles (224,000 km) of track crisscrossing the country. This is more than twice as much as the country with the second-largest network, China, which has 62,000 miles (100,000 km).

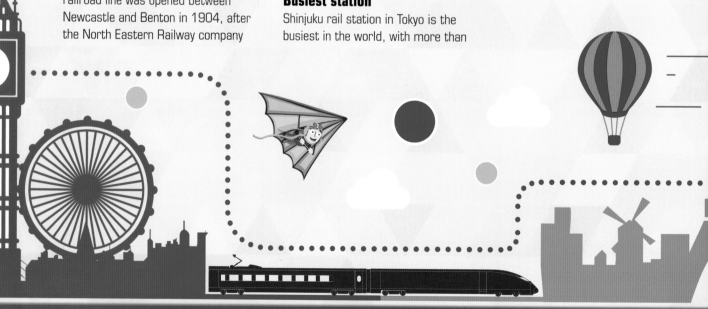

FAST TRAINS

375 mph (603 km/h)
Japan's LO series Maglev train reached this speed on a test track.

302 mph (486 km/h)
China's CRH380A is the fastest legal way to travel by land. It hit this speed in tests but generally travels at up to 236 mph (380 km/h).

268 mph (431 km/h)
Shanghai's Maglev train covers an 18 mile (29 km) trip to the airport in just eight minutes.

219 mph (352 km/h)
South Korea's KTX 2 is designed for this speed although normal speeds are nearer 190 mph (305 km/h).

199 mph (320 km/h)
The operating speed of Japan's Shinkansen train, called the "Duck-Billed Platypus" after its aerodynamic nose.

357 mph (574.8 km/h)
France's high speed train LGV Est reached this speed in tests in 2007.

279 mph (449 km/h)
The top speed of Germany's experimental Transrapid TR-09 which uses magnetic levitation (Maglev) technology.

224 mph (360 km/h)
Italy's AGV Italo's maximum operational speed, although it hit 357 mph (575 km/h) in testing.

217 mph (350 km/h)
The operating speed of Spanish AVE Talgo-350 on the Madrid to Barcelona line.

199 mph (320 km/h)
The Eurostar connects London and Paris, traveling under the English Channel.

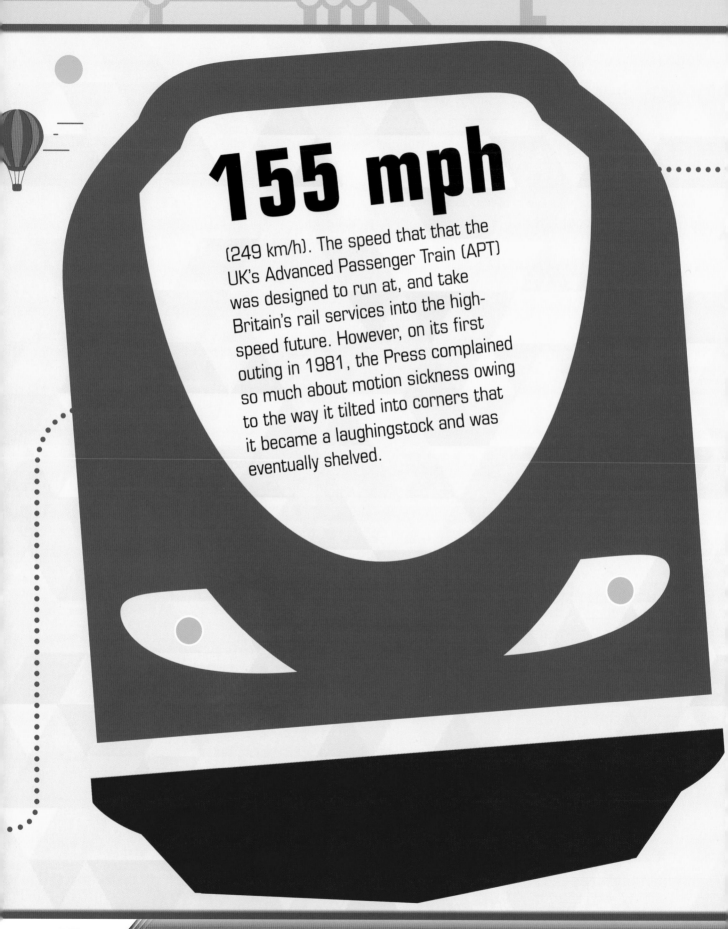

155 mph

(249 km/h). The speed that that the UK's Advanced Passenger Train (APT) was designed to run at, and take Britain's rail services into the high-speed future. However, on its first outing in 1981, the Press complained so much about motion sickness owing to the way it tilted into corners that it became a laughingstock and was eventually shelved.

1.3 MILLION

staff are employed by Indian Railways, making it the largest rail employer in the world. It is the seventh largest employer in the world overall.

Take a book

Not surprisingly given the size of the country, Russia is home to the three longest rail services in the world. The longest, the Trans-Siberian Express from Moscow to Vladivostok is 5,753 miles (9,259 km) in length, takes seven days to complete, and stops at 67 stations.

Long run

The longest passenger train ran in Belgium on April 27, 1991. The one-off service raised money for charity and consisted of 70 coaches pulled by one electric locomotive. It was 1 mile (1.6 km) long and traveled 39 miles (63 km) from Ghent to Ostend.

Iron horse

Freight trains can be much longer, with trains transporting ore and coal often more than 2 miles (3 km) long. The Guinness World Record for longest freight train is held by a BHP iron-ore train in Australia. The record, set on June 21, 2001, was for a train 4.569 miles (7.353 km) long, made up of 682 loaded iron ore wagons and eight locomotives with a total weight of 110,230 tons (100,000 tonnes). It traveled 171 miles (275 km) and was controlled by one driver.

Grand place

The largest train station by number of platforms is New York's Grand Central Terminal, which has 44 and occupies a site covering 48 acres (19 ha).

Secret source

Grand Central also has a secret subbasement, M42, which supplies electricity to the Terminal and was not acknowledged by the owners until the 1980s.

Cleaning up

Steam locomotives could return to the world if researchers are successful. Scientists at the University of Minnesota are studying the use of bio-coal to power a new breed of cleaner, more efficient steam engine.

Wired trains

Trains running between Sweden and Norway were the first in the world to have Wi-Fi onboard when the Linx trains offered the service in 2002.

1895

The first electric mainline service opened on the Baltimore Belt Line, a 4-mile (6.4-km) section of the Baltimore and Ohio Railroad.

346 feet

Arsenalna station on Kiev Metro is the world's deepest underground station at 346 feet (105.5m).

SUBWAY

Meet the Met
The world's first subway was the Metropolitan Railway in London, which opened in 1863 and ran from Paddington to Farringdon. It carried 38,000 people on the first day and 9.5 million in the first year.

Deep breaths
The tunnel for the first subway had little ventilation, resulting in noxious smoke. The owners of the railroad took to claiming that traveling in its smoky confines could cure ailments such as asthma.

Manners please
Tokyo's metro system has introduced women-only carriages during the morning rush hours. Its Subway Manners guidebook advises passengers to set their cells to silent and refrain from talking during journeys.

Pneumatic railroads
London is also home to the second-oldest underground railroad in the world, the London Pneumatic Despatch Railway (LDPR), which used air pressure to blow mail trains under the capital's streets from 1863 to 1874. Thrill-seeking passengers, including Napoleon III, enjoyed rides in its small cars.

Safety doors
The first station in the world with platform screen doors was Park Pobedy on the St. Petersburg Metro in 1961.

Wooden trains
Buenos Aires subway used wooden train carriages for nearly 100 years until they were phased out in early 2013 and replaced by modern Chinese carriages.

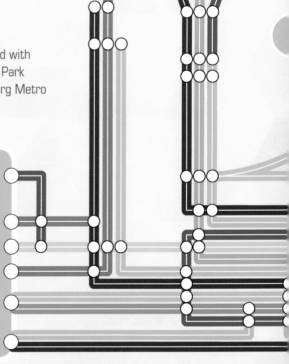

6.5 miles

For 76 years mail in London was transported 6.5 miles (10.5 km) on an underground mail railroad. The tiny trains visited eight sorting offices, collecting sacks of mail and avoiding traffic congestion above ground. The last collection was in 2003.

16 HOURS, 14 MINUTES, AND 10 SECONDS

is the record for visiting all 270 London Underground stations. It is jointly held by Ronan McDonald and Clive Burgess.

African first

Cairo Underground was the first subway in Africa and the Middle East when it opened in 1987.

Shanghai surprise

In 2010, Shanghai Metro overtook London Underground as the world's largest urban transit system, covering 260 miles (420 km) and 278 stations. New York's Subway has the largest number of stations at 468.

Art on the go

Moscow Metro has a moving art gallery. The Aquarelle train displays copies of renowned works of art every year to celebrate the opening of the Metro on May 15, 1935.

Not Bad!

Michael Jackson shot the music video for "Bad" at the Hoyt-Schermerhorn subway station in New York. However, the city's transportation chiefs have rejected proposals to install a memorial to the King of Pop at the station.

FUNICULARS

Balanced approach

Funiculars use a counterbalancing system where two cars, attached by cable round a pulley, minimize the amount of energy required to move the car up a slope. As one goes down, the other goes up.

Swiss leaders

Not surprisingly given its mountainous terrain, Switzerland has the greatest concentration of funiculars in the world, with more than 50 commercially operated lines.

Quick rise

The shortest funicular ride in the world is thought to be the Zagreb Funicular which is only 217 feet (66 m) long.

2.6 miles

On December 16, 1997, the two sections of the Sierre-Montana-Crans funicular were joined into a single section, making it the world's longest funicular at 2.6 miles (4.2 km). It links the Swiss town of Sierre, in the Rhône valley, to the Crans-Montana-Vermala resort, via a 12-minute ride.

155

people died in a fire on the Kaprun funicular in Austria on November 11, 2000. The car was transporting skiers to the nearby slopes.

Steepest

The steepest funicular in the world is the incline elevator, Katoomba Scenic Railway, in Australia, where the steepest part reaches 52 degrees. It was originally constructed to haul the coal and shale for a mining operation in the Jamison Valley in the 1880s.

Hot stuff

Active volcano Mount Vesuvius had its own funicular to transport daredevil travelers to the summit from 1880 to 1944, when it was destroyed by an eruption. Despite this, serious thought has been given to rebuilding a rail on Vesuvius.

Oldest ride

The Reisszug is believed to be the oldest funicular in the world, possibly dating back to 1495. The private funicular provides goods access to the Hohensalzburg Castle at Salzburg in Austria.

Subterranean funicular

While most funiculars provide fantastic views, the Carmelit Haifa Subway in Israel is entirely underground. It links six stations during an eight-minute ride, and is Israel's only subway.

11,674 STEPS

The Swiss Niesenbahn funicular has the world's longest stairway running alongside it. The service stairway runs beside the 2.2 miles (3.5 km) of the railroad and once a year is open to the public for a charity stair race up it.

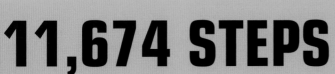

£399

($927) was the cost of the British electrical tricycle, the Sinclair C5, on its 1985 launch. Devised as an innovative, cheap form of transportation, the vehicle flopped, with only about 17,000 sold.

WEIRD AND WACKY TRANSPORTATION

Takes the cake

Two U.S. chefs created a car made entirely out of cake, apart from the tires, chassis, and brakes. The car could be driven and reached 28 mph (45 km/h) on March 4, 2012, when cake maker Carey Iennaccaro drove it down a street in Kansas City, Kansas.

Tight fit

The smallest roadworthy car was built by Austin Coulson of Phoenix, Arizona, and stands 25 inches (63.5 cm) high, 26 inches (65.41 cm) wide and 50 inches (126.47 cm) long. Its paintwork is themed after the P-51 Mustang military aircraft and the sides are inscribed with the tail numbers of a ship served on by Coulson's grandfather during World War II.

Quick breakfast

The world's fastest milk float runs on a 4,500 cc Rover V8 engine and can reach a speed of 84.556 mph (136.081 km/h). It was created by breakfast cereal company Weetabix to promote a new drink and includes BMW wheels, a chrome spoiler, a front bull bar, four roof-mounted spotlights— and a flamethrower.

Colin's creations

UK inventor—or, as he styles himself, "plumber"—Colin Furze has built a motorized pram capable of reaching a speed of 53.46 mph (86.04 km/h). Furze's creations also include a 25-seater motorcycle and a jet-propelled bicycle.

You've got to go

The fastest toilet traveling under its own power is the "Bog Standard," a motorcycle and sidecar hidden under a bathroom set consisting of bathtub, sink, and laundry bin, which can travel at up to 42.25 mph (68 km/h) and

119

The largest parade of Segways took place in Potsdam, Germany, on July 28, 2011. There were originally 120 of the two-wheeled electric scooters, but one dropped out.

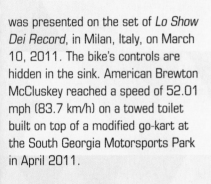

was presented on the set of *Lo Show Dei Record*, in Milan, Italy, on March 10, 2011. The bike's controls are hidden in the sink. American Brewton McCluskey reached a speed of 52.01 mph (83.7 km/h) on a towed toilet built on top of a modified go-kart at the South Georgia Motorsports Park in April 2011.

What's the tip?

The longest distance driven in a taxi is 43,319 miles (69,716 km) by the UK's Leigh Purnell, Paul Archer, and Johno Ellison. The three left Covent Garden, London, in the black cab (called Hannah) on February 17, 2011, and returned on May 11, 2012. The meter read £79,006.80 ($126,400).

1,700+

The world's worst rail disaster occurred in Sri Lanka on December 26, 2004, when a tsunami wave hit a crowded train. Exact numbers of dead are unknown as many bodies were swept out to sea before authorities could respond.

RAIL CRASHES

July 25, 1832

The first recorded rail accident in the USA happened on this date when four passengers were thrown from a coach and over a cliff in Quincy, Massachusetts.

Clean getaway

A train cleaner in Stockholm, Sweden, accidentally started the engine in January 2013 and was unable to stop it. The train jumped the tracks and crashed into a house. Apart from the cleaner, no one was hurt.

Bridge down

There were 59 victims from a train crossing the Tay Bridge near Dundee in Scotland on December 20, 1879, when the bridge collapsed in a severe storm. As a result of the disaster bridges were required to have a greater ability to withstand high winds.

Falling train

On October 22, 1895, a train overshot the buffers at Paris's Gare Montparnasse station, falling on to the street 33 feet (10 m) below, where it remained propped on its nose. The one fatality was a woman who was killed by falling masonry.

Wheel failure

A single fatigue crack in the wheel of a high-speed train led to 101 deaths at Eschede in Germany. The incident, on June 3, 1998, is Germany's worst rail accident.

Sacred beasts

Cows have been associated with a number of rail disasters. More than 500 passengers were killed on June 6, 1981, when an engineer braked to avoid hitting a cow, causing the train to plunge into the Baghmati River in India. Over 350 people were killed at Firozabad in 1995, when a train was hit from behind after stopping to avoid hitting a cow.

AFLOAT

27,000

The approximate number of men in the fleet of Chinese admiral—and eunuch—Zheng He, who led a fleet of 62 massive 417-foot (127-m) treasure ships and around 90 smaller ships on an expedition to east Africa in 1405. Zheng He had been castrated after being captured by enemy soldiers as a child.

AGE OF SAIL

World traveler

Portuguese explorer Ferdinand Magellan is often credited as being the first to circumnavigate the globe, but he was actually hacked to death during a fight with natives in the Philippines and never made it all the way round. Four ships and most of the 237-strong crew were lost on the voyage (1519–22), and only 18 men returned in the *Victoria*.

Cook's cabbage

Englishman Captain James Cook (1728–79) always took a supply of fermented cabbage (sauerkraut) on his voyages. He was one of the first to realize

that scurvy, a disease causing painful gums and bleeding beneath the skin, could be prevented if sailors ate plenty of fruit and vegetables.

Mystery solved?

The *Mary Celeste* is synonymous with mystery, but the actual facts may not be so mysterious. The ship was found deserted in December 1872. However, ships' crews often went missing in the 19th century and no one paid much attention until Sherlock Holmes author, Arthur Conan Doyle, wrote a story about the vessel. It is likely that the captain, his wife, daughter, and crew of seven abandoned ship when they feared their cargo of alcohol was about to explode and then died at sea.

Cannibal coincidence

Richard Parker was a 17-year-old cabin boy on board the yacht *Mignonette* when she sank in 1884—he was killed and eaten by the rest of the crew as they drifted on a lifeboat. By coincidence Richard Parker was also the name of a character in a novel by Edgar Allen Poe who is killed and eaten after a ship capsizes—the book was written nearly 50 years before the *Mignonette* disaster.

Lady pirates

The pirate ship *Revenge*, commanded by notorious English pirate Calico Jack, was unusual in having two women in the crew. Anne Bonny and Mary Read were both convicted of piracy in Jamaica in 1720, but both

escaped hanging, claiming they were pregnant by announcing to the judge, "Mi'lord, we plead our bellies." As British law forbade the killing of an unborn child, their sentences were temporarily stayed.

Picture this

Tattoos have been popular with sailors since Cook and his crew visited the tattooed Maori of the South Pacific in the 1700s. Tattoos had different meanings—an anchor showed a seaman had sailed the Atlantic Ocean, while a shellback turtle showed he had crossed the equator. A pig on one foot and a rooster on the other were supposed to save him from drowning.

99 DAYS

was the time taken by speedy clippers to carry tea 14,000 miles (22,530 km) from China to London. The Great Tea Race of 1866 saw three ships docked within an hour and a quarter of each other.

1854

The date of the construction of the PS *Skibladner*, the oldest steamship still in regular operation. Built in Sweden, the paddle steamer now carries tourists across Norway's Lake Mjøsa.

AGE OF STEAM

Speedy Sirius
The first ship to cross the Atlantic under steam power was the SS *Sirius*, a small 700-ton paddler. Brunel's SS *Great Western* began its crossing a few days after the *Sirius* but arrived in New York just a day later, having traveled at a higher average speed.

Doomed camel
The gymnasium in the ill-fated RMS *Titanic* had a mechanical camel that passengers rode for exercise. It cost a shilling to ride. On the fateful night of April 14–15, 1912, when the ship hit an iceberg, Thomas McCauley, the gym instructor, remained at his post in the gymnasium and went down with the ship.

Imprisoned inventor
The inventor of the first steamship was incarcerated in the same French prison as the mysterious Man in the Iron Mask. After his release in 1775—he had been locked up for dueling—the Marquis de Jouffroy built a steamship that floated for about 15 minutes. He wasn't able to continue his research though, as the French Revolution drove him out of France.

Last message
The SS *Pacific*, a transatlantic steamship, disappeared on a journey from Liverpool to New York. No one knew what had happened to her until a message in a bottle was discovered off a remote Scottish island seven years later. The note said the ship had sunk surrounded by icebergs.

Mississippi Mark
Writer Mark Twain, the creator of Tom Sawyer and Huckleberry Finn, piloted steamships on the Mississippi River before becoming a novelist. Born Samuel Clemens, he took his pen-name from the cry of "Mark twain!" often heard on the river— meaning that the water was two fathoms deep.

3 DAYS, 10 HOURS, AND 40 MINUTES

The time taken to cross the Atlantic by the SS *United States* on its maiden voyage in 1953. The liner was the last holder of the Blue Riband, an award for the fastest Atlantic crossing. Twenty-five winners were British, five German, and three American, with one each from Italy and France.

Engine driver

When steamships were introduced, they brought with them a whole new type of seafarer—the marine engineer, sometimes sarcastically called the "engine driver" by the rest of the crew. Many engineers had driven steam locomotives before working on ships.

Fact or fiction?

Fourteen years before the sinking of the *Titanic*, author Morgan Robertson wrote a novel called *Futility, or the Wreck of the Titan*. In it the "unsinkable" *Titan* strikes an iceberg on the starboard side 400 miles (644 km) from Newfoundland and sinks, with tragic consequences. Fourteen years later in 1912, the *Titanic* struck an iceberg on the starboard side 400 miles (644 km) from Newfoundland and sank, with tragic consequences.

19,224

The number of 20-foot (6-m) shipping containers that can be carried by MSC *Oscar*, the world's largest container ship. The Mediterranean Shipping Company vessel is 1,297 feet (395.4 m) long and 194 feet (59 m) wide—the size of four soccer pitches—and set sail in January 2015.

MODERN SHIPPING

Globetrotting

MS *The World*, a 644-foot (196.3-m) ship that launched in 2002, does not have passengers —it has residents. Rather than a ticket, residents buy one of 165 sets of rooms and make the boat their home. The ship travels around the globe—in 2014, destinations included Morocco, Iceland, the Seychelles, and Antarctica.

Pirate attacks

Along with the swimming pools and sun loungers, cruise liners are increasingly carrying weapons such as sonic devices and water cannons to ward off pirates. The luxury cruise ship, *Seabourn Spirit*, employed a long-range acoustic device in 2005 against Somalian pirates attacking with rocket launchers, while the *Spirit of Adventure* did the same in 2011 in the Indian Ocean.

Sibling rivalry

The world's largest cruise ship pips its sister to the title by only a couple of inches. The Oasis-class MS *Allure of the Seas* is said to be 2 inches (50 mm) longer than sister ship MS *Oasis of the Seas*, owned by Royal Caribbean International, although both are officially 1,181 feet (360 m) long. However, both vessels will be dwarfed by their younger sister—when she

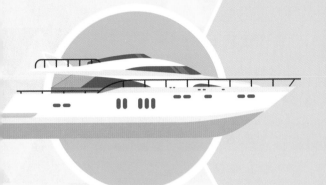

$605M

The estimated cost of the *Azzam* (Arabic for Resolute), the largest private yacht in the world at 590 feet (180 m) in length. Built by Lürssen Yachts and launched on April 5, 2013, the *Azzam* was commissioned by the president of the United Arab Emirates.

launches in 2016, this vessel will be 7 feet (2.1 m) longer.

Waste not
A cruise ship carrying 3,000 passengers generates approximately 176,000 gallons (800,000 liters) of raw sewage every week. Modern cruise ships usually recycle "blackwater" (sewage) and "greywater," such as waste from showers. The resulting liquid, although said to be "near drinkable," is for technical use only.

Huge hovercraft
The world's biggest hovercrafts are the Ukranian Zubr, known to NATO

as Pomornik, which are 187 feet (57 m) in length and have a full-load displacement of 555 tons. The craft are designed to move assault units from ship to shore, as well as transport and plant mines.

Polar explorer
The first surface ship to reach the geographic North Pole was the Soviet nuclear-powered ice breaker, NS *Arktika*, on August 17, 1977. Launched in 1974, and operational until 2008, she was able to break through sea ice 16 feet (5 m) thick.

Floating volcano
Yachts nowadays come in all shapes and sizes. The 295-foot (90-m) concept yacht, *Tropical Island Paradise*, is designed to resemble a floating tropical island and comes with its own volcano, with a cascading waterfall feeding an onboard swimming pool.

275.97 KNOTS

(317.58 mph)

The official world waterspeed record, held by Ken Warby in the unlimited class jet-powered hydroplane, *Spirit of Australia*. The record-breaking ride took place on Blowering Dam Lake, New South Wales, Australia, on October 8, 1978.

Fast ferry

The fastest car ferry in the world speeds across the estuary between Buenos Aires, Argentina, and Montevideo, Uruguay. The *Francisco* catamaran has a maximum speed of 58.1 knots (67 mph/107.6 km/h) and can carry up to 1,024 passengers and 150 automobiles.

Name game

The most popular boat name in the United States is *Serenity*, followed by *Second Wind* and *Island Girl*. In the UK, the most popular name for a canal boat is *Kingfisher*, followed by *Dragonfly* and *Phoenix*.

Beer boats

The annual Beer Can Regatta in Darwin, Australia, is a competition in which all boats have to be made from beer cans—or soft drink cans for the kids. Other odd boat races around the world include the U.S. Concrete Canoe Championship, the International Regatta of Bathtubs in Belgium, and the Milk Carton Boat Race, part of the Milk, Bread, and Honey Festival in Jelgava, Latvia.

Flag it up

Although Panama is a small nation of around three million people, it has the largest shipping fleet in the world—bigger than those of the United States and China put together. Around 8,600 ships fly the Panamanian flag. Worldwide, three quarters of ships are registered under the flag of a country not their own.

Scrap value

The largest ship ever scrapped—and until recently the largest ship ever built—was the Ultra Large Crude Carrier (ULCC) *Seawise Giant*, later renamed *Happy Giant*, *Jahre Viking*, *Knock Nevis*, *Oppama*, and *Mont*. She was 1,504 feet (458.45 m) long and could carry a weight of 623,000 tons (565,000 tonnes). She was scrapped at the Alang ship-breaking yard in India in 2010.

20 YEARS

The length of time the U.S. Navy's nuclear-powered *Nimitz*-class aircraft carriers can go without refueling. At 984 feet (300 m) long they are the biggest warships ever built, able to carry around 80 aircraft and more than 5,000 crew.

1,600 feet

The length of the biggest ship in the world, the *Prelude FLNG*, currently under construction in South Korea for energy giant Shell. At 1,600 feet (488 m) the vessel is longer than the Empire State Building is tall. It will act as the world's first floating liquefied natural gas platform, incorporating a factory and storage facility.

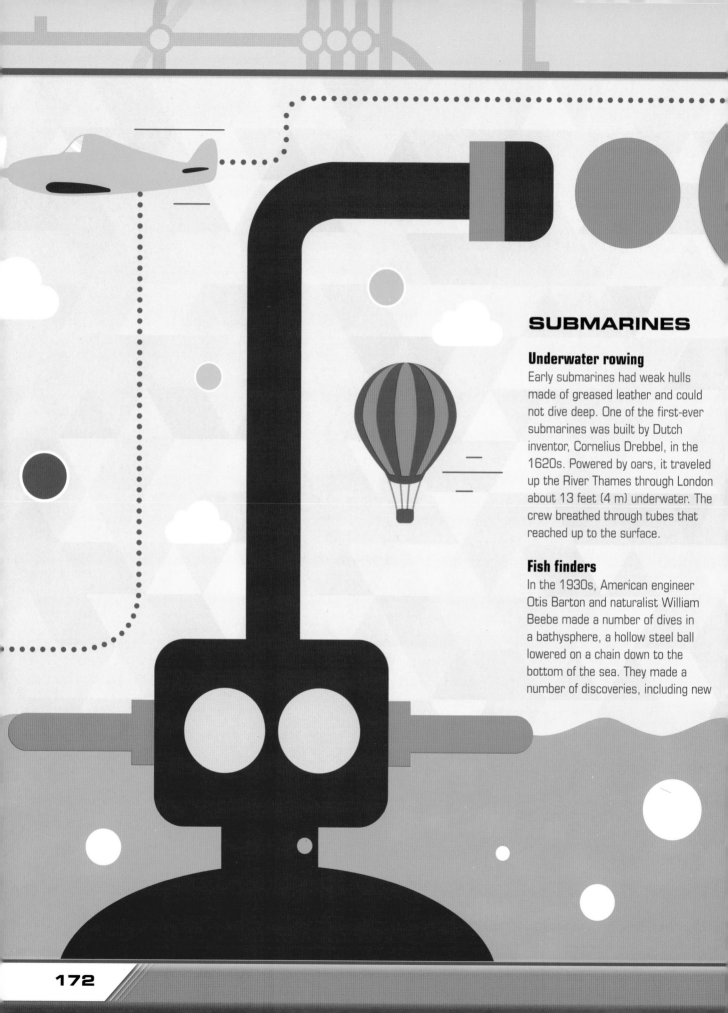

SUBMARINES

Underwater rowing

Early submarines had weak hulls made of greased leather and could not dive deep. One of the first-ever submarines was built by Dutch inventor, Cornelius Drebbel, in the 1620s. Powered by oars, it traveled up the River Thames through London about 13 feet (4 m) underwater. The crew breathed through tubes that reached up to the surface.

Fish finders

In the 1930s, American engineer Otis Barton and naturalist William Beebe made a number of dives in a bathysphere, a hollow steel ball lowered on a chain down to the bottom of the sea. They made a number of discoveries, including new

574 feet

(175 m). The length of the largest submarine in history, the Soviet *Akula*-class vessel, known to the West as Typhoons. With a submerged displacement of 48,000 tons, the nuclear-powered ballistic missile subs were designed to stay under water for 120 days, or more if necessary—in the case of a nuclear war for example.

sea creatures, some of which have never been seen again.

Titanic effort
In 2012, *Titanic* director James Cameron reached the deepest part of the ocean, the Mariana Trench, in a custom-made one-man submersible, the *Deepsea Challenger*. Cameron was the first to make the 6.8-mile (11-km), two hour and 36 minute descent alone. The first to reach that depth were Swiss oceanographer Jacques Piccard and U.S. Navy lieutenant Don Walsh in 1960.

First submarine death
In 1774, English wheelwright John Day invented a diving vessel which he tested out in Plymouth harbour.

He funded the process by getting a friend to place bets on whether he would be able to stay under for 12 hours—expecting to ascend after that time and rake in the cash. Sadly, despite a system of floats that was supposed to alert watchers to danger (red meaning "in indifferent health" and black "in immediate danger"), Day never came back up.

Mile Low Club
Newlyweds with £175,000 ($263,000) to spare can honeymoon in a luxury submarine. *Lovers Deep* can be moored anywhere the happy couple wish, but is usually in the Caribbean, giving spectacular undersea views from the glass-fronted living areas.

Toilet break
A German submarine in World War II was scuttled after it was forced to surface off the coast of Scotland because of a broken toilet, which caused a chlorine gas leak. Some U-boats had very complicated toilets, which needed a special operator to flush them. On surfacing, the U-1206 was bombed by British patrols.

It's for you
The U.S. Navy developed an underwater telephone to communicate with its submarines in 1945. The phone was called Gertrude.

194

The number of ships sunk by German submarine U-35 in World War I. Commander Lothar von Arnauld de la Perière holds the record for most successful submarine commander.

$500 million

The value of the silver and gold coins recovered from the ocean floor around 180 miles (290 km) off Portugal by U.S. company Odyssey Marine Exploration in 2007. The identity of the ship that was carrying the treasure, the most valuable haul ever recovered from a wreck, is uncertain. The coins have been returned to Spain to be held by museums.

SHIPWRECKS

Wartime disaster

The worst shipwreck in history was the sinking of German military ship, the MV *Wilhelm Gustloff*, in January 1945 with an estimated loss of about 9,400 people, including thousands of children. The ship, which was originally going to be called the *Adolf Hitler*, was evacuating refugees and military and technical personnel when it was sunk by a Soviet submarine.

Sunken giant

Ultra Large Crude Carrier, *Energy Determination*, is the world's largest shipwreck. The 322,000-ton vessel blew up and broke in two in the Persian Gulf, in December 1979. The ship was not carrying any cargo at the time but its hull value was $58 million.

133 days

The longest-ever time spent adrift alone at sea. Second Steward Poon Lim of the UK Merchant Navy spent more than four months on an 8-foot (2.5-m) wooden raft after his ship was sunk by a German U-boat in November 1942. Living on seabirds, fish, and rainwater, Poon Lim lost 20 pounds (9 kg) in weight during his ordeal but was able to walk unaided on being rescued.

Ancient wreck

The oldest shipwreck ever discovered was a wooden, single-mast sailing ship wrecked off Uluburun in southern Turkey and dated to the 14th century BCE. The vessel carried an extensive cargo of copper, tin, and glass ingots, jars of resin, gold and silver jewelry, nuts, and spices.

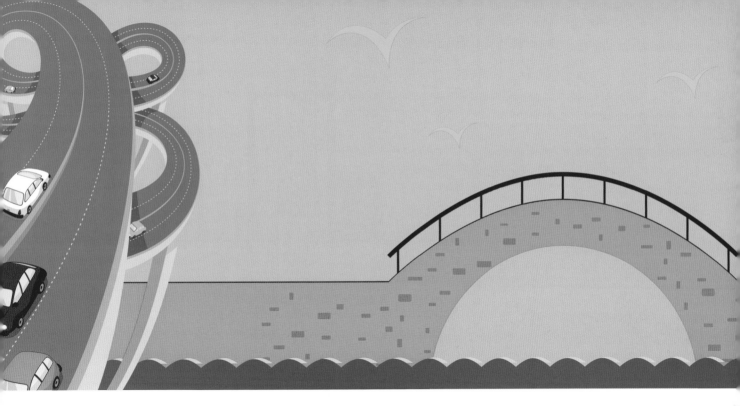

TRANSPORT
NFRASTRUCTURE

1919

Hounslow Heath Aerodrome, London, became the first airport to operate scheduled international flights.

AIRPORTS

Holding pen

In 2016, New York's JFK airport is set to open the world's first terminal for animals. The $48 million facility, The Ark, will be able to deal with cats and dogs, as well as larger animals such as horses and cattle.

Taxi to position

Qamdo Airport in China has the world's longest publicly used paved runway at 3.4 miles (5.5 km). The length is needed because of the airport's altitude (14,219 feet/ 4,334 m above sea level), which affects lift and requires higher than normal liftoff speeds.

Sandy landing

Barra Airport in the Outer Hebrides, Scotland, is the only airport in the world where scheduled flights land on a beach.

In transit

Mehran Karimi Nasseri, an Iranian who claimed he was expelled from his country in 1977, spent nearly 17 years living at Charles de Gaulle Airport outside Paris. He eventually left the airport in 2006 due to illness.

Stop for traffic

Gibraltar Airport is located between the city and a mountain. Its relatively short 5,900-foot (1,800-m) runway intersects Gibraltar's busiest road, which has to be closed every time a plane lands or departs.

Wings of delight

Changi Airport in Singapore houses the first butterfly garden to be found in an airport, with 1,000 species. It features an abundance of flowering plants and a 20-foot (6-m) waterfall.

Terminal art

Amsterdam's Schiphol Airport has its very own museum, which displays paintings by famous Dutch artists and features changing exhibitions. The airport also boasts a casino and a meditation center.

Big investment

The Kansai Airport, Japan, is the world's most costly airport at $20 billion since opening in 1994. It

1909

The world's oldest continually operating airport is thought to be College Park Airport in Maryland, established by Wilbur Wright.

96.2 MILLION

Hartsfield-Jackson Atlanta International Airport has been the world's busiest since 2000, clocking up 96.2 million passengers in 2014. Based on flight numbers, Chicago's O'Hare was the busiest, with 881,933 in 2014.

is built on a 2.5-mile (4-km) long artificial island with a large sea wall to protect it from waves.

Biggest hangar

Hangar One at Moffett Airfield in California is one of the biggest aircraft hangars ever. Built for airships in the 1930s, the structure covers 8 acres (3.2 hectares).

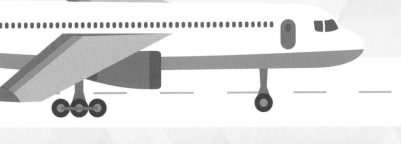

26.9 SQ MILES

Dallas-Fort Worth International Airport covers an area bigger than the island of Manhattan.

9¾

The famous platform where Harry Potter boards the Hogwarts Express can be found at London's King's Cross station.

STATIONS

High times

At 16,627 feet (5,068 m) above sea level, Tibet's Tanggula Mountain Station is the world's highest railroad station. It's so high that the waiting room is equipped with oxygen.

Mumbai marvel

Chhatrapati Shivaji Terminus in Mumbai is a UNESCO World Heritage Site. Formerly known as Victoria Terminus, construction began in 1887 and was completed in 1888. It was built in a traditional high Gothic style. More than 100 years later the station was featured in the movie *Slumdog Millionaire*.

0.84 miles

A platform at Gorakhpur Railway Station in the Indian state of Uttar Pradesh is the world's longest, measuring 0.84 miles (1.4 km).

$4 BILLION

The cost of New York's World Trade Center Transportation Hub, which will feature retractable glass and steel wings to allow natural light on to its platforms. The new station will provide access to nine subway lines.

Royal retreat

Thailand's Hua Hin railroad station has a special waiting room for royalty. The Royal Waiting Room was built during the reign of King Rama VI (1910–25) and is where he and his court would have been welcomed upon their arrival into the city.

It's a jungle

Estación de Atocha in Madrid was designed by Gustave Eiffel, of Tower fame, hence its many steel girders. These days it is more famous for containing a 43,055-square foot (4,000-m²) jungle complete with 500 species of animals and plants.

Glazed look

Formosa Boulevard Station, Kaohsiung, Taiwan, is known for its "Dome of Light," the largest glasswork in the world, covering an area of 22,690 square feet (2,108 m²) and made up of 4,500 colored glass panels shipped from Germany. It took artist Narcissus Quagliata almost four years to build.

Dead busy

Until 1942, London had its own railroad station for funerals. The London Necropolis Railway transported coffins for burial at a site outside the city. Its station had many private rooms, which could be used to hold funeral services, and a hydraulic lift to raise coffins to platform level. Railroad arches were used for the storage of bodies.

1830

The oldest railroad station in the world is the UK's Manchester Liverpool Road station, which opened on September 15, 1830, and closed to passenger services in 1844. The nearby Broad Green station opened on the same day and is still in use.

2500 BCE

The date of the earliest known docks, in Egypt. Archaeologists discovered anchors and storage jars at Wadi al-Jarf on the Red Sea coast.

DOCKS

Magnificent seven

Seven of the world's biggest ports are in China, with the others in Singapore, the Netherlands, and South Korea.

Heavy lifting

The largest quay cranes in the world are situated at London Gateway container port. Three of the 453-foot (138-m) tall cranes are able to pick up containers 25 rows across the deck of a ship.

Titanic berth

The largest dry dock in the world is the Thompson Dry Dock in Belfast, which was built to accommodate the building of the *Titanic*. It was opened on April 1, 1911, and is 850 feet (259 m) long and 128 feet (39 m) wide. When flooded, it held 21 million gallons (95 million liters) of water, which could be pumped out in one hour and 40 minutes to leave ships settled on their blocks.

Plenty of space

The longest wharf in the world is at the Port of New Orleans, Louisiana, which is 2 miles (3.4 km) long and can accommodate 15 ships at any one time.

Cruise capital

Miami is the world's busiest cruise port, with 4.8 million cruise passengers a year. It is also headquarters to many of the world's biggest cruise companies.

Bricked up

Stanley Dock Tobacco Warehouse in Liverpool is thought to be the largest brick warehouse in the world and the largest brick building in the world. The 14-story building could store 70,000 hogsheads of tobacco, each holding 1,000 pounds (454 kg).

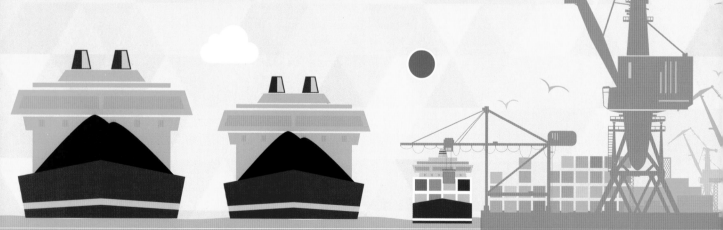

33.6 MILLION

Port Shanghai is the world's busiest dock, handling a record 33.6 million containers in 2013.

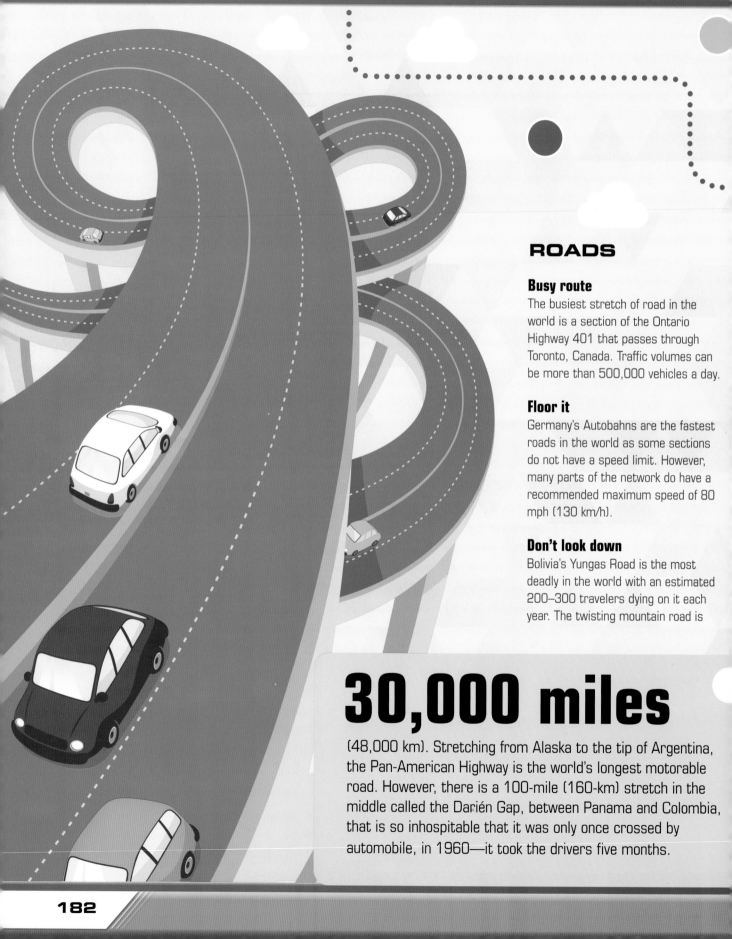

ROADS

Busy route

The busiest stretch of road in the world is a section of the Ontario Highway 401 that passes through Toronto, Canada. Traffic volumes can be more than 500,000 vehicles a day.

Floor it

Germany's Autobahns are the fastest roads in the world as some sections do not have a speed limit. However, many parts of the network do have a recommended maximum speed of 80 mph (130 km/h).

Don't look down

Bolivia's Yungas Road is the most deadly in the world with an estimated 200–300 travelers dying on it each year. The twisting mountain road is

30,000 miles

(48,000 km). Stretching from Alaska to the tip of Argentina, the Pan-American Highway is the world's longest motorable road. However, there is a 100-mile (160-km) stretch in the middle called the Darién Gap, between Panama and Colombia, that is so inhospitable that it was only once crossed by automobile, in 1960—it took the drivers five months.

1.24 MILLION

people die in road-related accidents every year, and the number is increasing. The Pulitzer Center on Crisis Reporting estimates that road deaths will rise to 3.6 million by 2030.

only a few yards wide in parts and has precipitous drops beside it of 2,300 feet (700 m).

Choose your lane

With 26 lanes in certain parts, the Katy Freeway, or Interstate 10, is the widest highway in the world. It serves more than 219,000 vehicles daily in Texas.

Handbrake start

Baldwin Street, Dunedin, New Zealand, is the world's steepest street, with an average slope of just over 1:5. For every 16 feet (5 m) traveled horizontally, you also travel 3 feet (1 m) vertically. The steepest part has a gradient of 1:2.86.

Cool drive

The McMurdo–South Pole Highway, Antarctica—also called the South Pole Traverse—is a 995-mile-long (1,600-km) snow road linking McMurdo Station to the Amundsen-Scott South Pole Station. It is marked by flags.

Jammed

The longest traffic jam on record was 109 miles (175 km) between Lyon and Paris on February 16, 1980. It occurred on an autoroute as a result of hundreds of skiers returning from holiday in poor weather.

Take the high road

At 15,397 feet (4,693 m), the Karakoram Highway is the highest paved highway in the world. The route was completed in 1986, following an agreement by Pakistan and China to ease travel between the two countries.

Sixteen feet

Elgin Street in Bacup, Lancashire, England, is the shortest street in the world at 16 feet (5 m).

1300–1200 BCE

The oldest surviving bridge in the world is thought to be an old Mycenaean bridge which is more than 3,000 years old. The Arkadiko Bridge is on the road between Epidavros and Nafplio, in Greece. It is built from massive Cyclopean stones and can still be used.

BRIDGES

High and mighty

The Danyang–Kunshan Grand Bridge is the world's longest bridge. The 102.4-mile-long (164.8-km) viaduct carries the Beijing–Shanghai High-Speed Railway over an area of the Yangtze River Delta that is mainly lowland rice paddies, canals, rivers, and lakes. Construction took four years and cost about $8.5 billion.

Over the sea

China opened the world's longest sea bridge in 2011. The 26-mile (42-km) structure could easily span the English Channel. Stretching across the waters of Jiaozhou Bay, the Y-shaped bridge connects the northern port city of Qingdao with an airport built on a nearby island and the industrial suburb of Huangdao.

3,000 feet

A wooden toll bridge across the Oi River in the middle of Shizuoka Prefecture, Japan, is nearly 3,000 feet (914 m) long. The Horai Bridge was first built in 1879 and was rebuilt in the 1960s because of flooding.

High anxiety

The world's tallest bridge is the Millau Viaduct in France. The cable-stayed bridge has one mast reaching a height of 1,125 feet (343 m). It crosses the valley of the river Tarn near Millau and on cloudy days appears almost to float on the clouds.

Suspend belief

The Akashi Kaikyo Bridge is the longest suspension bridge in the world, with a central span of 6,532 feet (1,991 m). It links the city of Kobe on the mainland of Honshu to Iwaya on Awaji Island, in Japan.

Shine on

The world's largest solar bridge opened at London's Blackfriars Station in 2014. The 4,400 photovoltaic

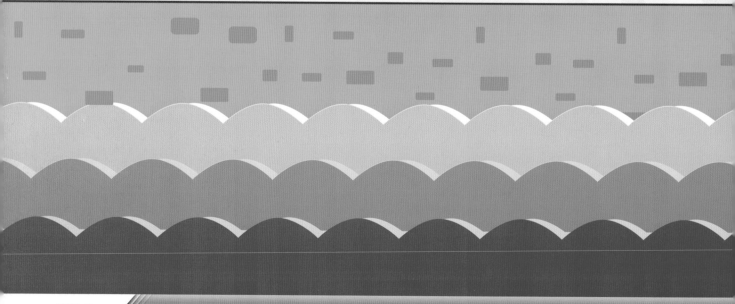

1,627 feet

The Sidu River Bridge (or Siduhe Bridge) is the world's highest bridge, at 1,627 feet (496 m). It spans a deep river gorge in Hubei Province, China, and was the first bridge in the world to use rockets to place the pilot cables. The main span of the bridge is 2,952 feet (900 m) long.

panels that cover the roof of the station span the River Thames, providing up to 50 percent of the station's energy. The panels reduce the station's CO_2 emissions by an estimated 563 tons (511 tonnes) a year, equivalent to around 89,000 average car journeys.

20 MINUTES

is the time it takes to drive through the longest road tunnel in the world. Drivers can stop for a break at any of three caves built in Norway's Laerdal Tunnel. It opened in 2000 and is 15.5 miles (25 km) long. The tunnel has a lighting system designed to mimic the sunrise, as drivers make their way from one end to the other.

TUNNELS

Digging history

London's Thames Tunnel was the first successful attempt anywhere in the world to construct a tunnel under a river. Engineer Marc Brunel designed the tunnel shield to protect workers as they dug, but it still took 18 years to complete by 1843. It is still in operation as part of the London rail network.

Joined-up thinking

The Channel Tunnel between England and France has the longest undersea portion of any tunnel in the world with 23.5 miles (37.9 km) running beneath the English Channel. The rail tunnel opened on May 6, 1994, but plans to go under the stretch of water date back to the 19th century.

Longest yet

The Seikan rail tunnel will be overtaken as the world's longest in 2016 by the Gotthard Base Tunnel in Switzerland. This rail tunnel will run for 35.4 miles (57 km) under the Alps, improving links between Germany and Italy.

Timber tunnel

A tunnel was dug through an ancient sequoia in America's Yosemite National Park in 1881, eventually enabling vehicles to drive through it. The Wawona Tree fell in 1969 under a heavy load of snow; it was estimated to be around 2,300 years old.

No way through

The longest canal tunnel in the world is France's Rove Tunnel, which is 23,360 feet (7,120 m) long. Following a collapse of one section it has been closed since 1963.

High five

The Yerba Buena Island Tunnel is the world's largest single bore tunnel. Completed in 1936, the double-decker roadway in the tunnel carries five lanes of traffic to and from the San Francisco–Oakland Bay Bridge.

33.46 miles

The Seikan railroad tunnel, linking Honshu to the island of Hokkaido in Japan, is the world's longest at 33.46 miles (53.85 km). It was opened in 1988.

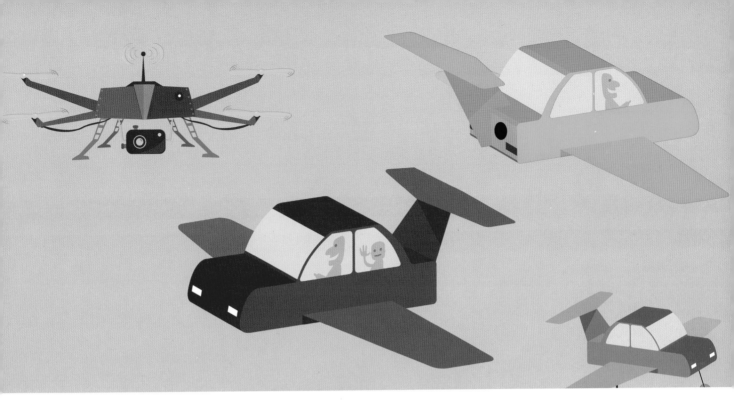

THE
FUTURE

€4.287 million

($4.6 million) The amount of money the European Union spent on looking into the feasibility of a system of personal small flying vehicles for use in urban areas, as a way of combatting congestion. The project was called myCopter.

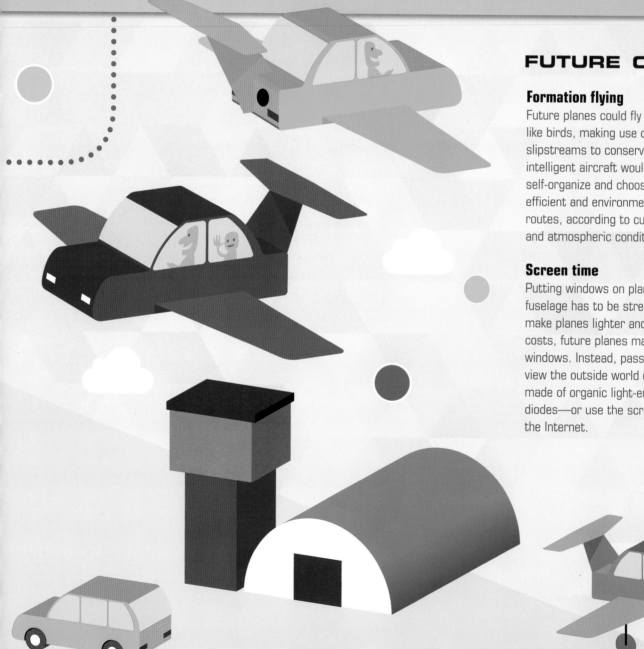

FUTURE OF AIR

Formation flying

Future planes could fly in formation like birds, making use of each other's slipstreams to conserve energy. The intelligent aircraft would be able to self-organize and choose the most efficient and environmentally friendly routes, according to current weather and atmospheric conditions.

Screen time

Putting windows on planes means the fuselage has to be strengthened. To make planes lighter and save on fuel costs, future planes may not have windows. Instead, passengers could view the outside world on screens made of organic light-emitting diodes—or use the screens to surf the Internet.

500 MILLION HOURS

The amount of time that could be saved if future aircraft used existing technology better, according to plane manufacturer Airbus. The company says this would make each journey an average of 13 minutes shorter, saving around 10 million tons (9 million tonnes) of fuel a year and generating 30 million tons (28 million tonnes) less CO_2 emissions.

Owl lessons

Airbus engineers are studying owls to unlock the secrets of silent flight. Ideas include a retractable brushlike fringe to mimic the owls' trailing feathers and velvety coating on aircraft landing gear.

Double drive

UK researchers have successfully tested the first aircraft to be powered by both an electric motor and gasoline-powered engine. The vehicle is able to charge its batteries in flight and uses up to 30 percent less fuel than a gas-only plane. Until recently batteries have been too heavy to make hybrid aircraft viable, but the advent of improved lithium-polymer batteries, similar to those found in a laptop computer, is driving development forward.

Hyper speed

The future isn't just supersonic—it's hypersonic. Technology firm Lockheed Martin's Skunk Works division— the department that focuses on innovation—is developing a hypersonic aircraft that will fly at up to six times the speed of sound. The company thinks the plane—called the SR-72— will be ready by 2030.

Transforming travel

BAE Systems has designed a plane that can transform into three separate aircraft at a moment's notice, saving on fuel while allowing it to be more flexible in different situations. The craft's two wings can break away to become two smaller support jets.

Printed planes

By 2040, military planes could be fitted with 3-D printers that could print out smaller drones while in the air, designed for whatever situation the plane finds itself in. Entire planes have already been printed out. In 2011, engineers from the University of Southampton in Britain developed the world's first printed aircraft.

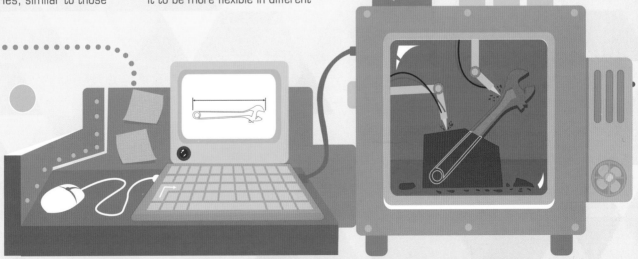

FUTURE AUTOMOBILES

Self-cleaning paint
Cleaning your car can be a bit of a chore—but luckily the automobiles of the future could clean themselves. Nissan has already produced a prototype electric vehicle with self-cleaning nano-paint technology.

Testing times
Legislation may be the main obstacle to the introduction of self-driving automobiles to the roads, but the State of California is leading the way with testing permits issued to a number of vehicles.

Curious cars
Like televisions that learn to record shows you like based on past preferences, cars will start to learn your preferred routes and track real-time traffic problems to suggest detours. They will even tune the radio to the right station for you, depending on the time of day.

No hands
Technology company Google is working on an automobile that drives itself. The vehicle has no steering wheel, just a start and stop button. It uses radar, cameras, and lasers to check for obstructions, and can recognize objects, people, other cars, road markings, signs, and traffic lights.

Panel power
Vehicles of the future may be fueled by their body panels. Toyota is developing lightweight body panels that would capture and store solar energy, while Volvo is researching panels that would capture energy produced during normal driving—for example, when a car brakes—and feed it back when needed.

Good to talk
The "Internet of things" is the idea that digital devices can communicate with each other—like your refrigerator telling you you're out of milk. Cars are set to join in with the advent of vehicle-to-vehicle (V2V) communications. They will be able to exchange messages about traffic, weather, and road conditions, as well as potential safety hazards.

331 mph

(533 km/h). The maximum speed of the Moller Skycar 400. Skycars don't need a landing strip—they take off and land vertically. They are a bit bigger than an SUV, five times as fast, and use the same amount of fuel.

FUTURE FUEL

Hydrogen-powered vehicles emit only water and heat rather than polluting gases. Manufacturers including Toyota and Hyundai have already released hydrogen-powered vehicles, but the technology is currently limited by the availability of filling stations—in the United States there are only around 12, ten of which are in California.

Park life

Some cars already boast features that help you park, like sensors in their bumpers. The next step is cars that park themselves. Honda recently demonstrated a driverless parking system that uses wireless communication between Wi-Fi-enabled automobiles and cameras placed in the four corners of a parking lot. Drivers get out of the car and watch as it steers itself into a free space.

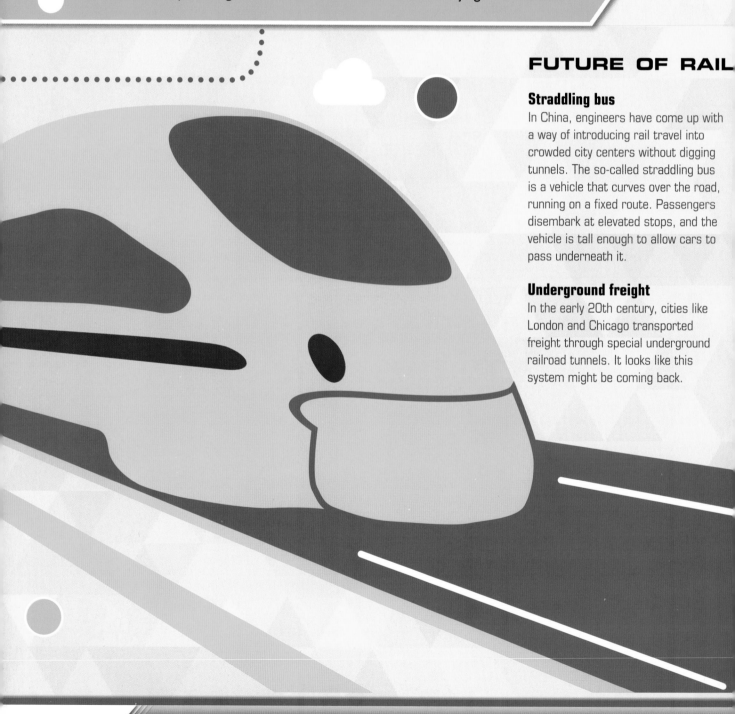

4,040 mph

(6,500 km/h). The speed a future maglev system could travel at, according to its inventors. The ET3 consortium says its system of automobile-sized capsules running in 5-foot (1.5-m) vacuum tubes is "space travel on Earth" and will allow passengers to travel from New York to Beijing in two hours.

FUTURE OF RAIL

Straddling bus

In China, engineers have come up with a way of introducing rail travel into crowded city centers without digging tunnels. The so-called straddling bus is a vehicle that curves over the road, running on a fixed route. Passengers disembark at elevated stops, and the vehicle is tall enough to allow cars to pass underneath it.

Underground freight

In the early 20th century, cities like London and Chicago transported freight through special underground railroad tunnels. It looks like this system might be coming back.

German company CargoCap proposes using an underground network of aerodynamic, electric-powered capsules to transport freight, while a project in southern California envisages automated freight trains running through underground pipelines originally designed for long-distance water transmission.

Virtual shopping

Passengers waiting for trains in the future could do some shopping in virtual supermarkets. Retailer Tesco Homeplus has already set up a virtual store along the platform of the Seonreung subway station in South Korea. Smartphone users scan the code of a product to order it. And China's biggest online retailer, Yihaodian, plans to open 1,000 virtual supermarkets in the country.

Drone assistance

Railroad companies will become increasingly dependent on drones to manage their infrastructure. Dutch railroad company ProRail uses drones with infrared sensors to check the heating systems on its tracks, while Germany's national railroad company is testing micro drones to tackle the problem of graffiti. The drones can hover 490 feet (150 m) above the company's depots and gather evidence on trespassers.

Pedestrian power

Future stations will be able to use electricity created by passengers walking over special energy floors. Trials have already taken place in Russia and France.

Hydrogen cells

By 2050, hydrogen could be a primary means of powering locomotives. Hydrogen fuel cells could replace the diesel engines and generators used in modern diesel-electric vehicles. The first hydrail passenger railcar was debuted in Japan in 2006.

IN THE LOOP

The Hyperloop is a solar-powered transportation system described by its inventor as a cross between Concorde, a rail gun, and an air hockey table. Passengers and cars are fired down a tube inside capsules, with a system of magnets acting as accelerators and brakes. The brainchild of billionaire entrepreneur, Elon Musk, the system could be up and running by 2025.

34

The number of fjord crossings per day made by the world's first nonpolluting electric vehicle ferry in Norway. A conventional ferry plying the same route would emit 2,680 tons (2,430 tonnes) of CO_2 and 37 tons (34 tonnes) of nitrogen oxide each year.

FUTURE OF WATER TRAVEL

Sci-fi robots

Space technology company SpaceX uses robotic ships as landing platforms for its rockets. The unmanned drone ships are named after sentient spaceships from late sci-fi author Iain M. Banks' *Culture* series. The first is called *Just Read The Instructions* and the second *Of Course I Still Love You.*

Back to sail

In the future, sail may once again rule the seas as oil becomes scarce and costly. German cargo ship, MS *Beluga Skysails*, is the world's first ship partially powered by a giant computer-controlled kite. This method saves up to a third of the fuel the ship would otherwise use.

Sea lab

The *SeaOrbiter* is a planned ocean-going research vessel. Half under and half above the water, the 190-foot (58-m) structure will drift with the ocean current, although it will also have two small propellers. The brainchild of French architect Jacques Rougerie, the project advisory team includes two astronauts, a former NASA administrator, and Prince Albert II of Monaco.

Sun shine

Future boats may draw their energy from the Sun. *The Tûranor*, the largest solar-powered boat to set sail, uses weather-data software to steer the ship into sunny areas, avoiding clouds. The boat can store as much as three

days' worth of sailing power in a huge rack of lithium-ion batteries, allowing it to sail at night.

Remote-controlled ships

Container ships of the future could be remote-controlled. Manufacturer Rolls-Royce has come up with designs for crewless cargo ships. The robot vessels, which would be controlled from dry land, would save space usually given over to crew facilities and would be able to travel more slowly, saving fuel without raised salary costs.

Water jet

The Jetlev-Flyer is a jet pack that propels thrill-seekers up into the air—about three stories high—over a body

of water by shooting jets of water out at high volume. But environmentalists are concerned about the impact the gadgets could have on fish and coral.

Underwater drones

Drones are not just for the air—underwater drones are increasingly being used for research and rescue operations. Unmanned underwater vehicles were used to search for the wreckage of Malaysia Airlines Flight 370, which disappeared in 2014.

50,000

The number of inhabitants housed by Belgian architect Vincent Callebaut's proposed floating city. Called the Lilypad, the eco-friendly structure comprises three marinas and three mountain regions. Constructed from polyester fibers coated in titanium dioxide, which would absorb atmospheric pollution, the ecopolis was designed as a solution to global warming.

CRIME
& PUNISHMENT

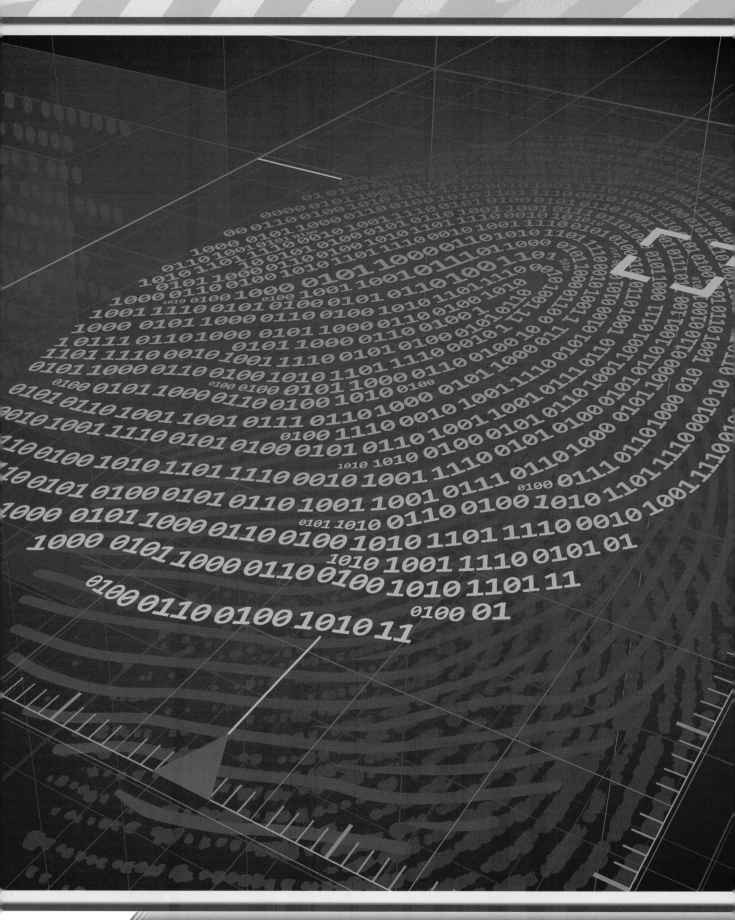

INTRODUCTION

"What do you think, would not one tiny crime be wiped out by thousands of good deeds?" This is the question posed by Russian novelist Fyodor Dostoyevsky in his famous book, *Crime and Punishment*.

Like many societies before and after, Dostoyevsky's novel is concerned with the nature of human behavior and how we determine what is permissible and what is not. He does this over a sprawling epic of more than 200,000 words.

For those with less time, and more of a hunger for fact-sized pieces of information, the stories we tell here will take you on a whistlestop tour through the history of crime and criminals, law enforcement, the legal system, punishment, and what crime and crime fighting could look like in the future.

Crime is a fact of life around the world, but it takes many different forms, and is judged in different ways. For example, did you know that your vehicle is more likely to be stolen in the United States if it is a Honda Accord, or that pine nut theft is so rampant in Italy that the nuts have to be fitted with special security tags?

These are just some of the fascinating facts that you will pick up in the following pages. They include some truly mind-blowing statistics about the scope of criminal activities, including the total value of fake goods around the world, and the biggest fraudster in the world—step forward Bernie Madoff—who scammed $65 billion in the biggest Ponzi scheme the world has ever known. You will also find out what a Ponzi scheme is, as well as who Ponzi was.

For as long as criminals have been plotting to carry out the perfect crime, law enforcers have been involved in a cat-and-mouse game to stop them, catch them, and bring them to justice. You'll find out all about their efforts here. The first electric burglar alarm was produced in 1853, and as early as 1933 an ingenious inventor had rigged up a security camera in his henhouse to find out who was pinching his eggs. It worked too!

The failed egg thief joins a long line of criminals who have been busted, some of whom deserve a special mention for their ineptitude, such as the would-be thief who was pictured by a security camera as he tried to rob a car. He might even have got away with it, if it hadn't been for the fact that he had his name and date of birth tattooed on his neck.

For those who do fall foul of the law, the next stage is the judicial system, where the scope for punishment is wide and varied. Find out why one man was sentenced to listen to classical music as his punishment, and what a group of teenagers did that ended with them taking off on an unintended ten-mile run. At the other end of the scale, discover some of the most "draconian" punishments, and also why they are so called.

Our brief tour of wrongdoing finishes with a look at how technology is shaping a new wave of criminality and also the way that it is fought. Robocops may be closer to reality than you think.

CRIME

Crime

(noun) An action that constitutes a serious offense against an individual or the state and is punishable by law.

Punishment

(noun) A penalty inflicted as retribution for an offense.

DEFINITIONS AND ORIGINS

Sumerian justice

All ancient civilizations developed codes that defined what was acceptable within their societies and what were crimes against the society. The Sumerian ruler Urukagina is thought to have produced the first legal code around the 24th century BCE. An actual copy has never been discovered but it is referenced in other writings and covered such crimes as theft, murder, and adultery.

57 varieties of crime

The oldest legal document is a Sumerian tablet dating from around the 21st century BCE to the rule of King Ur-Nammu. The tablet contains five laws, although a further discovery revealed that there were 57 laws in total. It outlines capital crimes such as murder, rape, and robbery, as well as fines for other lesser crimes.

Harsh punishment

Greek citizen Draco wrote a code of law for Athens in 621 BCE. The penalty for many offenses was death, leading to the description of "draconian" for a particularly harsh law. His laws were the first written laws of Greece and gave the state the role of punishing those accused of crime. The citizens adored Draco and upon entering an auditorium one day they showered him with their hats and cloaks as was the customary way to show appreciation. By the time they dug him out he had been smothered to death.

The 12 tables

The Romans wrote a legal code in the form of 12 tables that were attached to the walls of the Roman Forum, allowing common men, or plebeians, to become acquainted with it. This knowledge of rights helped put an end to arbitrary justice.

Old laws

The Laws of Aethelbert are believed to be the first laws written down in England. Written in Old English, the laws date from around 600 CE and detail compensations for crimes according to social status.

1215

The Magna Carta is one of the most important legal documents in history. Signed in 1215, it established for the first time that nobody, not even the king, was above the law. Of its 63 clauses, only three are still in use today, but its core principles echo in the U.S. Bill of Rights and the Universal Declaration of Human Rights.

Words for different types of murder:

Patricide
killing your father

Uxoricide
killing your wife

Vaticide
killing a prophet

Regicide
killing a king

Episcopicide
killing a bishop

Giganticide
killing a giant

Amicicide
killing a friend

CRIME IN STATISTICS

25%

The proportion of the world's prison population held in the United States.
5 percent: The proportion of the world's population resident in the United States.

Half of all global homicide victims are under 30 years old. But in Europe, males aged between 30 and 59 have a higher risk of being murdered than younger men.

50%

10

European Union member states saw the number of crimes increase between 2007 and 2012.

16

European Union member states saw a fall in crime between 2007 and 2012. Scotland saw recorded crimes fall by 29 percent, England and Wales by 25 percent, and Estonia by 19 percent.

50%

The estimated proportion of the world's homicides that occur in countries that make up just over 10 percent of the global population.

 **95%** of murderers worldwide are male. Almost eight out of every ten murder victims are also male.

 **45%** of criminals in prison in the UK commit another offense within a year of being released.

500,000
The estimated number of people who were murdered worldwide in 2012. More than a third of those (36 percent) were in the Americas, 31 percent in Africa, and 28 percent in Asia, while Europe (5 percent) and Oceania (0.3 percent) had the lowest number of murder victims. Around 36,000 children under the age of 15 were the victims of homicide in 2012.

5.2% The proportion of the world population aged 15–64 that has used an illicit drug.

30% The proportion of murders relating to organized crime and gangs in the Americas, compared to less than one percent in Asia, Europe, and Oceania.

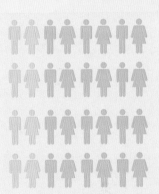 

 **1,567,100** The number of homes burgled in the United States in 2012: 493.6 burglaries for every 100,000 people.

20.9 MILLION The number of victims of human trafficking globally according to the International Labor Organization. This includes 5.5 million children, and 55 percent are women and girls.

 **43** murderers are convicted for every 100 killings worldwide. In the Americas the figure is 24; it is 48 in Asia and 81 in Europe.

6 YEARS OLD

Carl Newton Mahan is thought to be the youngest person to stand trial for murder. In Kentucky in 1929 he shot his friend Cecil Van Hoose after an argument about a piece of scrap iron that they wanted to sell. Initially sentenced to 15 years in reform school, the decision was later overturned and he was released into the care of his parents.

MURDER

Doctor Death
British doctor Harold Shipman may be the biggest serial killer of the modern age. He was convicted in 2000 of murdering 15 patients and an inquiry later identified 218 cases where he was held responsible. The true figure may have been as high as 250.

Victim profile
You are most likely to be murdered if you are a young man aged between 15 and 29 living in North or South America. More than one in seven of all homicide victims worldwide fit this profile.

Shooting sprees
In the United States between 2002 and 2011 there were an average of 32 acts of mass murder per year. Some 70 percent of all mass murders in that period involved firearms.

Murdering Mary
Mary Ann Cotton murdered 21 people in England in the 19th century, including her mother, children, and her husbands. Cotton poisoned them with arsenic, which made doctors mistake the cause of death for gastric ailments. She was eventually jailed and executed in 1873.

College killings
The worst school rampage killing was undertaken by Seung-Hui Cho, a student at Virginia Polytechnic Institute, on April 16, 2007. After mailing a "manifesto" explaining his actions to broadcaster NBC, he shot 32 students and himself at the college.

Work homicide
In the United States, you are most likely to be murdered at work if you work in retail—94 people working in the sector were murdered in 2013. The majority were employed by food stores (29) and gas stations (24).

Unhappy Monday
Brenda Ann Spencer claimed she was motivated to shoot dead two classmates and injure nine others at her San Diego school because she didn't like Mondays. Spencer was sentenced to 25 years to life for the crime, which inspired a song by Irish pop group, The Boomtown Rats.

MURDER WEAPONS (WORLDWIDE)

41%
Murders carried out using firearms

24%
Murders carried out using sharp objects

World's most prolific serial killers

Name	Proven Victims
Luis Garavito, Colombia	138
Pedro López Colombia, Peru, Ecuador	110
Daniel Camargo Barbosa Colombia, Ecuador	72
Pedro Rodrigues Filho Brazil	71
Kampatimar Shankariya India	70
Yang Xinhai China	67
Abul Djabar Afghanistan	65
Andrei Chikatilo Russia	53
Anatoly Onoprienko Ukraine	52

Happy ever after
An Argentine woman married the killer of her twin sister less than two years after he was convicted of the crime. Edith Casas married Victor Cingolani on St. Valentine's Day 2013. Cingolani claimed he was innocent of the killing.

35%

Murders carried out using other weapons

164,755,150 BRAZILIAN REALS
($69.8 MILLION)

The largest amount of money stolen from a bank by robbers. A gang dug a tunnel into the Banco Central in Fortaleza, Brazil, and in August 2005 they broke through 3 feet 7 inches (1.1 m) of steel-reinforced concrete to enter the bank vault.

THEFT

In accord
The most stolen automobile in the United States in 2013 was the Honda Accord, with 53,995 stolen, followed by the Honda Civic (45,001), and the Chevrolet Pickup (27,809).

Beach burglary
In 2008, thieves in Jamaica stole an entire beach. Some 500 truckloads of sand were removed from the beach at Coral Springs, in Jamaica's northern parish of Trelawny. Police carried out forensic tests on beaches along the coast to see if any of them matched the stolen sand.

92

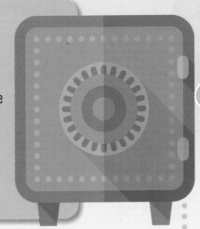

The age of the world's oldest convicted bank robber, J. L. Hunter Rountree, when he was sentenced to 151 months in prison on January 23, 2004. He pleaded guilty to robbing $1,999 from a bank in Texas. Rountree, nicknamed "Red," said he robbed his first bank when he was around 80 because he wanted revenge on banks for sending him into a financial crisis. He told reporters that prison food was better than what was served at some nursing homes.

Rhyming robbery

Black Bart was a robber in California who held up stage coaches. He was unfailingly polite and made a point of never robbing drivers or passengers of their personal money. His *modus operandi* was to leave a (badly written) poem at the scene of the crime. He was captured in 1883.

Hard cheese

In 2011 cheese was the most stolen food in the world. In the Asia Pacific region, however, high-quality seafood was the most stolen item, while in North America fresh meat and confectionery tied as the most stolen foodstuffs.

Merry Christmas

In 2012, English police in the West Midlands sent robbers and car thieves a Christmas card warning them to stay crime free. Those with a family received a card featuring a sad child while single robbers had a card showing an empty setting at a dinner table. The festive message was: "All the presents in the world won't make up for your lack of presence."

It's a scream

In 1994 two men broke into Oslo's National Gallery and stole famous artwork *The Scream* by Edvard Munch. They left behind a note saying "Thanks for the poor security" and demanded a ransom of $1 million for its return.

Nutty thieves

Italy has seen a rise in pine nut related theft, after poor harvests sent prices rocketing. Some supermarkets selling the nuts are adding antitheft devices to their stashes.

Light theft

In the 1980s owners of Volkswagen automobiles found that their VW badges were being stolen by fans of U.S. rappers, The Beastie Boys, attempting to emulate their heroes by wearing the logo around their necks.

$250 MILLION

Canadian counterfeiter Frank Bourassa printed a quarter of a billion in fake U.S. dollars but served only a month and a half behind bars. The going rate for $1 million in fake bills was $300,000—in the real thing.

FRAUD

Ponzi schemes

Italian Charles Ponzi established the Securities Exchange Co. in America in 1919, promising investors huge profits in just a few weeks. However, the profits came entirely from newly invested money and ever since this fraud has carried his name. Ponzi was charged with 86 counts of fraud in 1920 but pleaded guilty to only one.

Bernie tops the pile

New York money manager Bernard Madoff's $65 billion Ponzi scheme is the largest fraud ever by an individual. Madoff was exposed in December 2008 and is now serving 150 years in prison.

Tower going cheap

In 1925, con artist Victor Lustig tried to sell the Eiffel Tower. Presenting himself as a government official, he told French scrap-metal dealers that the Paris landmark was to be dismantled and took bids from the dealers before selecting André Poisson as the "winner." Poisson was too humiliated to report the incident to authorities, allowing Lustig to try and sell it again.

Catch him if you can

Con artist Frank Abagnale passed bad checks worth more than $2.5 million in the 1960s, while conning free flights from airlines dressed as a pilot. His story featured in the movie *Catch Me If You Can*. He eventually served 12 years in prison but now runs a successful financial fraud consultancy.

$1.7 TRILLION

The total value of fake goods around the world by 2015 according to the International Chamber of Commerce. That's two percent of the world's economic output.

1,000

Hungarian painter Elmyr de Hory is thought to have forged more than 1,000 artworks, by artists including Modigliani, Degas, Picasso, and Matisse. His productivity came to light only after his suicide in 1976. In his lifetime he was never charged with forgery.

Dear diary

In April 1983, the West German magazine *Stern* published excerpts from what it believed were the diaries of Adolf Hitler after paying nearly 9 million Deutschmarks ($3.8 million) for the 60 small books. The diaries fooled many eminent historians, but were actually written by Stuttgart forger Konrad Kujau, and sold by journalist Gerd Heidemann. In 1985, they were sentenced to more than four years in prison.

419

One of the most common types of confidence trick. The number refers to the section in the Nigerian Criminal Code that outlaws the practice of requesting upfront payment from gullible victims, usually in the hope of receiving greater riches. Many of these fraudulent scams purport to come from Nigeria, so they are sometimes known as Nigerian mail fraud.

$445 BILLION

The global cost of cybercrime in 2014, according to Internet security company McAfee. Germany had the highest incidence of cybercrime, accounting for 1.6 percent of its GDP.

CYBERCRIME

Looming change

The first recorded cybercrime according to some was in 1801, when weavers smashed the automated looms of French textile manufacturer Joseph-Marie Jacquard. He had produced an attachment for looms that allowed a series of steps in the weaving of fabrics to be repeated automatically. Weavers saw the automation as a threat to their livelihood.

Online separation

In October 2008, a 43-year old Japanese woman was arrested in Miyazaki, Japan, for killing her online husband, or avatar—a digital persona—after becoming angry at the fact that he had divorced her online in the interactive game, *Maple Story*. She was jailed on suspicion of illegally accessing a computer to "murder" her partner.

Whistle for it

In the early 1970s, John Draper discovered that the giveaway whistle in Cap'n Crunch cereal boxes reproduced a 2600 Hz tone that fooled phone systems into giving free calls. *Esquire* magazine published an article about the underground world of "phone phreaks" that went on to inspire hackers and computer entrepreneurs, including Apple founder Steve Jobs. Jobs and fellow computer enthusiast Steve Wozniak started their own phone-phreaking business before launching Apple.

$38 BILLION

2004 computer virus Mydoom was the most costly ever, infecting two million PCs via e-mail and spreading through the users' address lists.

Cheap rate

In 1981, Ian Murphy, or "Captain Zap," became the first felon convicted of a computer crime. Murphy broke into AT&T's computers and changed the billing clock so that people received discounted rates during normal business hours.

Movie mover

In November 2005, Chan Nai-Ming of Hong Kong was jailed for three months for uploading Hollywood movies on to the Internet using BitTorrent technology. Although the movie industry began targeting BitTorrent sites in December 2004, Chan Nai-Ming's case is the first in the world to lead to a prison sentence.

Virus alert

In 1986, Pakistani brothers Basit and Amjad Farooq Alvi produced Brain, the oldest virus created under unauthorized circumstances. It was an attempt to stop illegal copying of their software by slowing down PCs.

Radio ga ga

On June 1, 1990, hacker Kevin Poulsen and friends rigged the phone systems of radio station KIIS-FM to let only their calls through and win a Porsche in a phone-in. Poulsen, who was on the run from other computing charges, was guaranteed to be the 102nd caller. He subsequently served five years in jail and was banned from using computers or the Internet for three years on his release.

CRIME AROUND THE WORLD

Sweden

40 percent of homicides are family related, 11 percent are related to organized crime, and six percent to robbery and other criminal acts.

The USA

has the highest number of prison staff compared to the general population. The worldwide average is 115.4 prison staff per 100,000 people; the States have 138.3.

Vatican City

has the highest crime rate in the word. Although the population is just over 800, more than 600 crimes are committed there each year.

Honduras

is the country with the highest murder rate. With 90.4 homicides per 100,000 people, Honduras is an increasingly dangerous place.

Brazil

has the highest number of murders per year, with 50,108 in 2012.

Jamaica

44 percent of homicides are related to organized crime, 40 percent to robbery, and five percent are family related.

Uruguay

is the country where your car is most likely to be stolen—there were 437.6 car thefts for every 100,000 people in 2012.

San Marino

has the lowest prison population in the world, mainly because its few criminals serve their sentences in Italy. Its single jail has so few prisoners that it is cheaper to have meals sent in from a restaurant than to make them on site.

Japan

has seen its homicide rate decrease steadily since 1955 to reach one of the lowest levels in the world. Young men in Japan now commit only a tenth of the murders committed by their predecessors in 1955. According to researchers this decline could be caused by extremely low levels of gun ownership (one in 175 households), the stigma of arrest for any crime in Japanese society, and a greater chance of detection: 98 percent of homicide cases in Japan are solved.

Turkey

saw the total number of crimes recorded by the police increase by 96 percent between 2007 and 2012.

Cyprus and Greece

saw the number of robberies more than double between 2007 and 2012.

Australia

has specialist police squads to deal with the theft of cattle and sheep. "Duffing," as it's known locally, is a growing problem as cattle are worth around $1,200 per head.

1,698

The number of kidnaps in Mexico (2013), the country where you are most likely to be held to ransom, followed by India, Pakistan, Iraq, and Nigeria.

KIDNAP

Most wanted

Ruth Eisemann-Schier was the first female addition to the FBI Most Wanted list. On December 17, 1968, she and her lover Gary Steven Krist abducted 20-year-old student Barbara Jane Mackle and buried her alive in a remote forest in a fiberglass coffin. They demanded $500,000 ransom from Barbara's millionaire father, and she was released after 83 hours. Eisemann-Schier was apprehended on March 5, 1969, and sentenced to seven years in prison.

Royal fracas

The only living member of the British Royal Family to have undergone a kidnap attempt is Princess Anne. In March 1974, her car was held up by armed criminal Ian Ball, who demanded that she come with him because he wanted £2 million ($5 million). She replied: "Not bloody likely." After a fracas in which four people were wounded and 11 shots fired, Ball was apprehended.

Ransom refusal

U.S. oil tycoon and billionaire Jean Paul Getty refused to pay the $17 million demanded in ransom after his 16-year-old grandson John Paul Getty III was kidnapped in Rome in 1973. Even when the kidnappers sent his grandson's severed ear, and lowered the ransom to $3.2 million, Getty would only pay $2.2 million, because it was tax deductible. He loaned the rest to his son at four percent interest. John Paul Getty III was returned five months after he was taken.

Virtual kidnap

A scam known as "virtual kidnapping" is increasingly popular in Latin America. Criminals phone a family and tell them a loved one has been abducted, threatening to kill them if a ransom is not immediately paid. In reality the "victim" is happily going about their business, often temporarily out of reach in a place such as an airplane or movie theater.

$60 MILLION

The amount paid for the release of wealthy Argentine grain traders, brothers Jorge and Juan Born, kidnapped by the far-left terrorist group Montoneros in 1974. Equivalent to about $288 million today, the ransom is one of the highest ever paid.

MUSIC MAN

Jazz musician Fats Waller was kidnapped in Chicago in 1926 and forced to play piano at infamous gangster Al Capone's birthday party. It's said that he left the venue three days later very drunk, very tired, and with thousands of dollars in tips.

Guerrilla gangsters

When 19-year-old heiress Patty Hearst was kidnapped in 1974, her kidnappers, urban guerrilla group the Symbionese Liberation Army (SLA), demanded her father distribute $70 worth of food to every needy Californian—an operation that would cost an estimated $400 million. Hearst's father did distribute $2 million worth of food but his daughter was co-opted into joining criminal activities, ending up in prison for bank robbery. She eventually received a full pardon.

8,500 VOLTS

was the shock received by a security guard at a London hotel when he checked out a suspicious-looking automobile. The owner, Roderic Minshull, was cleared of common battery in 1994, having electrified the vehicle to create a homemade method of warding off thieves.

SECURITY

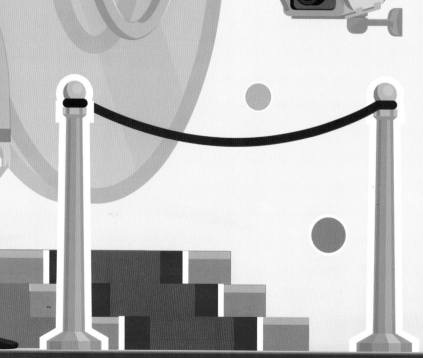

Don't panic

Safe rooms or panic rooms are fortified areas inside a building that provide refuge in the event of intrusion or emergency. One of the largest is rumored to belong to the Sultan of Brunei at 100,000 square feet (9,290 m²). The average U.S. home is about 2,150 square feet (200 m²).

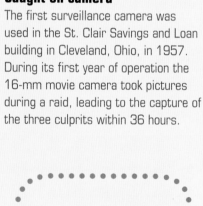

Smile please

An amateur photographer and chicken keeper invented the world's first security camera to try to catch an egg thief. A Mr. Norbury of London rigged up a box camera with a cord working the lever to take pictures of the culprit. It worked, and on July 27, 1933, Frederick William Barnwell was caught stealing eggs on film and the photos were used as evidence at his trial.

Caught on camera

The first surveillance camera was used in the St. Clair Savings and Loan building in Cleveland, Ohio, in 1957. During its first year of operation the 16-mm movie camera took pictures during a raid, leading to the capture of the three culprits within 36 hours.

1853

The first electric burglar alarm was patented by the American Reverend Augustus Russell Pope. The device worked by connecting doors and windows to an electric circuit. When a door or window was opened, it closed the electric circuit causing a brass bell to be rung.

Police support

In 1979, John Lennon donated $1,000 to help the cash-strapped New York police buy bulletproof vests. Ironically, Lennon was shot the following year by Mark Chapman as he entered his New York apartment.

Smoked out

A new deterrent to thieves is security fog, which fills the inside of a room, making it impossible to see or steal anything.

Bonkers bag

British boffins in the 1950s came up with a briefcase that helped trap a robber. When the miscreant grabbed the bag, it crushed his fingers, making it impossible to drop it, and then three long and unwieldy metal legs shot out, making further progress very awkward.

Vigilante Knobbers

The Bald Knobbers were a security force formed in lawless Missouri after the Civil War. Formed by the imposing Nathanial Kinney, who was 6 feet 6 inches (2 m) tall, the group vowed to fight lawlessness but rapidly devolved into a vicious vigilante group, which was eventually broken up.

Bling

The Federal Reserve Bank of New York contains 25 percent of the world's gold reserves, sunk three stories below ground. As well as American gold, bullion of other countries is stored in the vault. There are thought to be around 540,000 bars of gold locked behind its 90-ton (82-tonne) steel door.

2005

The year that Howard Stapleton invented a noise-emitting device that only people under 25 can hear. Nicknamed the Mosquito for its irritating high-pitched whine, the device is used to prevent youths hanging around in certain areas where they might commit crime.

$81 MILLION

The transport costs alone of moving cocaine through the Californian warehouse of drug boss Rafael Munoz Talavera. He was busted after police seized 21 tons (19 tonnes) of cocaine in 1989, in one of the biggest drug busts ever. It had a street value of $7 billion.

DRUGS

Low blow

In 2010, Mexican marijuana dealers built their own underground railroad to transport the drug under the border into California. The 1,800-foot (550-m) tunnel, was completed with a light rail system to move 30 tons (27 tonnes) of pot worth $20 million.

Losing battle

A report by the British Medical Journal found the purity of cocaine in the United States between 1990 and 2007 increased by 11 percent while its price dropped by 80 percent. Heroin purity increased by 60 percent while its price dropped by 81 percent, whereas cannabis herb saw an increase in purity of 161 percent and a drop in price of 86 percent.

Sneaky smugglers

Colombian drug smugglers have built their own submarines to get past U.S. coast guards and bring cocaine into the United States.

World-class deception

In 2010, Colombian police found a 24-pound (11-kg) replica of the soccer World Cup trophy made entirely of cocaine.

Light work

A cannabis grower in the Netherlands town of Haarlem was given away when snow on the roof of his house melted, thanks to his use of growing lamps.

116 TONS

(105 tonnes) of marijuana were seized following a gun battle in the Mexican city of Tijuana in 2010. It was the biggest drug seizure in Mexican history. The 10,000 bales were color coded and some featured images of Homer Simpson.

CRIMINALS

INFAMOUS CRIMINALS

Body of evidence

William Burke and William Hare became infamous after supplying human bodies for dissection in anatomy classes in Edinburgh, Scotland. The trade was lucrative enough for them to start killing people to ensure a supply. They killed 16 people in 1828 and Burke was hanged the following year, on evidence supplied by Hare, who escaped the gallows.

Scarface

More commonly known as Scarface, Al Capone was an American gangster and bootlegger. Capone was eventually brought to boot on tax evasion charges in 1931.

Armored robber

Ned Kelly was a 19th-century Australian bushranger who spent much of his life evading the police, for charges of robbery and murder. Kelly was eventually captured after a shoot-out in which he tackled police wearing homemade armor. He was shot in the legs, stood trial, and was hanged in November 1880.

Justice by wire

London doctor Hawley Harvey Crippen was the first criminal caught by wireless telegraph. Crippen poisoned his wife after starting an affair with his secretary, Ethel Le Neve, dismembering the body, and burying it under his cellar in February 1910.

1888

was the year of the so-called Jack the Ripper murders in Whitechapel, London. Over a period of about ten weeks, the killer murdered and butchered five East London women. His name was taken from a newspaper letter, which is now believed to be a hoax. The last murder was of Mary Jane Kelly on November 9, and despite many suggestions as to who the culprit was, an identity has never been conclusively proved.

$200,000

A "D. B. Cooper" hijacked a Northwest Orient flight on November 24, 1971, claiming he had a bomb in his briefcase. He released passengers after his demand for $200,000 and four parachutes was agreed to. The plane then took off and he jumped from it over Oregon, never to be seen again.

Crippen and his lover fled the country, but the captain of the ship on which they were fleeing to Canada recognized him and alerted Scotland Yard. Inspector Walter Dew jumped on a faster ship, boarded Crippen's vessel, and arrested him. He was hanged in Pentonville Prison, London, on November 23, 1910.

Live fast, die young

Bonnie Parker and Clyde Barrow were one of the more colorful gangs who wreaked havoc in the Depression of the 1930s. The couple carried out a string of robberies and nine murders before eventually being tracked down and killed in a hail of bullets on May 23, 1934, in Louisiana.

Last witch

Scottish medium Helen Duncan was the last person to be prosecuted under the British Witchcraft Act on April 3, 1944. She "materialized" a dead sailor wearing a cap of HMS *Barham*, a sunken ship about which the Admiralty had withheld information. The authorities became worried Helen knew and might betray details of D-Day preparations, and she was imprisoned for nine months.

Need change

Former bank worker John Wojtowicz tried to rob a New York bank to finance a sex-change operation for his boyfriend in 1972. He ended up surrounded by police in a 14-hour standoff before eventually being arrested. He was released from prison in 1978, by which time the movie *Dog Day Afternoon* had been made about the incident.

Time for lunch

French bank robber Albert Spaggiari spent two months digging from a sewer into Société Générale bank in Nice in 1976. His gang accessed the vault on the Bastille Day holiday and spent the weekend opening safety deposit boxes at their leisure and even drinking wine and dining. Although captured, Spaggiari escaped from the court by jumping from a window. He evaded further capture, possibly dying of cancer in 1989.

12

The number of times Charles Manson has been denied parole. Manson's warped philosophy predicted a race war, and he tried to speed things up by sending his followers to kill nine people in California in 1969. He will next be eligible for parole in 2027, age 92.

The Bandit Queen

India's Phoolan Devi became a female gang leader to avenge being assaulted. Her gang returned to the village where she had been attacked and rounded up and executed 22 men in 1981. After two years on the run, she gave herself up and spent 11 years in prison awaiting trial. Charges were eventually dropped and she went on to become an MP. She was assassinated in 2001.

Reagan survives

John Hinckley attempted to assassinate U.S. President Ronald Reagan in Washington, D.C., on March 30, 1981, in an effort to impress actress Jodie Foster. Hinckley shot four people including Reagan, who survived the attack.

Eight years a captive

Austrian kidnapper Wolfgang Priklopil abducted Natascha Kampusch at the age of ten and held her captive for more than eight years. She escaped on August 23, 2006, while Priklopil was distracted by a phone call. The kidnapper then killed himself by jumping in front of a train.

Drug baron

Colombian drug lord Pablo Escobar was named by *Forbes* magazine as one of the ten richest people in the world in 1989. He is also thought to have been responsible for thousands of deaths. After he was arrested in 1991, Escobar was housed in a prison of his own design, but continued to oversee his empire. When authorities tried to move him to a conventional prison, he escaped and was shot by police in 1993.

110 YEARS

The length of the sentence given to Robert Allen Stanford for conducting a massive Ponzi scheme and fraud. Stanford's company was charged by the U.S. Securities and Exchange Commission with the fraud, which totaled $7 billion.

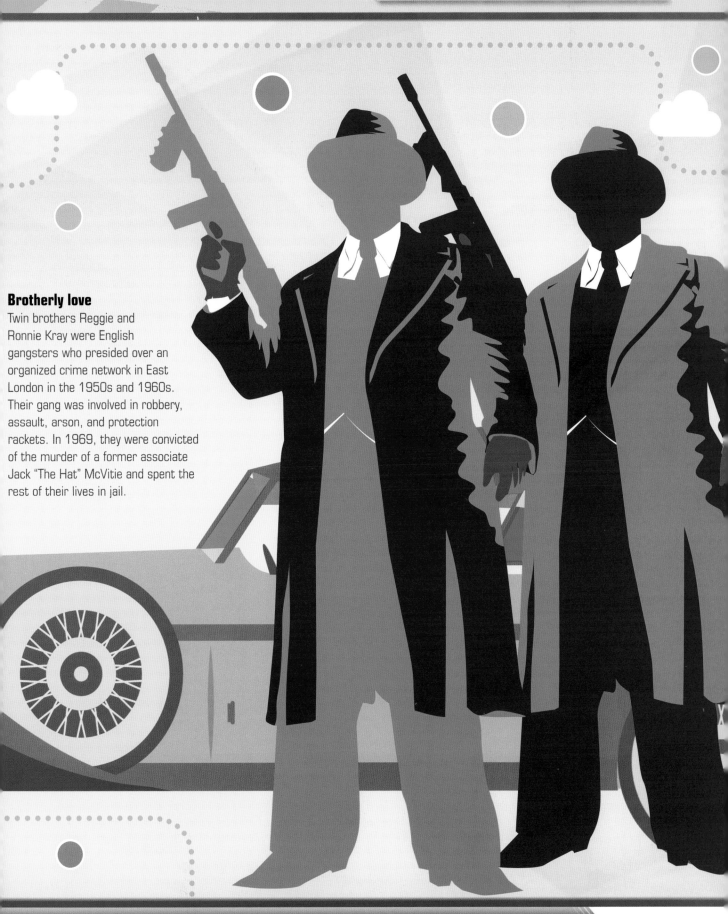

Brotherly love

Twin brothers Reggie and Ronnie Kray were English gangsters who presided over an organized crime network in East London in the 1950s and 1960s. Their gang was involved in robbery, assault, arson, and protection rackets. In 1969, they were convicted of the murder of a former associate Jack "The Hat" McVitie and spent the rest of their lives in jail.

CRIMINAL SUCCESSES AND FAILURES

They say that crime doesn't pay, but some make a go of it—for a time at least ...

SUCK IT AND SEE

In 2015, a French gang stole about £750,000 in 15 raids across Paris. The robbers worked out an ingenious way to use a modified vacuum cleaner to suck cash from the pneumatic tubes supermarkets use to transport notes from tills to safes.

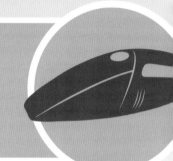

FRAMED

In May 2010, a thief broke into the Paris Museum of Modern Art and stole five paintings valued at 100 million ($123 million), by artists such as Picasso and Matisse. As the burglar alarm wasn't working, the thief simply smashed a window and removed the pictures from their frames before escaping.

BROUGHT TO BOOK

Former English soccer hooligan Cass Pennant emerged from four years in prison to write a successful memoir, *Cass*, which was made into a movie in 2008. He then started a publishing house, Pennant Books, which specializes in the stories of those who have ended up on the wrong side of the law.

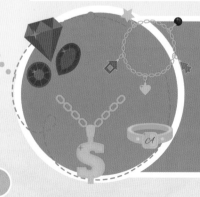

GLITTERING PRIZE

Serbian jewelry thieves the Pink Panthers are believed to have robbed more than 120 stores in 20 different countries. Renowned for their attention to detail and meticulous planning, their haul is in the billions, and with a revolving cast of criminals they have proved hard to catch.

For others, crime is a career dead end ...

STICKY BUSINESS

Kasey Kazee thought he had come up with the perfect disguise for robbing a liquor store in Michigan in 2007—a duct tape mask covering his entire head. Unfortunately for him, the covering simply made it impossible to deny he was the culprit when he was caught after running from the store empty handed.

COULD YOU SPELL THAT?

Wisconsin's Beezow Doo-doo Zopittybop-bop-bop made a big name for himself after he was busted for drug possession in 2012. Originally Jeffrey Wilschke to his friends, Beezow became national news due to his crazy name. His notoriety didn't stop him being arrested the following year for a similar offense.

TOO HOT TO HANDLE

In 2002, Australian thieves hoped to make a quick profit by using a blowtorch to open an ATM. However, the flames set the banknotes on fire and set off the alarm system.

INKED

Many people regret getting tattoos, none more so than Aarron Evans. The would-be car thief from Bristol, England, was caught on surveillance camera breaking into a car. It was handily positioned to capture his name and date of birth written on his neck.

ROBBER ROBBED

Brazilian Mauricio Fierro emerged from the pharmacy he had just robbed to find the getaway car, which he'd left with the engine running, gone. While figuring out what had happened, his loot was stolen from him. He reported the crimes at the local police station, where he was identified by the pharmacist he had held up, and arrested.

$870 BILLION

The estimated value of global organized crime activity in 2012 according to the United Nations. Narcotics account for more than one third of the figure, with counterfeiting and people trafficking the next two most lucrative crimes.

ORGANIZED CRIME

Open and shut case

Chicago mobster Samuzzo Amatuna is said to be the first mobster to hide a weapon in an instrument case. He was an accomplished fiddle player and originated the use of a violin case to hide a gun. He was also vain and violent and once killed a laundry horse in retaliation for the laundry scorching his embroidered shirts.

Fingers will point

Japanese Yakuza gangsters have to sever the top joint of their fingers with a knife and present it to their gang boss if they displease him. As the government has cracked down on the group, former Yakuza spend up to $3,000 for prosthetic fingers to hide their organized crime past.

Easy riders

Hells Angels are one of the biggest organized crime groups around the world. In the United States, Canada, Sweden, Germany, and Australia, police have special units just to deal with biker gangs.

Hippo hike

Colombian drug lord Pablo Escobar was so rich that he started his own private zoo, with elephants, giraffes, and other exotic animals. When he was finally killed by law-enforcement officers in 1993, the animals were dispersed to other zoos. However, nobody wanted the four hippopotamuses, which have subsequently bred and now number around 60, and possibly many more.

0.1 PER 100,000

In Italy, there has been a 50 percent decline in organized crime or gang killings since 2007, down from 0.2 per 100,000 of population.

THE BIGGEST ORGANIZED CRIME GROUPS BY REVENUE

YAMAGUCHI-GUMI

$80 BILLION

The largest known gang in the world is one of Japan's Yakuza groups.

CAMORRA

$4.9 BILLION

Italy's most successful mafia group is based in Naples and dates back to the 19th century, when it was formed as a prison gang.

SINALOA CARTEL

$3 BILLION

Mexico's largest drug cartel, with an estimated 60 percent market share.

SOLNTSEVSKAYA BRATVA

$8.5 BILLION

The biggest syndicate of the Russian mafia has around 9,000 members, and is involved in the drug trade and human trafficking.

'NDRANGHETA

$4.5 BILLION

Based in the Calabria region, the 'Ndarangheta is Italy's second largest mafia group, with strong ties to South American cocaine dealers.

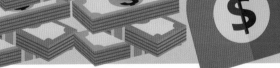

1,202

criminals were arrested after being featured on *America's Most Wanted*.

WANTED

Closing the net
Bank robber Leslie Ibsen Rogge surrendered to the FBI at the United States Embassy in Guatemala City, Guatemala, on May 19, 1996, after an individual saw his photo on the FBI website. He is credited as the first FBI Most Wanted criminal to be caught thanks to the Internet.

Picture perfect
In 1881, Percy Lefroy Mapleton was caught and convicted of murder on a train, following the first use of a composite picture of a suspect in Britain. An artist's impression of Mapleton was used on posters and in the *Daily Telegraph* newspaper.

54

The number of cards in the "Iraqi most wanted" playing card deck. During the Iraq war in 2003, the U.S. military gave troops a set of cards featuring pictures of the most wanted Iraqi leaders. Saddam Hussein was the ace of spades, and his two sons Qusay and Uday were the aces of clubs and hearts, respectively.

Band on the run

Former rocker Eric Franklin Rosser ended up on the FBI Ten Most Wanted Fugitives for the production and distribution of pornography. The former keyboardist with John Mellencamp's band was arrested in Bangkok in August 2001 and extradited to the United States.

First wanted poster

The FBI's first wanted poster was to help apprehend a deserting soldier, William N. Bishop, in 1919. Identification Order No. 1 featured a detailed description of Bishop, addresses he might visit, and a photo of him. He was subsequently captured on April 6, 1920.

Environmental criminals

In 2014, Interpol released a list of the nine most wanted environmental criminals, responsible for crimes costing hundreds of millions of dollars. They included animal smuggler Ahmed Kamran, illegal crab fisher Sergey Darminov, and Adriano Giacobone, who is charged with illegal transport and discharge of toxic waste, poisoning waterbeds, kidnapping, illegal detention, carrying of firearms, aggravated theft, and violence against a police officer.

Viral alert

The hunt for Ugandan warlord Joseph Kony went viral in 2012 when a movie detailing his crimes was released on YouTube. It went on to have more than 100 million views, although it was later criticized for being ineffective and misleading about money it raised.

23 YEARS

Fox TV's *America's Most Wanted* TV program ran for 23 years from 1988, making it the longest-running show on the network. It profiled the FBI's top ten fugitives and was a success from the start. Murderer David James Roberts was located in an apartment after hiding for four days after he had seen himself on the very first show.

414 YEARS

The length of time 28 criminals were sentenced to on the evidence of British supergrass Bertie Smalls in 1974 and 1975. He left the witness box to the songs "Whispering Grass" and "We'll Meet Again" sung by those he had helped convict. Smalls was given immunity from prosecution and lived to the age of 72 despite a price on his head.

POACHERS TURNED GAMEKEEPERS AND SNITCHES

Convicts please apply
An IT skills gap is forcing many UK companies to consider turning to hackers and ex-convicts in a bid to secure their IT networks. A report by consultants KPMG found that 52 percent of IT and HR professionals would use somebody with a criminal conviction.

Turning state's evidence
Accused criminals may turn state's evidence and provide information that helps convict others. Typically, this is done to make sentences more lenient, or for complete immunity and even a place in a witness protection scheme. In the UK it is known as turning Queen's evidence.

Security expert
Hacker Kevin Mitnick was on the FBI's Most Wanted list for hacking the computer system of Digital Equipment Corporation and stealing their software. He was a fugitive for nearly three years before being arrested in 1995 and serving seven years in prison. He now runs a company that helps other businesses discover security lapses in their systems.

Goodfella Hill
Arrested for drug trafficking in 1980, American gangster Henry Hill divulged information that led to 50 convictions. He entered the Witness Protection Program but was ejected in the early 1990s for continuing to commit crimes. His life inspired the movie *Goodfellas*.

Prison consultant
After serving ten years behind bars for conspiracy charges related to narcotics, securities fraud, obstruction of justice, and possession of automatic weapons, Larry Jay

1971

was the year that the USA launched its Witness Protection Program to encourage witnesses to speak out. Since then 18,400 people have been protected and the U.S. Marshals claim that nobody in the Program has ever been hurt or killed.

Levine used his experience and knowledge to become a federal prison consultant. His services include prison-survival education courses and legal services to lawyers and offenders.

Misleading statement

David Greenglass testified against his sister Ethel Rosenberg and her husband Julius in a trial that accused them of passing atomic secrets to the Soviets. He later stated that he had lied to protect his wife Ruth, who had typed the classified documents that he stole. Greenglass served nine and a half years in prison. The Rosenbergs were executed in 1953.

Frank admission

American drug dealer Frank Lucas was sentenced to 70 years for importing heroin from Southeast Asia to the United States during the Vietnam War. However, Lucas gained a reduction in his sentence after providing evidence that led to the conviction of 100 other criminals and was placed in witness protection along with his family. After he was released on lifetime parole in 1981, Lucas was again convicted of heroin possession in 1984 and was sentenced to a further seven years in jail.

THREE YEARS

The amount of time reporting restrictions were in place to cover trials associated with British "supergrass" Michael Michael. The drug dealer provided evidence that convicted 34 people for 170 years, and smashed 26 drugs syndicates. Michael provided evidence against his wife, his lover, and his own brother and was sentenced to a reduced period of six years in 2001.

GANGS

Fight the power

Jules Bonnot, the leader of a French anarchist crime gang, the Bonnot Gang, turned up at the offices of the daily paper *Petit Parisien* in 1912 to complain about its coverage of the gang. Brandishing a Browning pistol he boasted that he'd go down fighting the police. He did—they shot him a few months later.

Low pay

A 1997 study of American gang finances by economist Steven Levitt and sociologist Sudhir Venkatesh concluded that the average member of a drug-dealing gang would be financially better off taking a minimum-wage legal job.

1964

More than 1,000 members of Mods and Rockers gangs fought in the English seaside resort of Brighton. As well as indulging in running battles, the groups used bad language and kicked over deckchairs.

Policing the favelas

Brazil has introduced Pacifying Police Units (UPPs) to wrestle back control of *favelas*, or slums, in Rio de Janeiro, which have become the base for many organized criminal gangs. As of November 2013, 34 units were in operation in 226 communities, benefiting over 1.5 million people. The program has cut homicide and robbery rates.

Crips and Bloods

Notorious Los Angeles street gangs, the Crips and the Bloods, can be distinguished by their gang colors— Crips wear blue and Bloods wear red. Formed in the late 1960s and early 1970s, the groups have a long-standing animosity that often flares up into violence. There are thought to be around 50,000 members in the two gangs.

Prison breakout

Starting as a prison gang in St. Quentin jail in 1964, America's Aryan Brotherhood grew as U.S. prisons desegregated. When the system disbanded, prisoners started to group along racial lines. The group is now also active outside prisons, undertaking crimes such as moving stolen automobiles, motorbikes, and industrial machinery, armed robbery, and providing hit men.

Dance to the beat

Two Thai gangs in Bangkok decided to settle things with a "Gangnam Style"-like dance-off when they found themselves in the same restaurant in 2012. However, the slick moves soon gave way to violence and around 50 shots were fired.

Too cool for school

The *sukeban* is a gang composed of Japanese schoolgirls. Dating back to the 1970s, these delinquents are a female-only group who are reported to indulge in bouts of stimulant use, shoplifting, theft, and violence.

33,000

The number of violent street gangs operating in the USA in 2012, according to the FBI. They had around 1.4 million members, which was a 40 percent increase since 2009.

46664

The prison number of Nelson Mandela. Before he became the president of South Africa, Mandela spent 27 years in prison—18 of them on Robben Island—after being convicted of charges relating to sabotage against the apartheid state.

THEY FOUGHT THE LAW

Stealing the scene
French actor Gérard Depardieu was involved in petty crime as a youth and served three weeks in prison for stealing an automobile before being spotted as having acting potential by a talent scout.

Hard drive
Although he's now one of the world's richest men, Microsoft founder Bill Gates has a naughty past. On April 29, 1975, aged 19, he was arrested by the Albuquerque police department and charged with speeding and driving without a license.

Wesley's woes
Actor Wesley Snipes spent almost three years in prison after being convicted on charges of federal tax evasion in 2010.

Taxing times
Former Italian Prime Minister Silvio Berlusconi has been no stranger to legal scrapes. The politician has somehow managed to escape jail time, but he was ordered to carry out a year of community service at a care home in 2014 for tax fraud.

Stock recipe
American businesswoman and TV cook Martha Stewart was sentenced to five months in prison in 2004 for charges relating to the sale of shares.

Tale to tell
British novelist and politician Jeffrey Archer was jailed for four years in 2001 after being found guilty of perjury and perverting the course of justice. On his release, the prolific author published three volumes of prison diaries based on his experiences.

Stoned Stones
In 1967, Mick Jagger was sentenced to three months' imprisonment for possession of four over-the-counter pep pills he had

480 HOURS

Actress Winona Ryder was sentenced to three years on probation and assigned 480 hours of community service after she was caught stealing more than $5,000 worth of designer clothes and accessories from a Beverly Hills store.

purchased in Italy. His fellow Rolling Stone, Keith Richards, was sentenced to one year for allowing his house to be used for smoking cannabis. The convictions were later quashed on appeal.

Hot shot

In 1998, World Cup winner Diego Maradona was sentenced to two years in jail after firing a gun at journalists outside his home. The beloved Argentinian soccer legend has yet to serve the sentence.

EIGHT MONTHS

The length of the 1995 trial of former American footballer and actor, O. J. Simpson, before he was acquitted of murdering his ex-wife Nicole Smith and waiter Ronald Goldman. He was sentenced to 33 years in prison in 2008 for his role in a robbery in a Las Vegas hotel.

1974

The year in which mediation between victims and offenders started in Canada. Two accused vandals met their victims face to face to explain themselves.

REHABILITATION

Corrective action

In 16th-century London, Bridewell was established as a house of correction in a former royal palace. Originally part of the machinery of the Poor Law, houses of correction were intended to instill habits of industry through prison labor.

Model behavior

Supermodel Naomi Campbell was sentenced in New York to five days of community service after pleading guilty to striking her housekeeper with a cell phone in 2007. On her last day at the city sanitation department she turned up in a Dolce & Gabbana sequin dress and stilettos, and left in a silver Rolls-Royce.

On parole

Alexander Maconochie, a captain in the British Royal Navy, introduced the idea of parole in 1840 when he was appointed superintendent of the British penal colonies in Norfolk Island, Australia. To prepare inmates for a return to society, he developed a system where privileges were earned through good behavior, labor, and study. This built to conditional liberty outside of prison while obeying rules.

Borstal begins

At the end of the 19th century, there was recognition in Britain that young people should have separate prison establishments, leading to the development of the borstal system in 1908. Borstal training involved a regime based on hard physical work, technical and educational instruction, and a strong moral atmosphere. A young person in borstal would work through a series of grades, based on privileges, until release.

Puppy love

Inmates of the Shimane Asahi Social Rehabilitation Promotion Center in Japan help train guide dogs for the blind, raising the puppies and attending classes on dog walking and obedience training.

Highly strung

Musicians Billy Bragg and Mick Jones—guitarist with The Clash—started a rehabilitation program to teach British prisoners how to play

1933

The year Britain's first open prison was built, at New Hall Camp near Wakefield, Yorkshire. The theory behind the prison was summed up by penal reformer, Sir Alexander Paterson: "You cannot train a man for freedom under conditions of captivity."

16 PERCENT

The proportion of prisoners from Norway's Bastøy Island prison who are rearrested—one of the lowest rates in Europe. Prisoners live in cottages rather than cells, get themselves up in the morning, operate the island's ferry service, have access to saunas and sunloungers, and train for life after prison.

guitar. Jail Guitar Doors, named after a Clash B-side, started in 2007 and has donated more than 350 guitars to prisons.

Debt to society

Prison doesn't rehabilitate everyone. Armed robber Sean Bradish held up banks and building societies while on day release from prison. Londoner Bradish had been convicted of 100 raids in 2002.

1802

The first U.S. state prison library was established.

2%

The proportion of the population of Cabot Cove, fictional sleuth Jessica Fletcher's hometown, estimated to have been murdered during the run of U.S. TV series, *Murder She Wrote*.

CRIMINALS AND COPS IN CULTURE

Bored now

Crime writers have a tendency to grow weary of their detectives. Agatha Christie described her Belgian detective Poirot as "an embarrassment" and wrote the novel in which he died in the 1940s—but locked it in a safe until 1974. She saddled another of her characters, crime writer Ariadne Oliver, with a vegetarian Finnish detective, and made her frequently lament his existence.

Fact meets fiction

Real-life detectives have often inspired those in fiction. Wilkie Collins based the police officer in his novel *The Moonstone* on Scotland Yard inspector Jonathan Whicher, while Charles Dickens' Inspector Bucket was inspired by Inspector Charles Frederick Field. The 1950s' British TV series *Fabian of the Yard* was based on the memoirs of real-life detective Robert Fabian.

Ancient apples

One of the earliest known detective stories is "The Three Apples," one of the tales in the ancient Arabic collection, *One Thousand and One Nights*. In this story a king discovers a body inside a locked chest and orders his vizier to solve the murder in three days or face execution.

254

The number of times fictional detective Sherlock Holmes has been brought to life on the screen, making him the most portrayed human literary character in motion pictures and TV. He's not the most frequently portrayed character overall though—that's Dracula, with 272 appearances.

LAW
ENFORCEMENT

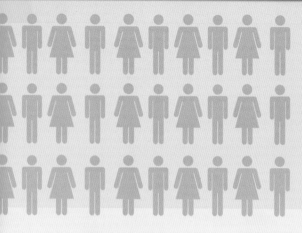

1,619.1

The number of police officers per 100,000 people in Bahrain, the country with the highest ratio of police to population.

POLICE

First force

The world's first independent police force was set up in Paris in 1667, and the first chief of police was Gabriel Nicolas de la Reynie, who served in the role for almost 30 years. The force moved into the world's first police station, close to Pont Neuf in Paris, in 1698. Before that they had been sharing premises with the judiciary.

Facial hair

Police in the Madhya Pradesh region of India were paid to grow moustaches to make them command more respect. The district's police chief came up with the idea, which saw moustachioed policemen earning 30 extra rupees a month, in 2004.

Drunk on duty

In the first six months after the Metropolitan Police was established in London, in 1829, just over half of the officers were sacked for drunkenness. They must have done something right though—four years later loot from robberies had been reduced from £1 million to £200,000 a year.

Small station

The smallest police station ever was located inside a lamppost in Trafalgar Square, London. It had room for one police officer and a telephone. It is still there today but is no longer used.

Cop car

The first police car was an electric wagon built by the Collins Buggy Company, bought by the police force in Akron, Ohio, in 1899, at a cost of $2,400. It had a top speed of 18 mph (29 km/h) and could run for 30 miles (48 km) without recharging. At one point it ended up in the Ohio River after being hijacked by a criminal mob, but was rescued and went on for a few more years of service.

4.4

The number of police officers per 100,000 people in Rwanda, the country with the lowest ratio of police to population.

1,600,000

The number of police officers in China, the country with the largest police force worldwide. Next on the list are India (1,585,353), Russia (782,001), and then the United States (780,000).

Polar police

In Hawaii, U.S. law-enforcement officers with jurisdiction over the South Pole were sworn in. The U.S. Marshals Service is the official law-enforcement entity for Americans in Antarctica, including those resident at research center McMurdo Station.

341.8

The average number of police officers per 100,000 people worldwide.

5 FRANCS

What Frenchman Eugène François Vidocq charged per interview when he founded the world's first private detective agency, Le Bureau des Renseignements. His services were available for an annual subscription of 20 francs or the five francs rate plus a percentage of any goods recovered. At its peak he was dealing with 40 clients a day.

DETECTIVES

The all-seeing eye

Although women were not allowed to be a part of a U.S. police force until 1891, and could not be detectives until 1903, the private Pinkerton National Detective Agency employed Kate Warne as the country's first woman detective in 1856. It is said she inspired the agency's slogan "We never sleep," which was displayed under a picture of an eye—supposedly the origin of the term "private eye."

Forced out

Inspector Jonathan Whicher was a founder member of the Scotland Yard detective branch and was known as the Prince of Detectives. He had a nervous breakdown after his theories about the murder of a three-year-old child, whose body had been stuffed down an outside toilet, were reviled by the press and public. He was proved right five years later but by then he had retired from the force.

Sniff test

Detectives in Northern Ireland are distributing scratch and sniff cards to members of the public to teach them what cannabis smells like. The police hope this will help people detect cannabis factories—forces using the cards have seen a 33 percent increase in reports from the public.

Seal of approval

The motto of the FBI, which appears on the investigation agency's seal, is "Fidelity, Bravery, Integrity." The two laurel leaves on the seal have exactly 46 branches because there were 46 states when the FBI was established in 1908.

Real-life inspiration

Chang Apana, a Chinese-Hawaiian detective working for the Honolulu Police Department at the turn of the century, was the inspiration for the fictional detective, Charlie Chan. He was successful in solving many cases—he is said to have arrested 40 gamblers in one night with no backup, armed only with a whip, and to have landed on his feet when thrown out of a second story window by drug dealers.

1811

The establishment of the first plainclothes unit, the Brigade de la Süreté. The first full-time professional detective was an ex-criminal who had spent time in jail for forgery and theft. Vidocq betrayed his band of highwaymen to the police and offered his services as an informer. He headed the group of 28 detectives, all former criminals.

FORENSICS TIMELINE

1248

The first forensics textbook was published in China, and was entitled *Hsi Yuan Chi Lu* (*The Washing Away of Wrongs*) by lawyer and death investigator Sung Tz'u. Investigating a fatal stabbing in a rice field, Sung Tz'u noticed blowflies were attracted to one sickle covered in invisible traces of blood, compelling its owner to confess to the crime.

1910

Edmond Locard, French professor of forensic medicine at the University of Lyon, France, set up the first police crime laboratory in Lyon.

1850

March 1850: The trial of John Webster, a professor at Harvard University, was one of the first to use dental evidence to identify a body. Webster murdered his colleague Dr. George Parkman, a man with glittering false teeth and an abnormally protruding lower jaw. Webster spent five days dismembering and burning the body, so no head or hands could be found with which to identify it. However, Parkman's dentist testified that teeth found matched the wax cast from which they had been made—evidence that sent Webster to the gallows.

1987

November 13, 1987: The first time DNA evidence was used to convict someone was in the case of rapist Robert Melias in Bristol, England. He was sentenced to 13 years in prison.

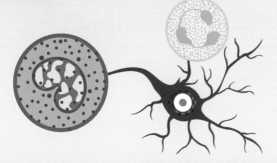

2004

April 2004: In Britain, Craig Harman was the first person to be arrested and convicted after police found a family member through a DNA search. Harman threw a brick from a motorway bridge, killing a truck driver. DNA evidence was found on the brick—Harman's DNA was not on file but that of a close family member was, and as a result Harman was tracked down and sentenced to six years for manslaughter.

2000

July 12, 2000: The first time that forensic gait analysis (the analysis of a person's style of walking as a method of identification) was considered admissible as evidence in criminal law. A consultant podiatrist was able to identify a jewelry thief at the Old Bailey Central Criminal Court, London, from earlier police surveillance footage. The expert confirmed that less than five percent of the British population walked in the same way as the suspected thief, who had stolen goods worth £750,000 ($1.1 million).

2012

Ecuador deployed the world's first biometric identification platform at a national level. The system combines voice and face identification capabilities to assist the security services' fight against crime. The database holds voice recordings or photographs of suspected criminals and allows them to be rapidly compared to identify individuals. According to the Russian developer of the system, the voice biometric identification system provides 97 percent reliability. Supplementing voice biometrics with face biometrics brings it closer to 100 percent.

734 MILLION

The number of fingerprints held by the Unique Identification Authority of India, the world's largest fingerprint database.

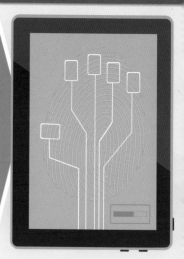

FINGERPRINTS

Prison break

In 19th-century India locals had a practice of hiring substitutes to take their place in prison. The guards didn't care as long as the head count was right, but British government official Sir William Herschel (1833–1917) of the Indian Civil Service insisted that convicts were fingerprinted in court to prevent anyone else from taking their place in jail.

Ancient evidence

The Chinese, Japanese, and Iranians were collecting hand, foot, and fingerprints from crime scenes as early as the year 300 and using them in subsequent court proceedings.

Print pioneer

The first Westerner to publically advocate the use of fingerprints in criminal identification and detection was Scottish missionary Henry Faulds (1843–1930), after he saw Japanese archaeologists matching up broken pieces of pottery by using the fingerprints of the ancient potters still visible on the clay. He was able to save a colleague from arrest after a break-in at a hospital by showing his prints did not match those found at the crime scene.

Murder solved

The first criminal conviction by fingerprint alone was secured by police in Buenos Aires, Argentina, in 1892. A mother who claimed to have been attacked and her children murdered by her neighbor was shown to have committed the crime herself. She was sentenced to life imprisonment.

Balls up

Burglar Harry Jackson was the first UK criminal to be convicted on fingerprint evidence alone, in 1902. He left a thumbprint on a freshly painted window frame after stealing a set of billiard balls. He had previously served time for burglary, so police had a copy of his prints.

28,000

The number of times law-enforcement professionals searched Interpol's database of more than 195,000 fingerprints from 178 countries in 2013. There were around 1,200 positive matches.

Acid test

Notorious 1930s' American gangster John Dillinger used acid on his fingertips to try to get rid of his prints. In the 1940s, burglar Robert Philipps, also known as Roscoe Pitts, went a step farther, getting a doctor to graft skin from his chest onto his fingers to get rid of his prints. Unluckily for him, he was identified by his palm prints.

Background check

Using the latest molecular-mapping technology, police can now use fingerprints to tell whether a criminal is male or female. They can also test fingerprints to find out whether the criminal takes drugs, what hair and cleaning products they use, and even what food they have been eating.

$30 MILLION

The largest amount paid by Rewards for Justice to one individual, for information leading to the location of Uday and Qusay Hussein, the sons of former Iraqi president Saddam. It is thought to be the largest reward ever handed out.

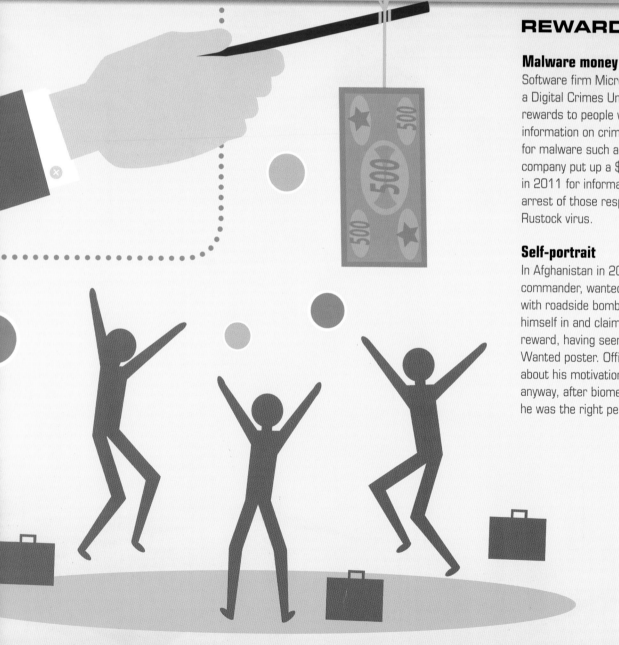

REWARDS

Malware money
Software firm Microsoft sponsors a Digital Crimes Unit which offers rewards to people who provide information on criminals responsible for malware such as viruses. The company put up a $250,000 bounty in 2011 for information leading to the arrest of those responsible for the Rustock virus.

Self-portrait
In Afghanistan in 2012, a Taliban commander, wanted in connection with roadside bomb attacks, handed himself in and claimed the $100 reward, having seen himself on a Wanted poster. Officials were unsure about his motivation but arrested him anyway, after biometric scans proved he was the right person.

$125 MILLION

The amount the U.S. Government's Rewards for Justice program has paid out to people who have provided information on terrorist suspects since 1984. More than 80 people have received rewards under the scheme.

Reward scheme

The Crimestoppers anonymous tip-off and reward scheme was started by Detective Greg MacAleese in New Mexico, following the murder of a gas-station worker in 1976. In the UK, businessman Michael Ashcroft (now Lord Ashcroft) stepped forward to provide a reward for information on the murder of police officer Keith Blakelock during riots in 1985—he founded the UK Crimestoppers organization three years later.

Thief takers

The development of daily newspapers in 18th-century England allowed the government and private individuals to better publicize rewards, leading to the rise of the so-called "thief taker" profession. Thief takers used their knowledge of the criminal underworld to profit from rewards, and some even encouraged gullible men to commit crimes so they could catch them and claim the reward.

No claims

Crimestoppers UK, the charitable organization that offers rewards for information that helps the police to make an arrest, says fewer than two percent of people eligible for a reward actually claim one.

Bounty hunter

Robert Ford, a member of Jesse Jame's Wild West outlaw gang, shot him in 1882 for the $10,000 reward offered by Governor Thomas T. Crittenden ($232,600 in today's money). However, he only got $500. He later earned money by posing for photographs as "the man who shot Jesse James" and reenacting the murder as part of a traveling show, but the public was not happy with the way he had shot the unarmed James from behind.

DOG GONE

In 2012, a British woman remortgaged her house so she could put up a £10,000 ($15,000) reward for the return of her dog Angel—thought to be the highest reward ever offered for a pet. The German short-haired pointer was thrown into a van by thieves while being walked by her owner.

POLICE KIT

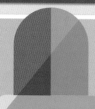

HELMETS

British police have worn the so-called custodian helmet since 1863, when it replaced top hats worn by the London Metropolitan Police at the time. As well as providing protection for the head, the helmets made police officers seem taller.

BODY ARMOR

The development of new tough materials such as Kevlar has made body armor much lighter and able to be worn for longer periods. The British Home Office was reported to be developing special protective vests for female officers who have had breast implants.

CAMERAS

Officers can now collect evidence at the scene of an incident with small body-fitted cameras that record incidents for future reference.

BATON

Police use batons or nightsticks as weapons of compliance and for self-defense. They are made from different materials and come in many different designs, such as expandable and side-handle batons.

GUNS

Many police forces routinely carry handguns. French police are issued with SP 2022s, New York police can choose between the Glock 19 and the SIG Sauer P226, while South Africa's force generally uses Vektor Z88s.

HANDCUFFS

The first modern handcuffs were invented by W. V. Adams in 1862. Since then they have become standard issue for police officers. In fact, they were originally called "handcops," from the Old English "cops," meaning chain or shackle.

TASER

Electrical stun guns were used by police as early as the 1960s. The TASER was patented in 1974 by NASA researcher Jack Cover. The design has developed since then, but its use remains the same—to incapacitate someone where a gun cannot be used, or to make an arrest without causing excessive injury.

RADIO

Detroit police-car patrols were the first in the world to receive radio communications in 1928, but it was only one way. Two-way communication didn't arrive until 1933. Personal radios now keep police in contact with HQ and other officers. It is legal to listen to police radio in Norway, and there are online streams to do so.

TABLET COMPUTERS

The fight against crime is increasingly hi-tech. The London Metropolitan Police force has tested the use of iPads by its street patrols, replacing notebooks and collecting witness statements.

TEDDY BEARS

Dutch traffic police often carry soft toys in case they come across children who have been traumatized.

60,000

The approximate number of Kinder Surprise eggs seized by United States authorities in 2011, a big year for chocolate-egg smuggling in the country. The Italian candy eggs with a toy inside are banned: U.S. Border and Customs Patrol describes the treats as "dangerous and potentially life-threatening."

STRANGE LAWS

No kissing
In Dubai kissing in public is illegal. In 2012, a couple were sent to jail for a year for kissing on a beach, despite the man's claim that he was giving his girlfriend the kiss of life because she was having an asthma attack.

Camouflage veto
If you are traveling to Barbados, you need to leave your camouflage clothing at home. It is an offense for anyone, even children, to wear anything made of camouflage material.

Street life
In the UK, it is illegal to carry a plank along a pavement. It is also illegal to fly a kite, play annoying games, sing rude songs, or slide on ice in the street. It is against the law to beat or shake a rug or carpet in the street, but beating or shaking a doormat is OK as long as it is before 8 a.m.

Driving ban
Legislation introduced in Russia in 2015 bans men from driving an automobile if they are wearing a dress. You are also not allowed to drive if you are a compulsive gambler or a kleptomaniac.

Hands off
In the UK, it is illegal to handle a salmon in suspicious circumstances.

Name game
In France it is illegal to call a child Nutella or Fraise (Strawberry). In New Zealand banned names include Justice, Christ, Senior Constable, and Stallion.

3,565

The number of names—1,853 female and 1,712 male—that Icelandic parents must choose from when naming their child. In Iceland, it is illegal to call your baby Harriet or Duncan—but Elvis and Jagger are fine.

Space election

In 1997, the State of Texas passed a law allowing American astronauts to vote in elections from space. A few of them have since taken advantage of this legislation and cast their vote from orbit.

Fishy business

Under a 14th-century law that has never been repealed, all whales and sturgeons found off the British coasts belong to the reigning monarch. However, when a sturgeon was caught in Swansea Bay, Wales, in 2004, Queen Elizabeth II decided she didn't really fancy it and it ended up in the Natural History Museum in London.

£120,000

($180,500) The amount handed out by UK police in compensation for police dogs biting innocent people between 2011 and 2013.

ANIMALS

Hero hounds

Some 11 police dogs have been awarded the PDSA Gold Medal for bravery and devotion to duty since its launch in 2001. New Zealand police dog Gage was awarded the medal posthumously for taking a bullet aimed at his handler, Senior Constable Bruce Lamb, during a drugs search. Spanish explosives search dog Ajax received the medal in 2013, after detecting a hidden bomb on the island of Majorca in 2009.

Failed experiment

The first experiment with official police dogs took place in 1888 in London, when Metropolitan Police Commissioner Charles Warren hoped to track infamous Victorian serial killer, Jack the Ripper, using two bloodhounds. However, one dog bit the commissioner and then both hounds ran off, requiring a police search to find them.

Police pigs

In the 1990s, police in Portland, Oregon, had an unusual colleague—a pot-bellied pig called Harley. The porker was used to sniff out illegal drugs.

Musical mounts

The Royal Canadian Mounted Police, known as the Mounties, have not used horses for regular duties since the 1930s. Horses are still used for special occasions such as the Mounties' equestrian event, The Musical Ride—they must be black, and all horses born in a particular year have names starting with the same letter.

Mind your language

Most United States police dogs are imported from Europe, which is why they are often given their commands in a language other than English.

Police officers say it is easier for them to learn 30 or 40 phrases in German, than for the dog to relearn its commands.

LEGAL SYSTEM

17 YEARS 8 MONTHS

The age of the youngest-ever judge, Marc Griffin of Greenwood, Indiana, who was appointed a justice of the peace on February 19, 1974. He presided over civil and criminal cases as well as performing weddings.

COURTS

Court statistics

The country with the highest number of judges compared to the general population is Slovenia, which has 50 judges for every 100,000 people. The lowest rate can be found in Ethiopia, which has 0.2 judges for every 100,000 people. Among the 20 countries with the highest rates of professional judges, 19 are from Europe, with Costa Rica being the only exception.

War crimes

The first person to be tried at the International Criminal Court (ICC) was Congolese warlord Thomas Lubanga Dyilo in 2009. Lubanga appeared on war crimes charges for his role in the civil war in the Democratic Republic of Congo. He faced charges of using children as weapons of war for his Union of Congolese Patriots, and recruiting and commanding a militia that committed atrocities. The ICC is based in The Hague, the Netherlands.

Cell phone madness

When a cell phone went off in Judge Robert Restaino's courtroom in New York State in 2005, he demanded to know who was responsible. When the offender didn't step forward to confess, Restaino sent all 46 people who were in the court that day to prison.

Queen's justice

The British Royal Coat of Arms appears in every courtroom in England and Wales, showing that judges and magistrates are official representatives of the Queen. Lawyers and court officials bow to the judge or magistrates' bench when they enter the room, to show respect for the Queen's justice.

104

The age reached by Judge Wesley Brown, from Kansas, who continued to work until a few weeks before he died in 2012. He used an oxygen tube in court to help him during hearings.

Court costume

In 1635, the correctly dressed High Court judge in England would have worn a black robe faced with miniver (a light-colored fur) in winter, and violet or scarlet robes, faced with shot-pink taffeta, in summer. A black girdle, or cincture, was worn with all robes.

Digital justice

The UK's Civil Justice Council has recommended the government should set up an online court service to deal with civil cases worth less than £25,000 ($37,600). This would include the appointment of online judges—full-time and part-time members of the judiciary who could pass judgment on cases via the web.

LAWYERS

Celebrity lawyers

Famous people with law degrees include talk show host Jerry Springer, comedian and actor John Cleese, singer Julio Iglesias, and Scottish actor Gerard Butler. Dave Rowntree, drummer in British band Blur, has qualified as a solicitor, as has former England soccer player Stuart Ripley.

Red tape

The phrase "red tape", meaning excessive bureaucracy, comes from the traditional use of red or pink tape to tie up official documents. Lawyers in England and Wales still use pink tape to tie up briefs relating to cases from private citizens. White tape is used for briefs from the Crown.

Courtroom drama

Ohio lawyer Clement Vallandigham died in 1871 while defending a man who was accused of murder during a barroom brawl. To show the jury how the victim might have accidentally killed himself with his own gun, Vallandigham staged a re-enactment. Unfortunately, while doing so he shot himself and died of his wounds. The defendant was acquitted before Vallandigham died.

18

The age of Gabrielle Turnquest, the youngest person ever to qualify as a barrister in England and Wales. The average age of lawyers passing the exams is 27. Turnquest was born in the Bahamas and raised in Florida.

245

The number of successful murder-charge acquittals in a row gained by Guyana-born lawyer, Sir Lionel Alfred Luckhoo (1914–97). Senior partner of law firm Luckhoo and Luckhoo, his acquittal rate led to him being described as the world's most successful lawyer.

Formal food

Eating dinner is part of the training for barristers in England and Wales. The law students have to take part in 12 "qualifying sessions," which can be formal dinners, before they can be called to the bar. For the dinner to count the student must remain seated until coffee has been served.

No nicknames

The State of New York tried to ban lawyers from using nicknames in their advertisements in 2007, but the ban was overturned. Popular nicknames include "The Hammer" and "The Heavy Hitter." In South Africa, Gerrie Nel, lead prosecutor in the murder trial of athlete Oscar Pistorius, is known as "Bulldog" for his tenacity.

Internet investigators

Two Australian lawyers created Internet legal history in 2008 when they used the Facebook social networking site to serve court documents on a couple who had failed to keep up repayments on their mortgage. Attempts to track the couple down in the real world, including private investigators and advertising, had already failed. A Supreme Court Judge ruled that court notices served on the site were binding.

Big law

In 2015, the world's largest law firm was created by the merger of American Dentons with the Dacheng Law Offices of China. The firm has more than 6,500 lawyers in more than 50 countries.

26%

26%

The proportion of UK jurors in high-profile cases who admit to having seen information related to the case on the Internet—something that is strictly banned.

JURY

Jury members

We think of juries as composed of "twelve good men" (or women) but the prescribed number of jurors varies across the world. In Gibraltar juries consist of nine people, in Hong Kong juries are generally made up of seven members, and in Norway there are ten people on a jury.

Spirit guidance

A UK man convicted of double murder in 1994 won the right to a retrial because four members of the original trial jury consulted a Ouija board before finding him guilty.

Justice game

A three-month-long drugs trial costing $1 million had to be abandoned in Australia in 2008, after it emerged

that jurors had been playing Sudoku for almost the entire duration of the hearing.

Judge not

Some religious groups, including Jehovah's Witnesses and Plymouth Brethren, are not supposed to judge other people's actions, so can excuse themselves from taking part in jury service.

1,501

The number of jurors in important trials in ancient Greece. More run-of-the-mill cases had juries with a mere 500 members.

64%

64%

The proportion of cases in which a jury finds the defendant guilty in the UK. When the defendants are male, juries convict in 77% of cases but, when the defendants are female, juries convict in 47% of cases.

Jurors are supposed to decide the guilt or innocence of the accused, but sometimes they are the ones who end up on the wrong side of the law.

In 2001, British grandmother Joanne Fraill caused a drugs trial to partially collapse after she contacted one of the defendants on Facebook. She was sentenced to eight months in prison.

Canadian juror Gillian Guess was sentenced to 18 months in prison in 1998, after it came to light that she had started an affair with the accused during the trial itself. The court clerk said Guess would flip her hair and smile at the defendant, who was on trial for murder.

In Britain, 51-year-old juror Janet Chapman was jailed for 56 days in 2012 for abandoning a robbery trial three weeks in, and flying off to Malta on holiday. She claimed she couldn't come to court as she had a bad back, but was caught when an official noticed she was calling in sick from a foreign number.

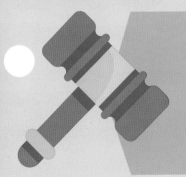

In 2004, two U.S. jurors received five-year prison sentences for accepting bribes in a 1996 cocaine-smuggling trial. Jurors Gloria Alba and María del Carmen Peñalver accepted $300,000 and $20,000, respectively. Alba promptly quit her job, took expensive vacations, and fixed up her house.

NOTABLE CASES

War law

The 1945 Nuremberg Trials of 23 high-ranking Nazis were a landmark in legal history, establishing a new international law of war. The prosecution team consisted of 23 U.S. attorneys, seven British barristers, five French advocates, and 11 Soviet lawyers. Twelve of the defendants were sentenced to death and three acquitted, while the rest received prison sentences.

Bad book?

The accused generally stands "at the bar" in British courts. But in the 1960 case of The Crown vs Penguin Books, the dock was empty, because it was a book that was on trial. The authorities failed to prove that D. H. Lawrence's

56

The number of countries in which the trial of war criminal Adolf Eichmann in Israel in 1961 was shown on TV. Israelis could watch live broadcast of the trial, while videotape was flown daily to the United States for viewing the next day. Eichmann was found guilty seven months after the trial began and sentenced to death.

313 DAYS

The length of the so-called McLibel trial, which saw fast-food chain McDonald's sue two environmental campaigners for libel. The longest-running trial in English legal history, it ended with McDonald's awarded £60,000 ($90,000) by the court, later reduced to £40,000 ($60,000).

seminal work *Lady Chatterley's Lover* was obscene and should not be published—the prosecutor famously showing himself to be out of touch when he asked the jury: "Is this a book you would wish your wife and servants to read?"

Famous speech

The Rivonia Trial in South Africa (1963–64) led to the imprisonment of future president Nelson Mandela. One of ten leaders of the African National Congress on trial for sabotage, Mandela—a lawyer himself—opened defense proceedings with a four-and-a-half-hour speech outlining his defense to the all-white jury, despite the prosecutor's efforts to prevent him from speaking.

Dingo death

One of Australia's most sensational trials was that of Lindy Chamberlain, who was accused of murdering her nine-week-old daughter in 1980. Chamberlain's claim that a dingo had eaten her child was dismissed by a jury who found her guilty, and she was sentenced to life imprisonment with hard labor. But in 1987 she was pardoned, and in 2012, 32 years after the tragic event, a coroner ruled that the dingo had taken baby Azaria.

Evil weevils

In 1587, the people of the French village of St. Julien instituted legal proceedings against the weevils that were destroying their grape crop. The weevils were appointed a defense counsel who argued they were only doing what came naturally, while the prosecution demanded the weevils be banished and excommunicated. We don't know the outcome of the case as the last page of the report was destroyed—perhaps by weevils.

SENTENCES

161

The number of life sentences handed to Terry Lynn Nichols, who took part in the preparations for the Oklahoma City bombing in April 1995, in which 168 people, including 19 children, were killed.

72

The number of criminals sentenced to death in the United States in 2014. This was a decline from the previous year in which 79 people received a death sentence. The majority of the sentences were handed out in California (14), Texas (11), and Florida (11).

15.6 MONTHS

The average length of a prison sentence in England and Wales.

$290,000

The world-record speeding fine handed out to a Swiss motorist who was caught driving at 85 mph (137 km/h) in a 50-mph (80-km/h) zone in 2010. He was driving a red Ferrari Testarossa and the fine was calculated based on his wealth, assessed at $22.7 million. It was also increased because he was a repeat offender.

9,000 YEARS

The amount American Darron Bennalford Anderson's 2,200-year sentence was extended by after he put forward an appeal and was reconvicted in 1994. This was later reduced by 500 years.

60 SECONDS

The length of the sentence handed out to U.S. soldier, Joe Munch, in 1906. Munch was charged with being drunk and disorderly but the judge decided that the offense only merited this token sentence.

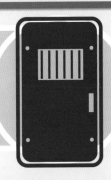

10,000 YEARS

The length of the prison sentence handed down in Alabama to Dudley Wayne Kyzer in 1981 for killing his wife. It is thought to be the longest single sentence in U.S. history. Kyzer also received two life sentences for murdering his mother-in-law and a student.

€1.06 BILLION

The record-breaking amount ($1.14 billion) microchip manufacturer Intel was fined in 2009 by the European Commission for anticompetitive practices and abusing its dominant position in the market. The company appealed the fine but the European General Court upheld the decision in 2014.

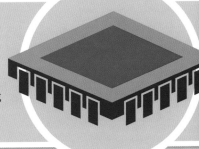

1,150,303

The number of criminals sentenced in England and Wales in one year to June 2014. Eight percent were immediately taken into custody, ten percent received a community sentence, and 69 percent were fined.

42,924 YEARS

The prison sentence given to Moroccan Otman el-Gnaoui, who helped to transport the dynamite used to blow up trains during terrorist attacks in Spain in 2004, which killed 191 people. His countryman Jamal Zougam, who planted at least one bomb, received a sentence of 42,922 years. However, under Spanish law the maximum sentence that can be served is 40 years.

SOME FAMOUS PARDONS

President Gerald Ford pardoned his predecessor Richard Nixon for any crimes he might have committed when in office.

Some 306 British men shot for cowardice during World War I were pardoned posthumously in 2006.

APPEALS AND PARDONS

Half-hanged Smith
In 1705, John Smith was hanged for burglary at Tyburn Tree in London. After he had been hanging for 15 minutes a reprieve arrived and he was cut down, still alive. He was known for the rest of his life as "Half-hanged" Smith. His near-death experience didn't seem to teach him anything however, and he returned to a life of crime, ending up with a sentence of transportation to Virginia.

Third time lucky
John Lee gained a similar reputation as "The Man They Couldn't Hang." In 1885, he was due to be hanged at Exeter Gaol in Devon, England, for the murder of his employer. The hangman tried three times to hang Lee, but each time the lever failed to operate, despite working fine when checked between attempts. Lee was returned to his cell. He was later given a reprieve by the Home Secretary.

Electric chair
Convicted murderer Michael Godwin, serving time in a prison in South Carolina, had his sentence reduced from death to life imprisonment. Although he escaped the electric chair he died in prison in 1989 after being accidentally electrocuted by sitting on his steel lavatory seat while biting a wire. He was trying to fix his TV set.

Alan Turing, pioneering British computer scientist and World War II codebreaker, was granted a posthumous pardon by Queen Elizabeth II in 2013 after being prosecuted in 1952 for homosexual acts, when such behavior was still criminalized in the UK. Turing killed himself two years after receiving the conviction.

Infamous English pirate Blackbeard, real name Edward Teach, took advantage of a royal pardon offered to any pirate who turned themselves in by a certain date. He subsequently settled in North Carolina in 1718, but died shortly afterward.

In 1977, President Jimmy Carter offered pardons to everyone who had evaded the draft during the Vietnam War.

PUNISHMENT

368

The estimated number of people burned alive as witches during the 16th-century Witch Trial of Trier in Germany, probably the biggest witch trial in Europe. Academics estimate the total number of people executed as witches in Europe and North America is between 40,000 and 60,000.

HISTORICAL PUNISHMENTS

No quarter

To be sentenced to be hanged, drawn, and quartered was particularly horrific, and reserved for men convicted of high treason in Britain. They were hanged until almost strangled, had their genitals cut off, their intestines ripped out, their head cut off, and their body cut into four pieces. The sentence was first recorded during the reign of Henry III (1216–72) and was officially abolished in 1870. Those hanged, drawn, and quartered include Scottish leader William Wallace, but would-be regicide Guy Fawkes cheated the executioner by jumping from the scaffold, breaking his neck.

Honey trap

The ancient Persians used to execute prisoners using a method called "the boats." The victim was placed between two boats fastened together with their head, hands, and feet sticking out of holes, and force-fed milk and honey, while also having the mixture smeared on his body. He was then left to be covered by flies and insects and to rot.

Wheel of fate

The prison treadmill was introduced in Britain by Suffolk engineer, Sir William Cubitt, in 1818. The labor needed to turn the wheel was agonizing and it achieved absolutely nothing.

Elephant executioner

Execution by elephant was a common practice in South Asia, particularly in India. Trained elephants would crush victims to death underfoot or, in some cases, slice them with blades attached to their tusks. Elephant executions were still taking place in India and Vietnam in the 19th century.

Stock punishment

The pillory and the stocks humiliated victims and made them a target for ill-treatment from the public. The pillory held victims by their head and hands in a wooden frame while the stock held them by their feet. Perjurer Peter James Bossy, 31, was the last person ever convicted to stand in the pillory in England, in 1830.

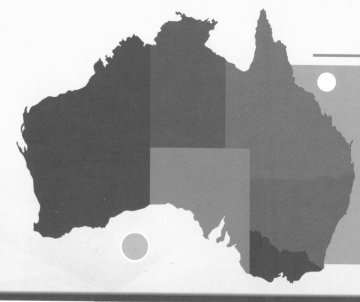

162,000

The number of prisoners transported from Britain to Australia over 80 years in the 18th and 19th centuries. There were around 137,000 men and 25,000 women.

Antismoking

Sam Mirza, the Shah of Iran between 1629 and 1642, strongly disapproved of smoking. He is reported to have had those caught smoking in public executed by pouring molten lead down their throats.

Pond life

The ducking stool was used in Europe and North America for punishing scolds and gossips. Victims were paraded around the streets before being tied to a chair on the end of a beam and ducked a number of times in a pond or river. The last victim of the ducking stool in Britain was one Jenny Pipes, in Leominster, in 1809.

779

The number of prisoners who have been held in Guantanamo Bay Detention Camp since 2002 according to the American Civil Liberties Union. As of January 2015, 122 were still there; 54 were cleared for release, and 36 lacked enough evidence to prosecute but were considered too dangerous to release.

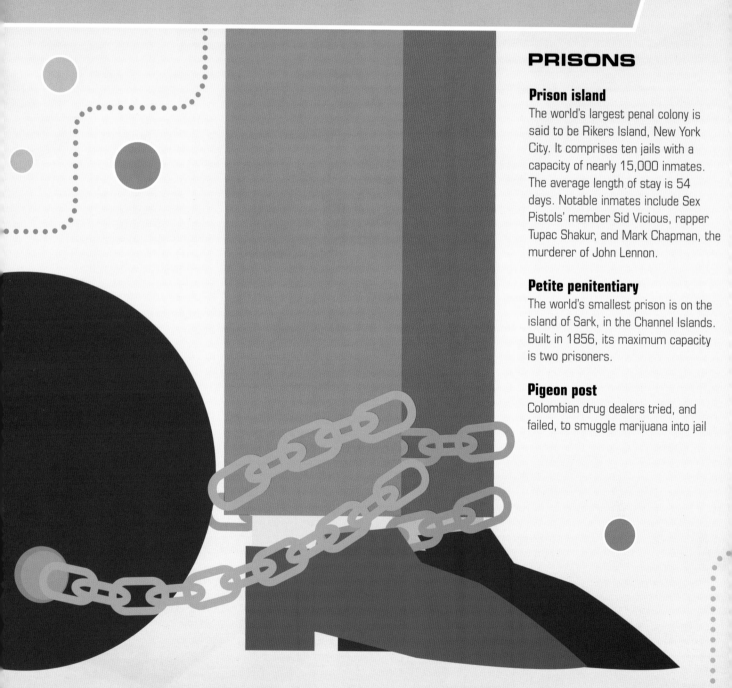

PRISONS

Prison island
The world's largest penal colony is said to be Rikers Island, New York City. It comprises ten jails with a capacity of nearly 15,000 inmates. The average length of stay is 54 days. Notable inmates include Sex Pistols' member Sid Vicious, rapper Tupac Shakur, and Mark Chapman, the murderer of John Lennon.

Petite penitentiary
The world's smallest prison is on the island of Sark, in the Channel Islands. Built in 1856, its maximum capacity is two prisoners.

Pigeon post
Colombian drug dealers tried, and failed, to smuggle marijuana into jail

using a pigeon as a carrier. A 1.6-oz (45-g) package was strapped to the pigeon and it was released in the direction of Bucaramanga jail. Inmates of the jail probably trained the bird but the package proved too heavy for the bird and it was easily captured by police officers outside the prison.

Life sentence
120 inmates of Carandiru prison, Sao Paulo, Brazil, married their fiancées in a mass ceremony on June 14, 2000. The brides wore white—the grooms wore prison pants.

Great escape
The largest jail break in history took place on February 11, 1979, when some 11,000 inmates escaped from

Ghasr prison in Tehran, Iran. The mass breakout was sparked by an Iranian employee of the Electronic Data Systems Corporation who led a mob into the prison to rescue two American colleagues.

Big mack
Some U.S. prisoners use mackerel as a form of currency, since a smoking ban led to a shortage of cigarettes. Foil packets of the oily fish, known as "macks," make a good cash substitute because hardly anyone wants to eat them and they are easy to store.

Bright spark
John "Ruby" Sparks was the first to escape from both Dartmoor and Strangeways prisons in the UK.

To escape Strangeways, Sparks made a dummy out of a stool, a blanket, and a chamber pot, donned a suit made from another blanket, and sawed through the cell bars, leaving a badly written poem behind him. In Dartmoor, Sparks memorized the design of the five keys he needed to escape and made them over the course of a year from metal secretly taken from the machine shop.

10.2 MILLION

The number of people held in prisons throughout the world, including those waiting for trial. If those reported to be held in "detention centers" and prison camps are included, the total is more than 11 million.

2,220,300

The number of prisoners in the United States, the country with both the most people in prison, and the highest percentage of the population incarcerated. There are 716 prisoners for every 100,000 Americans. The country with the lowest prison population rate is San Marino, where the rate is effectively zero.

Eton mess

To keep someone in prison for a year in the UK costs £45,000 ($68,000)—one and a half times as much as it would cost to send them to Eton, the public school attended by British Princes William and Harry.

Pay to stay

At San Pedro prison in Bolivia inmates have to pay for their stay. There are no guards inside the prison, no uniforms or metal bars on the cell windows. However, inmates have to pay for their cells, so most of them work inside the jail, selling groceries or working on the food stalls. In the past, tourists were allowed in on tours and to buy drugs.

Aliens detained

New York's Ellis Island, the gateway for millions arriving in the United States from Europe in the 18th and 19th centuries, became a detention center for enemy aliens during World War II. A total of 7,000 Germans, Italians, and Japanese were detained at Ellis Island during the war.

Cuba says "No"

Guantanamo Bay Detention Camp is located inside the U.S. naval base on the island of Cuba. The location is the result of a 1934 treaty that allowed the USA to rent the naval base for as long as it liked. The Cuban government has declined to accept payment since the Cuban revolution.

Family friendly

Aranjuez prison in Spain allows inmates to live as families in order that children can bond with their parents while toddlers. However, beyond the age of three the children must leave the prison.

Super secure

ADX Florence is a supermax prison in Colorado designed for the most dangerous inmates, including terrorists such as September 11 plotter Zacarias Moussaoui, Ramzi Yousef, who carried out the 1993 World Trade Center bombing, and "Unabomber" Ted Kaczynski. The maximum security unit houses around 410 inmates.

25 DAYS

Rioting prisoners in Manchester's Strangeways prison took to the roof in 1990, after wrecking most of the prison in Britain's longest-ever prison riot.

Thrilling spectacle
Inmates at the Philippines maximum security prison in Cebu undertake daily dance sessions to keep fit. These elaborate dances have become Internet sensations, with a movie of them enacting Michael Jackson's "Thriller" video clocking up more than 54 million views on YouTube.

36

The number of prisoners who tried to escape from Alcatraz Federal Penitentiary during its 29 years of operation. Most were recaptured, killed, or presumed drowned in San Francisco Bay, but it has never been definitely resolved whether the 1962 escape attempt by John and Clarence Anglin, and Frank Morris, was successful or not.

CAPITAL PUNISHMENT

Sharp shock

Dr. Joseph-Ignace Guillotin, who gave his name to the guillotine, did not invent the device. In fact, he was opposed to the death penalty. The machine was already in use—and known in France as a Louisette or Louison after the French surgeon who designed it—when Guillotin suggested it be used on humanitarian grounds for all executions, not just for aristocrats. He hoped this would be the first step toward abolition of capital punishment.

Hang it

Four English hangmen were hanged themselves. Cratwell was executed in 1538 for robbery, Stump-leg in 1558 for thieving, Paskah Rose in 1686 for housebreaking and theft, and John Price in 1718 for the murder of an old woman.

Lethal injection

The first prisoner to die by lethal injection was Charles Brooks Jr., at Huntsville Prison, Texas, in December 1982. He was sentenced to death for killing an auto mechanic whom he tricked into going with him on a test drive. Because of ethical problems surrounding a doctor deliberately causing death, the injection was administered by a medical technician.

4.1 PERCENT

The proportion of U.S. prisoners sentenced to death who are innocent, according to research from the University of Michigan.

80%

80 percent of all known executions in 2013 were recorded in three countries—Iran, Iraq, and Saudi Arabia. China keeps its execution numbers secret.

Final executions

The last men hanged in Britain were murderers Gwynne Owen Evans and Peter Anthony Allen. Both executions took place at 8 a.m. on August 13, 1964, but in different prisons. Ruth Ellis was the last woman executed in Britain, age 28, on July 13, 1955. A former model, she shot her lover four times outside *The Magdala* pub, in Hampstead, London, where the bullet holes can still be seen. Hangman Albert Pierrepoint said she was the bravest woman he ever hanged.

Medical check

Prisoners on Death Row in the United States are given a physical beforehand to make sure they are healthy enough to execute.

No warning

In Japan, prisoners on Death Row are not told when their execution is to be until a few hours before it takes place—some are given no warning at all. Families are usually only informed after the event.

Second thoughts

Albert Pierrepoint, Britain's last executioner, hanged more than 400 people in his macabre career but campaigned for the abolition of the death sentence on retirement. He said he didn't believe any of the executions he carried out acted as a deterrent against future crime.

Capital crimes

By the end of the 18th century, there were 220 crimes punishable by death in Britain. These included sheep stealing, damaging London's Westminster Bridge, living with gypsies for a month, and blacking your face in a forest. A 1723 law made more than 50 offenses subject to the death penalty and was known as the Black Act.

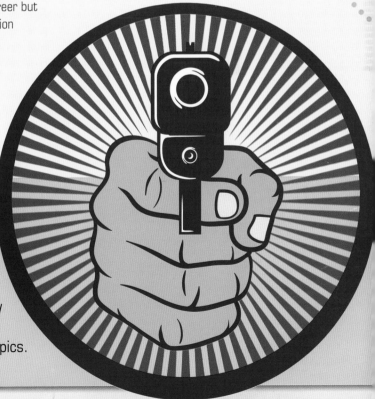

FIRING SQUAD

Murderer John Albert Taylor was the last man to be executed by firing squad in the United States, in Utah on January 26, 1996. He chose the firing squad to annoy state politicians who were worried about bad publicity because Utah had applied to host the 2002 Winter Olympics.

MUSIC MARATHON

An Ohio judge offered to cut a fine for noise violations from $150 to $35 if the defendant agreed to listen to classical music for 20 hours. The hip-hop fan, accused of playing loud music on his car stereo, lasted only 15 minutes before agreeing to pay the full fine.

STRANGE PUNISHMENTS

Speedy retribution

A group of UK teenagers who scammed sponsorship money for a charity run they had no intention of doing were made to complete the full 10-mile (16-km) run alongside a police officer after being caught. The police said it was a way of keeping them out of the youth court.

Silent justice

Officials in Venezuela sent 120 mime artists into the streets of capital Caracas to mock dangerous drivers and law-breaking pedestrians in 2011. The mimes, dressed as clowns, silently rebuked drivers jumping red lights and shamed careless pedestrians with elaborate gestures.

Activist's apology

A Malaysian activist had to tweet an apology 100 times over three days, as part of a settlement with a magazine publisher who accused him of defamation.

Slum sentence

A Beverly Hills landlord and neurosurgeon was sentenced to 30 days' house arrest in one of his own vermin-infested slums. The 63-year-old had been convicted for failing to improve conditions in four buildings that he rented to low-income tenants.

Swine sign

Ohio judge Michael Cicconetti is known for his creative approach to sentencing. He once sentenced a man who shouted "pigs" at police officers to stand on a corner next to a pig, holding a sign reading "This is not a police officer." He also sentenced a woman who abandoned kittens to spend a night alone in the woods.

THIS IS NOT A POLICE OFFICER

LAST WORDS

LAST WORDS OF MEN ABOUT TO BE EXECUTED

British serial killer Dr. William Palmer, also known as the Rugeley Poisoner, stood on the gallows in 1856 and asked officials:

IS THIS THING SAFE?

WELL, FOLKS, YOU'LL SOON SEE A BAKED APPEL

As George Appel was being strapped into the electric chair in 1928 he said this to the witnesses. Appel was executed for murdering a police officer.

Before being hanged in 1946, Englishman Neville Heath—known as the Lady Killer—asked for a whisky.

CONSIDERING THE CIRCUMSTANCES, YOU MIGHT MAKE THAT A DOUBLE.

I HAVE A TERRIFIC HEADLINE FOR YOU IN THE MORNING: FRENCH FRIES.

In 1966, James French did an attending newspaper reporter's job for him on his way to the electric chair. French, already in prison for life, had murdered his cell mate.

In 1987, Louisiana convicted murderer Jimmy Glass said this. Then he was electrocuted, at age 25.

I'D RATHER BE FISHING.

LAST MEALS OF CONDEMNED MEN

Thomas Grasso was executed in 1995 for using Christmas tree lights to strangle an 85-year-old woman. His last meal request included 24 steamed mussels, half a pumpkin pie with whipped cream, and a can of SpaghettiOs with meatballs, served at room temperature. Unfortunately, kitchen staff made a crucial mistake. Grasso's last words were: "I did not get my SpaghettiOs, I got spaghetti. I want the press to know this."

In September 2011, the State of Texas abolished all special last-meal requests after condemned prisoner Lawrence Russell Brewer requested a massive last meal and then refused it, saying he wasn't hungry. The repast included two chicken-fried steaks, a cheese omelet with ground beef, three fajitas, a pizza, ice cream, fudge, fried okra, a triple bacon cheeseburger, and a pound of barbecued meat with half a loaf of bread.

German serial killer Peter Kürten, known as the Vampire of Düsseldorf, consumed Wiener schnitzel, fried potatoes, and a bottle of white wine before his execution by guillotine in 1930. He requested a second helping and received it.

Nazi war criminal Adolf Eichmann declined a special meal before he was hanged in Israel in 1962. Instead, he drank half a bottle of a dry red Israeli wine, Carmel.

Until 2003, the last meals of inmates in Texas could be viewed on its Death Row website.

FUTURE CRIME

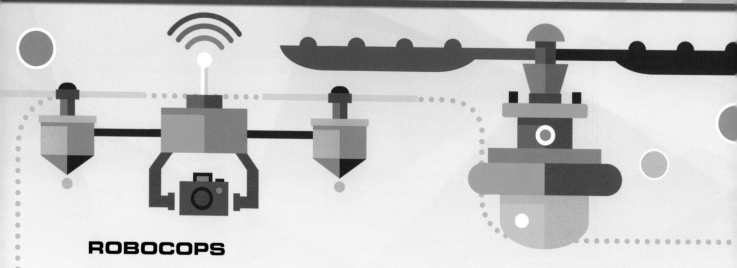

ROBOCOPS

Remote control

Students at Florida International University have created robots that could carry out community policing tasks, as well as surveillance activities. The wheeled, 6-foot-tall (1.8-m) telebots have three cameras and can be remotely controlled. They also have an "emotive display" allowing them to express simple emotions.

Giant robots

In Kinshasa, capital of the Congo, two 8-foot (2.4-m) tall robots are directing traffic and helping children cross the road. The solar-powered robots use lights, raised and lowered arms, and a voice—they can say "Drivers, you should make way for pedestrians," and "Don't touch me."

No driver

Driverless vehicles will likely present a challenge to law enforcement. Who is responsible when one driverless car crashes into another? Law and engineering academics at Stanford University are working on a project to understand how the law will apply to automated vehicles.

Drone arrest

The first arrest performed by an automated drone in the UK occurred in 2010. The Air Robot was deployed by Merseyside police officers when they lost a suspected car thief they were tracking through thick fog. The device's thermal-imaging camera led officers to the 16-year-old suspect hiding in bushes beside a canal.

Tactical partner

The latest addition to police Special Weapons and Tactics (SWAT) teams across the world is the Avatar III Tactical Robot. The robot, which is fitted with cameras and sensors, can open doors, move objects, and allow two-way communication, and is designed to be sent into dangerous situations to see what obstacles may be present.

Safety first

High-speed chases can be dangerous for police and for innocent bystanders. Now police can use a system that fires a GPS-equipped dart that attaches to a fleeing vehicle and then track the criminal car from a safe distance. The darts are aimed using a laser and stick using magnets and a special glue.

50 FEET

(15 m) The distance U.S. police officers can see through walls, using handheld radar units. The sensors can detect the slightest movements, including breathing, through concrete and brick. First designed for use in Iraq and Afghanistan, the devices show officers if movement has been detected inside a building and how far away it is.

900

The number of extra officers London's Metropolitan Police estimates its new mobile technology is worth in terms of freeing up existing officers to fight crime.

Smart tech

The Dubai police force has been experimenting with smart glasses. Traffic patrol officers will use the wearable technology to take photos of traffic violations, which will be instantly added to the traffic system, and to identify stolen automobiles just by looking at the license plate. The device can also link into a database of wanted criminals and alert officers when it recognizes one in real life.

30 PERCENT

Crime in Memphis, Tennessee, was reduced by this amount through the use of predictive analytics. By drawing on criminal records, statistics, and other data, police map crime hot spots and place officers in areas where crimes are more likely to take place.

FUTURE CRIME AND FIGHTING IT

Smart paper

It might not sound very exciting, but paperwork is an important part of the fight against crime, and technology will help police keep on top of it. Michigan police are planning a one-stop records management system that will incorporate all common administrative needs, including time accounting, report writing, form completion, and data collection, by 2022.

Sounds awesome

An acoustic stun gun is being developed by a British firm that will emit a directional beam of intense sound to target suspects up to 425 feet (130 m) away. A human guinea pig described the experience as making them feel as if their brains were rattling around.

Safety in numbers

Software can be used to help crowd control. Tech firm CrowdVision used a digital camera to overlook the crowds gathered on the beach to watch events on giant screens. The camera was connected to a computer, which ran software to predict movement. This allowed police to preempt the effects of crowd surges.

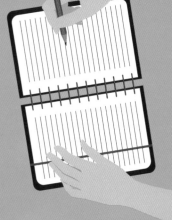
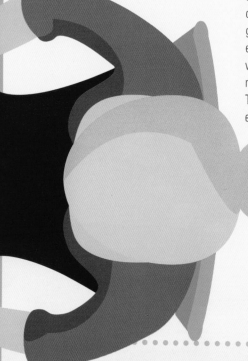

3-D PRINTING HAS BEEN SEIZED ON BY CRIMINALS

In Germany, a member of a lock-picking group released designs for a 3-D printed key that unlocks handcuffs used by Dutch police officers. He calculated the dimensions by looking at a photograph.

In Texas four men were indicted for using a 3-D printed skimmer that reads debit card details. It netted them more than $400,000 from an ATM machine. Bulgarian and Spanish police also arrested a gang who were 3-D printing skimmers on a huge scale in 2014.

Yoshitomo Imura, 27, of Kawasaki, Japan, was arrested by authorities for possession of five 3-D printed guns, two of which could fire real bullets.

Printing of illegal drugs by combining chemicals will soon be possible, experts predict. The University of Central Lancashire, England, has already devised a way of printing off customized medicines.

Online vigilance
Spanish researchers have developed a chatbot, or virtual presence, that could be used to police chat rooms. Software identifies suspect behavior and uses game theory to work out what tactics to use to keep individuals talking in order to gain enough information for a possible conviction.

Location locator
Researchers from the Ramón Llull University in Barcelona, Spain, have created a system capable of geolocating videos by comparing audiovisual content with a global database. In future, it could identify locations of images on social networks or kidnap videos to help locate missing individuals.

CRIME MOVES WITH TIMES.
HERE ARE SOME POSSIBLE FUTURE CRIMES

CYBER-JACKING

Technology could interfere with a plane's flight-management systems or ground-based flight-control systems to control flights or blackmail airlines.

HUMAN VIRUSES

WiFi-enabled medical devices, such as implants, could be attacked to harm individuals.

THE INTERNET OF THINGS

Wearables and future home Internet devices, such as smart refrigerators or controllable heating systems, could be controlled by hackers.

RANSOMWARE

Viruses that lock users out of their computers until they pay a fee will become more prevalent and more dangerous, as they target the plethora of devices controlled by the Internet, including our vehicles.

BIOLOGICAL HACKING

In the same way that computer hackers went from bedrooms and basements to affecting huge numbers of computers, biotechnologists will increasingly be able to synthesize materials that could cause chaos.

2054

The year in which police were able to predict who would be a criminal in Steven Spielberg's dystopian movie, *Minority Report*. In reality, they are not that smart yet, but predictive analysis is becoming ever more sophisticated, so who knows what the future will hold?

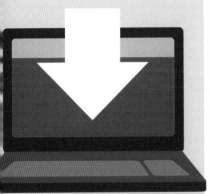

Spy in the office

Technology firms in Japan are using software to predict whether a rogue employee could steal from the company. NEC and security consultancy UBIC are looking at ways of mass data-mining employees' digital output, both inside and outside of the workplace. NEC's Mental Health Check tool can even measure your psychological state, mental fatigue, and aptitude and is already being used by some blue-chip companies in Japan.

Biological giveaways

Biometrics are unique physical characteristics that identify us. Fingerprints are one example, but in future, others could be used, including vein-pattern analysis, ear shape, gait analysis (the way we walk), and facial thermography, which indicates heat patterns on the face. All will make it easier to identify individuals.

Spoofing

As biometric security measures have become more sophisticated, criminals have become more determined to undermine them. So-called spoofing involves tricking biometric readers. Tsutomu Matsumoto, a graduate student at Yokohama National University, fooled fingerprint detectors by imprinting a random fingerprint on to a gelatin mold. Other biometric ID spoofing techniques use everyday materials, such as makeup, photographs, and voice recordings, to subvert or attack identification systems.

$100 MILLION

Suspected value of virtual currency Bitcoin stolen in November 2013 from online illicit goods marketplace, Sheep Marketplace. It is thought that the coins were processed and converted to cash, but no funds were recovered or culprits identified.

20.6 PERCENT

The average amount that gun crime fell by in a year in cities using electronic sensors to pinpoint the exact source of gunfire. Gunfire detection systems like ShotSpotter alert police when shots are fired. One area in the United States saw a fall of 80 percent in the number of gunshot incidents over a year.

CRIME PREVENTION

Fight cameras

British scientists have developed "fight cameras," which automatically alert police when violence is about to break out in public. The CCTV system can analyze crowd movements and predict where a brawl is about to happen, so officers can defuse the situation before it escalates.

Image share

A London wine-bar owner designed a system allowing businesses to share CCTV images of criminals with the police and each other, because he was fed up with his customers being victims of petty crime. Facewatch also provides an app allowing members of the public to identify and report criminals.

Hidden weapons

U.S. police are looking to develop a scanner that could use radiation emitted by the body to check for concealed weapons. Terahertz Imaging Detection can detect energy radiating from a body up to 16 feet (4.9 m) away and flag up anything blocking it, like a gun.

Danish design

The Sibelius estate in Copenhagen is Denmark's first estate designed especially to prevent crime. Built in the 1980s, it was designed without alleyways and other hiding places, with low hedges so residents can keep an eye on the area from their yards, and with public spaces that encourage natural surveillance.

Bench mark

Some cities use design to discourage homeless people—a luxury block of flats in London put metal studs in its doorways, while a French city enclosed its benches with cages over Christmas, so no one could sleep on them. But in Vancouver, Canada, the opposite approach is taken—some benches fold out at night to become temporary shelters.

121 cameras, six listening outposts, and 35 gunfire-detecting microphones guard the city of Camden, New Jersey, at a cost of $4.5 million. Crime has fallen by nearly 30 percent since the installation of the Real-Time Tactical Operations & Intelligence Center.

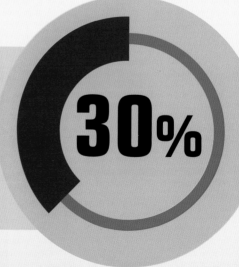

30%

42 PERCENT

There were 42 percent fewer burglaries on a social housing area in Nottingham, UK, after new secure windows and doors were fitted.

700,000

burglaries could be prevented in the UK every year if appropriate security devices were installed. That's an annual saving of almost £2 billion ($3 billion).

WAR
&
BATTLES

INTRODUCTION

Ever since the first cavemen began to bash each other over the head with rocks—and archaeologists are increasingly finding that ancient skeletons show evidence of violent assaults by clubs, axes, and arrows—warfare and battles have been part of our world. Throughout history man has developed ingenious ways of creating ever bigger bangs and killing his fellow man.

Those early battles may have been fought with primitive tools, but inventiveness quickly produced new and more powerful weapons. We think of chemical weaponry, biological warfare, and rocket-propelled missiles as horrors of the modern age, but they can all be dated back to olden times in one form or another—whether that's throwing plague victims over the walls of a besieged town or poisoning the enemy's

well. Of course these weapons have gradually been refined as time has gone by, with few, if any, war-free years to lull human beings into a sense of security.

Ancient writers tended to make grandiose claims for the numbers killed in particular battles, but the bloodiest wars have been without a doubt those of the relatively recent past. World Wars I and II produced some of the most fearsome fighting in history. They also spurred innovations that have helped us in peacetime, such as blood transfusions, plastic surgery, the jet engine, and plastics.

Nuclear missiles are just one of the astonishing weapons that you can read about in the following chapters. From the terrifying, such as the kamikaze planes and submarines of World War II, to the ever-so-slightly crazy, like the Great Panjandrum, a rolling drum of explosives that had an unfortunate habit of veering wildly off course. They are all here.

But weaponry is only one aspect of warfare. Uniforms have always been important for distinguishing troops. Did you know that although today's uniforms aim to camouflage troops, soldiers in the early days of gun fighting wore brightly colored outfits so combatants could identify their own comrades on smoky battlefields and cut down on "friendly fire" incidents? When it finally saw the need for jungle camouflage in the Pacific in World War II, the U.S. Army turned to the editor of a gardening magazine to produce its first design.

Men and women are not the only ones to go to war. Animals have been a crucial part of war efforts, from battle elephants in Mughal India and messenger pigeons in World War I, to bomb-carrying dogs and mine-clearing dolphins, our feathered and flippered friends have played a role, too. There is even a war memorial to the animal victims of war.

Wars have taken place on land, sea, and in the air, and we cover them all. You can learn about the world's biggest tank, and the role that inflatable tanks had in World War II. Or find out about the strange names that warships have taken through the years, or which army was the first to use paratroopers. It's all in here.

The names of some battles reverberate through history—Waterloo, Gettysburg, and Agincourt—while others are less well known, and frankly weirder—like the War of the Oaken Bucket. We cover both types, as well as the men and women who fought in them, from famous generals to rank-and-file heroes. And to round it all off, there's a glance into the future—from robot soldiers to space weapons, sci-fi warfare is just around the corner.

HISTORY OF
WAR

WAR TIMELINE

More than 120000 BCE

Bones have been found in Croatia dating from this period with marks made by stone spearheads—the oldest signs of warfare.

Around 2250 BCE

The first permanent army—some 5,400 soldiers—was created by Sargon of Akkad, the first great conqueror of the Sumerian cities of Mesopotamia.

490 BCE

Persian invaders were defeated by Athenian armored troops at Marathon in Greece. Legend has it that a runner carried news of the victory to Athens—the first marathon run—and promptly died

Around 3000 BCE

Organized warfare began.

900–600 BCE

The Assyrians (from modern-day Turkey) were the first society to introduce compulsory military service for all male citizens. Their armies were often considered unbeatable in the field.

June 27, 1743

George II was the last British monarch to lead his troops into battle at Dettingen, Bavaria.

1890

The Battle of Wounded Knee between the U.S. Cavalry and the tribal Sioux Indians was the last battle on American soil.

June 28, 1914

Archduke Franz Ferdinand, heir to the Austro-Hungarian throne, was assassinated in Sarajevo, Bosnia, setting in motion the events leading to World War I.

1863

The three-day Battle of Gettysburg, a key moment in the American Civil War, left the Confederate army in disarray. They had entered Gettysburg looking for shoes but suffered an attack by Union troops.

November 12, 1899

The earliest footage of war that still exists was shot during Britain's campaign at Orange River, South Africa, during the Boer War.

1066

An army of around 7,000 men under the command of William of Normandy met the 9,000-strong Saxon army of King Harold of England in Hastings. Harold was killed, and William took the throne.

1532

Spanish conquistador Francisco Pizarro landed in Peru with around 200 men and confronted the 40,000-strong Inca army at Cajamarca. The Spanish captured the Inca emperor and soon gained his empire.

636 CE

Muslim Arab forces met a Christian Byzantine army by the Yarmouk River in Syria. A massive sandstorm allowed the Arabs to mount a surprise attack and defeat the Byzantines.

1095–1291

The series of battles known as the Crusades, in which Christians and Muslims fought for control of the Holy Land.

8.16 a.m., August 6, 1945

The first nuclear bomb to be used in combat was dropped over Hiroshima, Japan. Approximately 80,000 people were killed as a direct result of the blast, and another 35,000 were injured. At least another 60,000 were dead by the end of the year from the effects of the fallout.

1990–1991

In 1990 Iraq invaded oil-rich Kuwait. The following year a U.S.-led force made up of troops from 29 different countries began a six-week aerial bombardment of Iraq, before ground troops liberated Kuwait in a four-day battle.

March 20, 2003

Coalition forces from the United States, Britain, Australia, and Poland began the invasion of Iraq.

September 1, 1939

Germany invaded Poland, initiating World War II—Britain and France declared war on Germany two days later.

1968

The only year of the 20th century in which no member of the British armed forces was killed on active service.

5,000–6,000

The number of chariots involved in the Battle of Kadesh, which pitted the Egyptians, led by Pharaoh Ramesses II, against the Hittite people (from modern-day Turkey) in around 1275 BCE. Although the battle is well-documented, nobody knows who won, since both sides claimed victory.

ANCIENT WAR

Toxic fumes

Chemical warfare was being used long before modern times. During the Peloponnesian War in the fifth century BCE, Spartans used sulfur and pitch to create toxic fumes to overcome their enemy.

Fungus attack

Biological weapons also have a long history. The Assyrians, in what is now Iraq, used rye ergot, a fungus blight, to poison enemy wells in the sixth century BCE. The poison caused delusional and paranoid behavior and even death among their attackers.

Early navy

The first recorded sea battle can be dated to around 1210 BCE. The king of the Hittites, Suppiluliuma II, defeated a fleet from Cyprus and burned their ships at sea.

Ancient weapon

The earliest recorded use of a crossbow was in 341 BCE at the Battle of Maling in China, although crossbows were probably used as early as the Stone Age, by people in Africa and Southeast Asia. Crossbows were introduced to England by the Normans in 1066.

War poem

The first formal declaration of war is found in the poem known as *The Epic of Gilgamesh*, from Mesopotamia (modern Iraq). The poem describes the deeds of Gilgamesh, king of Uruk in Mesopotamia, in approximately 2500 BCE. It is thought to have been composed in 1800–1700 BCE, nearly 1,000 years before Homer is believed to have written *The Iliad* and *The Odyssey*.

Battle books

The Romans helped formalize the art of war with military manuals that passed on best practice to future soldiers. Writers such as Frontinus collected successful stratagems from Greek and Roman campaigns in their works.

Gassed out

Ancient Persians used gas warfare when attacking a Roman garrison town in eastern Syria in around

1,178

The estimated number of vessels involved in the Battle of Salamis (480 BCE), thought to be the greatest naval battle of the ancient world. Oar-powered warships from Greece defeated a much larger fleet from Persia during the battle, which took place between the island of Salamis and the port city of Piraeus, Greece. The victorious Greeks sank about 300 Persian vessels and lost about 40 themselves.

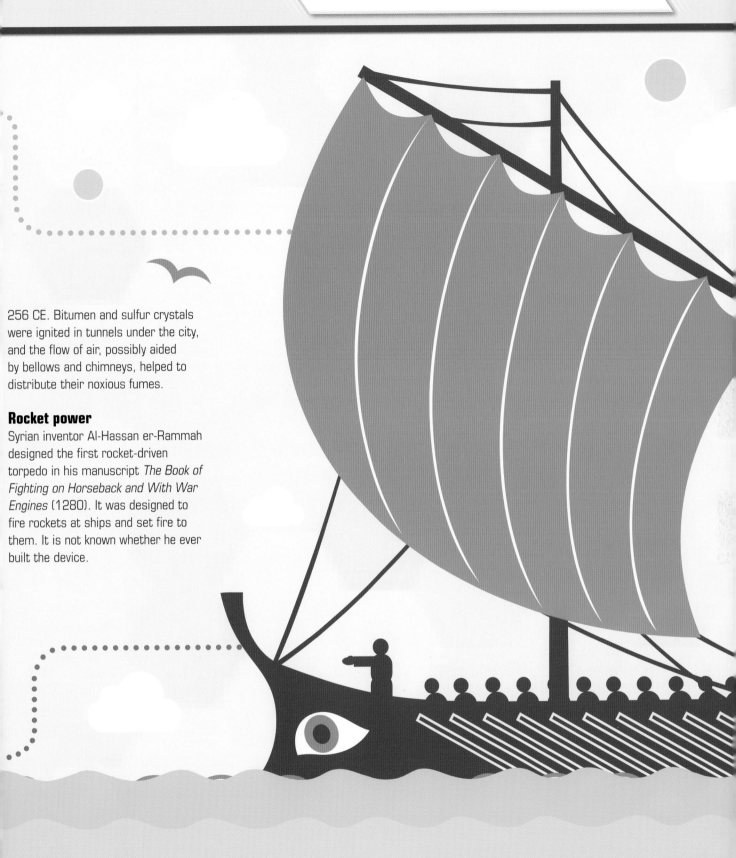

256 CE. Bitumen and sulfur crystals were ignited in tunnels under the city, and the flow of air, possibly aided by bellows and chimneys, helped to distribute their noxious fumes.

Rocket power

Syrian inventor Al-Hassan er-Rammah designed the first rocket-driven torpedo in his manuscript *The Book of Fighting on Horseback and With War Engines* (1280). It was designed to fire rockets at ships and set fire to them. It is not known whether he ever built the device.

38

The shortest war ever fought was between Britain and Zanzibar on August 27, 1896. Zanzibar surrendered after around 38 minutes.

 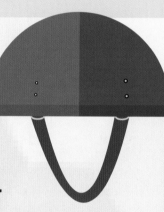

116 YEARS

The duration of the longest war, the confusingly named Hundred Years War, between English and French monarchs over claims to French land and the French throne.

46%

The proportion of the population of Paraguay that was killed in the Paraguayan war of 1864–70 against Brazil, Argentina, and Uruguay. Fewer than 30,000 of the survivors were adult males.

38%

The proportion of global military spending attributed to the U.S. in 2014. This was down from 47 percent in 2010.

ELEVEN

The number of countries not involved in armed conflict in 2014, out of 162 countries worldwide. These were Switzerland, Japan, Qatar, Mauritius, Uruguay, Chile, Botswana, Costa Rica, Vietnam, Panama, and Brazil.

$4 TRILLION

The estimated material cost of World War II far transcended that of the rest of history's wars put together. In the case of the UK the cost of £34.42 billion ($136 billion) was over five times as great as that of World War I and over 150 times that of the Boer War of 1899–1902.

1.1 MILLION

The number of casualties in the kingdom of Serbia during World War I, representing around 27 percent of the population. As well as casualties as the result of fighting, the country was hit hard by a typhoid epidemic. According to estimates by the Yugoslav government in 1924 Serbia's military dead (265,164 soldiers) accounted for 58 percent of the regular army.

26%

The proportion of armed conflict in Africa that Somalia was responsible for in 2014. Sudan and Libya were each responsible for ten percent, Nigeria for nine percent, and South Sudan for eight percent.

250,000

The estimated number of child soldiers in the world today. It is thought that 40 percent are girls and one in ten are found in the Democratic Republic of Congo. The UN believes that 15–30 percent of all new recruits in the D.R.C. army are under 18.

23 MILLION

The number of landmines estimated to be buried in Egypt, with most planted during World War II and the Egypt–Israel wars of 1956, 1967, and 1973. Egyptians refer to the minefields as "the Devil's garden."

4 YEARS, 3 MONTHS, 2 WEEKS
DURATION OF WORLD WAR I (28 JULY 1914-11 NOVEMBER 1918)

THE WAR TO END ALL WARS

Radio waves
The first battle between Germany and Britain in World War I was in Togo in East Africa, where British forces attacked a radio station used to relay information about British shipping. The Germans burned the station to the ground to prevent its capture and surrendered on August 26, 1914.

Main feature
In fall 1916, 20 million British people—half the population—went to see a silent movie, *The Battle of the Somme*, in theaters. The picture used real-life footage from the big push and turned it into a feature. It remains one of the most viewed British pictures ever. A second movie, of the Battle of Ancre, was released in 1917. In

2005 the Somme movie was digitally restored and released on DVD.

America goes to war
The US entered World War I on April 6, 1917, prompted by German attacks on US ships and the 'Zimmermann Telegram', a coded telegram to Mexico promising to restore to it pre-1836 territory, including Texas, if it allied with Germany.

Sausage time
As mayor of Cologne, future German chancellor Konrad Adenauer invented the vegetarian sausage because of wartime shortages. He was refused a patent for it in his own country, but Britain's King George V granted the soy sausage a patent on June 26, 1918.

Brazil backs the allies
Brazil was the only Latin American country to be directly involved in World War I. It declared war in 1917 due to German submarine attacks on its merchant ships.

The Somme
The British suffered 60,000 casualties on the first day of the Battle of the Somme on July 1, 1916, the worst toll for a single day in military history. Allied forces advanced 6 miles (9.7 km). Over the five months of the battle, more than one million people were killed.

U.S. hard line
Before the war, German had been the second most widely spoken language

17 MILLION
The total number of people killed in World War I—ten million troops and seven million civilians.

25,000 MILES (40,000 KM)

of trenches were dug on the Western Front.

in the USA. However, suspicion of Germans was so high during World War I that German shepherd dogs were killed and the names of frankfurters, hamburgers, sauerkraut, and dachshunds were all changed.

Shifting alliances

Although Japan fought alongside Axis forces in World War II, it was drawn into World War I on the side of the Allies because of the Anglo-Japanese Alliance, first signed in 1902.

No whistling

The British Defence of the Realm Act of 1914 included a ban on whistling for cabs in the street, in case it was mistaken for an air-raid warning.

INNOVATIONS OF WORLD WAR I

- Tanks
- Machine guns
- Zeppelins
- Bombing by plane
- Metal helmets
- Flame throwers
- Plastic surgery
- Blood transfusions

250,000

The number of underage British boys who served in the war. Soldiers were supposed to be 19, but the youngest, Sidney Lewis, was discovered to be just 12. The oldest person was William John Paxton, who enlisted at 68.

80%

80 PERCENT

Four out of five German troop deaths were on the Eastern Front in World War II.

6 YEARS AND ONE DAY

The length of World War II. It ran from September 1, 1939, until September 2, 1945.

ANOTHER WORLD WAR

Blitzkrieg

The German army tactic of blitzkrieg, or "lightning war," was developed to prevent the trench deadlock of World War I. Large mobile formations directed by radios could achieve rapid results. With these tactics, Poland was overwhelmed in just over a month in September 1939.

Radio assistance

British engineer Robert Watson-Watt was trying to develop a "death ray" that would destroy enemy aircraft using radio waves. However, it eventually became "radio detection and ranging," or RADAR, and was successfully used to give Britain advanced warning of attacks by German aircraft.

Bloody Stalingrad

The Battle of Stalingrad (1942–43) is believed to be the bloodiest battle in modern history, with anywhere between 800,000 and 1,600,000 casualties. It also marked the turning point of World War II in Europe.

Sounds familiar

The Nazis copied a Harvard American football song, *10,000 Men of Harvard*, to compose their Sieg Heil march. Harvard graduate Ernst Sedgwick Hanfstaengl, who composed Harvard football songs, became a confidant of Hitler. He claimed to have turned the chant "Fight Harvard! Fight! Fight! Fight!" into "Sieg heil! Sieg heil! Sieg heil!"

60 MILLION

The number of people thought to have died during World War II, the highest number in any conflict. Actual numbers are disputed and could be even higher.

INNOVATIONS OF WORLD WAR II

Atomic bomb
Computers
Jet engine
Napalm
Penicillin

Plastics
Radio navigation
Rockets
Synthetic oil and rubber

Tora! Tora! Tora!

The Japanese launched a surprise attack on 96 ships of the U.S. Navy at Pearl Harbor on December 7, 1941. Nineteen were sunk or seriously damaged, including eight battleships, 350 aircraft were destroyed or damaged, and 2,403 Americans killed. Britain and the U.S. declared war on Japan the following day.

War declared

On December 11, 1941, Germany declared war on the USA, the only nation it formally declared war on.

Winston rewinds

Winston Churchill's wartime speeches are said to have galvanized the British nation, but the versions that can be heard today were re-recorded by Churchill in 1949.

It's over

In 1974, a Japanese soldier named Hiroo Onoda came out of the jungle of the Pacific island of Lubang, 29 years after the war ended. He did not believe that the war was over and was only persuaded to emerge after his aging former commanding officer was flown in to see him.

D-Day

The Normandy landings of June 6, 1944, were the largest seaborne invasions ever, with 156,000 Allied troops landing on five separate beaches across 50 miles (80 km) of the coast. By late August 1944, northern France had been liberated, and by the following spring the Allies had defeated the Germans.

Her Hitler

The Allies hatched a plan to slip female hormones into Hitler's food to feminize him and curb his aggressive impulses.

1/4

The proportion of the Belarus population that died during World War II (2,290,000)—the highest in any country.

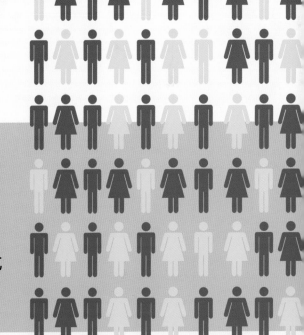

MODERN WAR

Shock and awe
The second Gulf War of 2003 saw 466,985 Coalition personnel deployed, 1,801 aircraft employed, and 41,404 sorties flown. The first Tomahawk missile strike on Baghdad was on March 20, 2003, and on May 1 President Bush announced that major combat operations were over. However, the last U.S. troops did not leave Iraq until December 2011.

Vietnam
During the Vietnam War, the U.S. sprayed more than 16.5 million gallons (75 million litres) of herbicides such as Agent Orange to deforest the Vietnamese jungle and deprive the North Vietnamese of cover. Thousands of people, including many children, still suffer disabilities as a result of the chemical usage.

Six-day war
A preemptive strike by the Israeli Air Force on June 5, 1967, destroyed almost the entire Egyptian Air Force, as well as destroying many Jordanian, Syrian, and Iraqi planes. The air victory provided a platform to allow Israel to seize the Gaza Strip, the Sinai Peninsula, the West Bank, and the Golan Heights by the time a ceasefire was agreed on June 11.

Ongoing conflict
Since the end of World War II there have been some 250 major wars, in which more than 50 million people have been killed, tens of millions made homeless, and countless millions injured and bereaved.

Falklands War
In 1982, Britain sent a taskforce of more than 100 ships and 28,000 troops 8,000 miles (13,000 km) to the Falkland Islands, which had been invaded by Argentinian troops. The task force set off on April 5, 1982, arriving at the islands on April 22. Troops liberated the capital Port Stanley on June 14.

Environmental disaster
The Iraqi army set fire to more than 600 oil wells in Kuwait as international troops moved to expel them from the country they invaded in 1990. Around one billion barrels of

58,148
Americans died in the Vietnam War, and 2.7 million Americans served in the war between 1955 and 1973; 1,642 Americans are still unaccounted for.

38TH PARALLEL

The line that split North and South Korea following the three-year Korean War in 1953. President Eisenhower threatened China, which was supporting communist North Korea, that the United States would drop the atomic bomb if a peace couldn't be achieved. A demilitarized zone stretching across the Korean peninsula was established as the new border.

oil are estimated to have been burned between the first oil-well fires on February 8, 1991, and the final well being capped on November 6.

Harry's war
Britain's Prince Harry served two tours of duty in Afghanistan. His first tour in 2007 was subject to a media blackout in an attempt to protect him.

War on terror
President George W. Bush first referred to the "global war on terror" on September 20, 2001, as an initiative to destroy al-Qaeda and other extremist groups.

NINE

The total number of Crusades

CRUSADES AND RELIGIOUS WARS

Sign in the sky
Roman Emperor Constantine was supposedly inspired to win the Battle of Milvian Bridge in 312 CE by a vision of the cross in the sky with the inscription *In hoc signo vinces*, meaning "In this sign you shall conquer." Constantine subsequently became a Christian, an event that helped cement the faith as the state religion of the Roman Empire.

Crusader foes
Although the Crusades are often portrayed as being between Christians and Muslims—or Saracens as Crusaders called them—other groups, such as the pagan tribes of Lithuania and Prussia, were considered legitimate opponents.

Dutch triumph
The Netherlands was established in 1648 as an independent state following the Eighty Years War against Spain. Among the causes of the war was growing resentment from the followers of Protestantism that reform did not reflect their faith.

The Reconquista
Spain was Islamic territory for more than 1,000 years, until a series of campaigns recovered the Iberian Peninsula from the Moors. Beginning in 718, the wars continued intermittently for 774 years until 1492, when Granada, the last Moorish stronghold, was finally conquered.

1095 CE

Pope Urban II initiated 500 years of conflict between Christians and non-Christians when he called for the recovery of Jerusalem from the Turks. Crusading armies took the city in 1099, but it was subsequently lost, resulting in further Crusades.

150,000 MARKS

The ransom demanded for the release of King Richard "the Lionheart" of England by Leopold V, Duke of Austria, in 1192. The vast sum was the equivalent of two to three times the annual revenue of England, but it was raised. Richard returned to England in 1194, only to head off to Normandy to fight with the French until he was killed by a crossbow bolt in 1199.

Religious freedom

Eight wars of religion were fought in France (1562–98) between the majority Catholic population and the growing numbers of Huguenots who sought greater religious freedom. The Edict of Nantes in 1598 provided this, but was revoked in 1685 by Louis XIV, resulting in the emigration of around 400,000 Huguenots from France.

Peace walls

"The Troubles" in Northern Ireland pitted Unionist Protestants, who wanted to remain part of the UK, against Republican Catholics, who saw their future as part of a united Ireland. More than 3,500 people have died in the conflict and so called "peace walls" continue to divide communities in the capital, Belfast.

Sneaky entrance

The ten-month siege of Antioch in 1098 was ended when the Crusaders bribed a guard who controlled one of the city's towers. He let them in, the gate was opened, and the Crusaders stormed the city, killing thousands of Christian civilians as they couldn't tell them apart from Muslim citizens.

ONE-FIFTH

The proportion of Mississippi's budget spent on artificial limbs for wounded soldiers in the year after the American Civil War ended in 1866.

CIVIL WAR

Uncivil war

In 1850, southern China was torn apart by the 14-year Taiping Rebellion. Conservative estimates of the dead start at between 20 million and 30 million.

Bloody end

Czar Nicholas Alexander, his wife Alexandra, and their five children, were shot by Bolsheviks on July 17, 1918, as the Russian Civil War raged. As well as the former royal family, 1.5 million combatants and around eight million civilians died between 1917 and 1922.

4 PERCENT

of the population of England and Wales are thought to have been killed in the English Civil War in the mid-17th century. This makes it the bloodiest war in British history relative to population size. Less than two percent of Britain's population died in World War I.

93,000

Pakistani troops surrendered in 1971, following the civil war between East and West Pakistan. As a result, East Pakistan declared independence and became Bangladesh.

Bosnia

The Bosnian War of 1992–95 came about as a result of ethnic tensions between Serb and Croat groups. Bosnian Serbs grabbed almost 70 percent of Bosnia Herzegovina. A process known as "ethnic cleansing" saw almost two million people displaced and around 100,000 killed.

Lengthy conflict

The ongoing internal conflict in Burma is one of the world's longest-running civil wars. It began shortly after the country gained independence from the UK in 1948.

Submarine first

The Civil War Confederate ship, *H.L. Hunley*, became the first submarine ever to sink another vessel during wartime, when she successfully "torpedoed" the Union Navy's USS *Housatonic* off Charleston harbor, South Carolina, on February 17, 1864. The torpedo consisted of a barrel of gunpowder attached to a spear, which the sub rammed into an enemy ship and detonated remotely by pulling a rope.

No surrender

There was no treaty signed to end the American Civil War. The surrender at Appomattox Court House on April 9, 1865, was a military surrender. Even if the Confederate government had surrendered, the U.S. government would not have accepted. To do so would have been to legally acknowledge the existence of the Confederate States.

Killing fields

More than 800,000 members of the Tutsi group in Rwanda were killed in just over 100 days in 1994. Most of the killings were carried out by the Hutu group using machetes. The government had imported one machete for every third male the year before, leading some to think that the genocide was planned.

5,819

The number of UN personnel in Africa's oldest state, Liberia, following the end of the second civil war in 2003. At its peak there were 15,000 UN peacekeepers.

16,300

The estimated number of nuclear warheads in the world. Around 4,280 are considered operational.

NUCLEAR WAR

History making

Only two nuclear weapons have ever been used in the course of warfare, dropped by the United States on the Japanese cities of Hiroshima and Nagasaki on August 6 and 9, 1945. The bombs were codenamed Little Boy and Fat Man.

Serial survivor

Tsutomu Yamaguchi was the longest lived of over 150 "double survivors"—those who survived both nuclear attacks. The Japanese man was 1.9 miles (3 km) from Ground Zero in Hiroshima, where 140,000 died. He was badly burned, but survived to return to his home in Nagasaki—where a second bomb was dropped three days later and more than 70,000 died. Mr. Yamaguchi died in 2010, age 93.

Hibakusha

Atomic-bomb survivors are known in Japan as *hibakusha* or "explosion-affected people." They are entitled to special medical and financial assistance.

Nuclear powers

The only countries known to have detonated nuclear weapons are the United States, the USSR (now Russia), Britain, France, China, India, Pakistan, and North Korea.

Animal testing

Pig 311 was a celebrated survivor of the U.S. nuclear tests at Bikini Atoll in 1946. One of 146 pigs placed on target ships to test the effects of the explosions, she was found swimming gamely across the lagoon and ended up being adopted by a zoo. As well as the pigs, 57 guinea pigs, 109 mice, 176 goats, and 3,030 white rats were used in the tests: 10 percent were killed by the air blast, 15 percent were killed by radiation, and 10 percent were killed by the researchers as part of later study.

Biggest bomb

The largest nuclear weapon ever exploded was the Czar Bomba ("King of Bombs"), detonated above a large island test site north of the Arctic Circle by the USSR in 1961. The 60,000-pound (27-tonne) bomb had

31,255

Number of nuclear weapons in the U.S. nuclear stockpile at its peak in 1967.

140

The number of nuclear tests that took place in 1962, the biggest year for nuclear explosions. Nuclear powers have conducted more than 2,000 nuclear-test explosions.

40,159

Number of nuclear weapons in the Soviet nuclear stockpile at its peak in 1986.

an estimated yield of more than 50 megatons. The explosion resulted in a fireball 5 miles (8 km) in diameter and a seismic wave that registered more than five on the Richter scale.

Forceful fashion
The bikini swimsuit gets its name from U.S. nuclear testing at Bikini Atoll. Paris swimwear designer Louis Réard, who registered the name, explained that "like the bomb, the bikini is small and devastating."

No laughing matter
An engineering company owned by the youngest Marx brother, Zeppo, was responsible for the design of the clamping device that held the atom bombs in place before they were dropped on Hiroshima and Nagasaki.

Chicken mines
In 1954 the British Army planned to place live chickens inside remote-controlled nuclear weapons, which it intended to bury in Germany in case of Soviet invasion. As it gets very cold underground, the chickens, which would be supplied with food and water, would keep the weapons warm enough to keep all the components working.

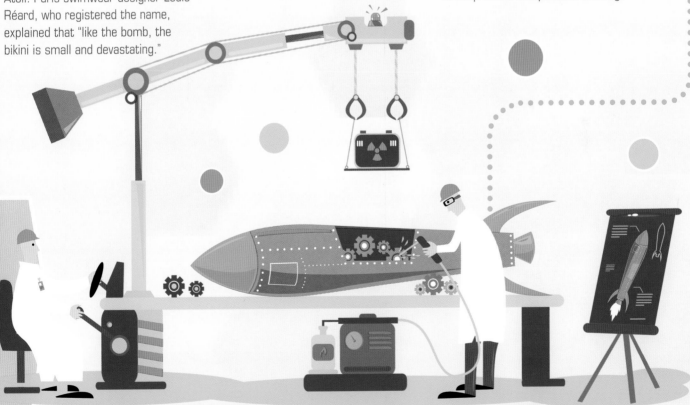

279 feet

(85 m) The height of *The Motherland Calls* memorial to Russian soldiers who fought the Germans at Volgograd in World War II. When it was completed in 1967, it was the tallest statue in the world. The female figure holds a sword that is 108 feet (33 m) long.

WAR MEMORIALS

Arched comment
The Romans built triumphal arches to commemorate their victories. The earliest known date to about the second century BCE but are no longer in existence. The 2,100-year-old Triumphal Arch of Orange in France is thought to be the oldest surviving triple arch and commemorates Gallic and Germanic wars.

Mountainous memorial
One of the biggest war memorials is on Stone Mountain, Georgia. Carved into the face of the mountain are three figures of the Confederate States of America on horseback. The carvings of Stonewall Jackson, Robert E. Lee, and Jefferson Davis, cover an area of about 3 acres (12,000 m²).

Remembered
The Arlington National Cemetery in Virginia is home to the remains of 400,000 soldiers from conflicts stretching back to the Civil War.

Beasts of war
In 2004, Britain erected a monument in Park Lane, London, to honor animals that had suffered and died while serving in war.

To the unknown
The Douaumont Ossuary contains the bones of at least 130,000 unknown French and German soldiers from the 1916 Battle of Verdun.

20,000

Cyclists gathered at Meriden Green, England, in 1921 for the inauguration of a memorial to cyclists who died during the Great War.

888,246

The number of Allied casualties of World War I commemorated by *Blood Swept Lands and Seas of Red*, an installation of 888,246 ceramic poppies in the moat of the Tower of London in 2014.

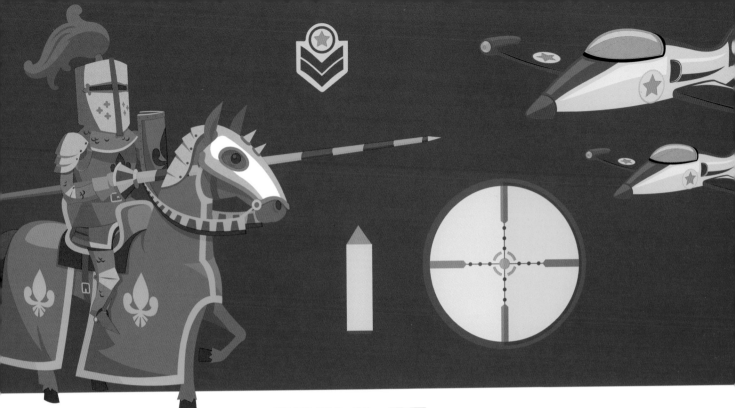

TOOLS OF
WAR

34

The number of battles won by what is thought to be the first standing army, formed by Sargon of Akkade in about 2250 BCE. The army consisted of around 5,400 soldiers.

ARMIES

King's shilling
In the 18th and 19th centuries, joining the Forces was said to be "taking the King's shilling." Lady Jane Gordon, the wife of the colonel of one of the Scottish regiments, toured Scotland in 1793 with a shilling between her lips—any young lad who wanted to join could have a shilling and a kiss. She recruited 940 men to fight the French.

Sausage song
The official song of the French Foreign Legion, *Le Boudin* (*The Sausage*), refers to Belgians as "lazy shirkers," because the Belgian king asked the French government not to commit Belgian Legionnaires in the Franco-Prussian War in the 1870s.

Seeing double
Zulu warriors in southern Africa carried their shields to one side to make it seem as if a man was standing next to them and fool the enemy into thinking the army was twice the size.

National service
The Bermuda Regiment is the only part of the British Army that still has conscription, based on a random lottery of 18–23-year-old men. Some 35 countries worldwide practice a form of conscription or national service.

Native force
Australia's Northern Territory is the largest military area of operations in the world at 700,000 square miles (1.8 million km²). It is largely defended by Aboriginal troops of Norforce (North-West Mobile Force). Britain's Prince Harry went on patrol with the native troops in 2015, as one of his final acts as a soldier before returning to civilian life.

Sleeve swastika
The U.S. Army 45th Infantry Division's shoulder sleeve insignia was a swastika from 1924. It was replaced in 1939 by a golden eagle, leading to the division's nickname, Thunderbird.

No protection
When Egyptian parents started blinding their children in one eye to

100

Roman centurions did not originally command 100 men. A *centuria* totaled 80 before a structural reorganization.

104,235

The number of uniformed personnel engaged in 16 UN Peacekeeping operations in 2015. They came from 128 countries. The UN has been engaged in 69 peacekeeping operations since 1948.

protect them from military service in the 1840s, the ruler Muhammad Ali set up a special corps of disabled musketeers.

Rock race

The Royal Ghurkha Rifles is the British Army's Nepalese regiment. Potential recruits are gathered from remote villages in Nepal, and have to complete a 2-mile (3.2-km) race up a near-vertical hill carrying 77 pounds (35 kg) of rocks in a basket attached to their head—in 20 minutes. Successful candidates are flown to North Yorkshire, England, to be trained for eight months.

Defense budgets 2014 (in billion U.S. dollars)

USA 581

CHINA 129.4

SAUDI ARABIA 80.8

RUSSIA 70

UK 61.8

Army sizes (active military)

China (2,285,000)

USA (1,325,000)

North Korea (1,190,000)

Russia (845,000)

Defense budgets as percentage of GDP

SOUTH SUDAN	10.32%
OMAN	8.61%
SAUDI ARABIA	7.98%
ISRAEL	5.69%
AZERBAIJAN	5.2%

Victorious armies against impossible odds

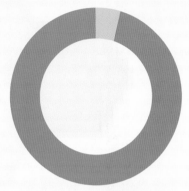

Thermopylae
480 BCE

300 Spartans
vs
around 200,000 Persians

Shayuan
537 BCE

Around 10,000 Chinese
troops under Yuwen Tai
vs
200,000 men under Gao Huan

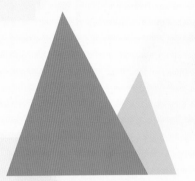

Kaithal, India
1367 CE

40,000 Muslim soldiers
vs
540,000 Hindu troops

Agincourt, France
1415

6,000 English and Welsh
troops
vs
20,000 French troops

Cajamarca
in modern-day Peru
1532

about 150 Spanish troops
vs
8,000 Incas

Rorke's Drift, South Africa
1879

139 British troops
vs
4,000 Zulus

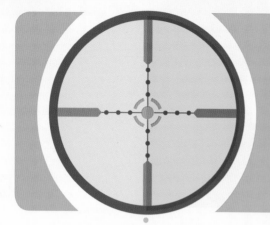

300

The earliest use of infrared technology in battle was in the 300 electric sniperscopes that were shipped to the Pacific during World War II. The scopes were mounted on top of rifles and converted the infrared energy of enemy soldiers into visible light, enabling the shooter to fire accurately in darkness.

WEAPONS

Bladed glove
In the 16th century, the Mughals of India developed the *pata*, an iron glove that extended to the elbow, attached to a sword blade.

No returns
Boomerangs were not all designed to come back. The lighter designs were for hunting birds but the heavier ones were weapons.

Fruit hit
Fiji island warriors often used a club shaped like a pineapple to attack their enemies.

Blessed blades
Samurai swords could take months to make, as they were produced by

4,000

The number of men required to fire the largest guns ever made. The German Dora and Gustav rail cannons of World War II had to be assembled and mounted on a prepared track. They also required an antiaircraft regiment and troops to protect them. Only Gustav saw active service, firing 42 of its 31.5-inch (80-cm) caliber shells during the 1942 siege of Sevastopol. The shells weighed 11,560 pounds (5,244 kg) and could travel 90 miles (145 km).

$400 BILLION

The Lockheed F-35 jetfighter is the most expensive weapon ever developed. The system has already doubled its original budget and depending on how many of the jets are sold, each one will cost between $80–115 million.

blending different types of steel and shaping them to create a blade. Each was made by a master craftsman and included prayers and religious rituals.

Oldest pistol

The oldest surviving gun has been dated to 1288. It was found in China in the modern Acheng district.

Gas attack

Mustard gas was discovered by Cesar-Mansuete Despretz in 1822 as a way to eradicate locusts. It was perfected in 1913 when the British biochemist Hans Thacher Clarke, working in Berlin, replaced one of the chemicals with hydrochloric acid and dropped the flask, hospitalizing himself for nearly three months. The German Army had

the gas in production before Clarke was back on his feet.

Balloon bombs

During World War II, the Japanese launched 9,000 "wind ships" against the USA. These paper and rubberized-silk balloons carried incendiary and antipersonnel bombs and more than 1,000 hit their targets, reaching as far east as Michigan.

Lock, stock, and barrel

This term refers to the three major components of early guns. The stock is the wooden holder in which the gun barrel is mounted, allowing it to be fired. The lock is the mechanism that ignites the charge of gunpowder in the chamber of the barrel.

Groovy guns

A rifle is a spiral groove inside a gun barrel, a series of which causes a bullet to spin and improves accuracy. Rifled guns became known as "rifles."

Blackout bombs

Nonlethal graphite bombs were used by NATO in May 1999 to successfully disable 70 percent of Serbia's power supply. The so called "soft" bombs work by exploding a cloud of thousands of ultrafine carbon-fiber wires over electrical installations, short-circuiting the electrical systems. It is thought they were also used in the Gulf War.

904 CE

Use of fire arrows—elementary rockets filled with gunpowder—was recorded as early as the tenth century. Chinese warriors were familiar with the explosive nature of gunpowder for celebratory fireworks and moved on to using it for military purposes.

100 MILLION

AK-47s have been produced since its invention by Mikhail Kalashnikov in 1947, making it the most widely used firearm in the world.

Blanket of death

The earliest documented use of the smallpox virus being used as a biological weapon was during the French and Indian Wars of 1754–63. British soldiers distributed blankets that had been contaminated with smallpox among the Native Americans, killing more than 50 percent of the affected tribes.

Kamikaze

The Japanese Kamikaze—meaning "divine wind"—tactic was suggested in October 1944 by Vice-Admiral Onishi in a desperate attempt to hit back at American forces. As many as 4,000 kamikaze pilots died, sinking 34 U.S. ships and damaging 368. Onishi committed suicide on August 16, 1945, leaving a note that apologized to those pilots who had been sent to their deaths.

Growth of IEDs

The use of improvised explosive devices (IEDs) is increasing as weapons of war. According to UK charity, Action on Armed Violence, they are second only to firearms as a cause of death. In 2013, it recorded 22,735 civilian casualties resulting from IED incidents. Where IED attacks occurred in populated areas, 91 percent of the casualties were civilians.

2 MILLION

The number of extra bullets that the British army overordered for its troops in Afghanistan in 2013. The bullets would not be fired by their "use-by" date and had to be recycled.

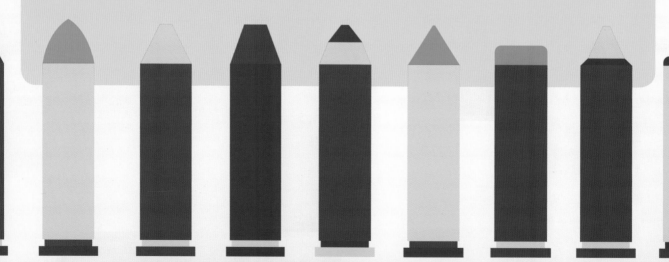

617

The number of the British "Dambusters" squadron that destroyed two Ruhr dams on May 16, 1943. Conventional bombs powerful enough for the task would have been too big to carry, but English inventor Barnes Wallis deduced that a smaller bouncing bomb placed at the foot of the dam would do the trick.

BANNED
MILITARY WEAPONS

DUMDUM BULLETS

Expanding bullets banned by the 1899 Hague Convention.

CHEMICAL WEAPONS

180 nations signed the Chemical Weapons Convention in 1997.

ANTIPERSONNEL MINES

162 nations have signed the Ottawa Convention.

WHITE PHOSPHORUS AND NAPALM

These burning weapons are also covered by the Ottawa Convention.

UNIFORMS

Garden designer
Norvell Gillespie, the garden editor of *Better Homes and Gardens* magazine, designed the camouflage print for U.S. service uniforms in World War II.

Germ-fighting pants
British troops are issued with germ-fighting underwear, designed to be worn for days at a time. The unisex pants have antimicrobial silver nanoparticles incorporated into the material. Troops in Afghanistan were issued with waterproof bacteria-zapping socks.

Bright colors
When soldiers started using muskets and other firearms in battle, battlefields became very smoky. Troops began wearing brightly colored uniforms to stand out against the smoke and combat the danger of being fired on by their own side. British soldiers started wearing red coats in 1645.

Safety helmet
The Israeli army provides its soldiers with a *mitznefet* helmet cover that disguises the shape of the soldier's head. It looks a bit like a militarized chef's hat.

Feathered friends
The Italian *Bersaglieri* (sharpshooters) wear a ceremonial wide-brimmed hat trimmed with feathers from wood grouse. They sometimes add feathers on to their combat helmets as well.

Belt up
The Sam Browne belt is used to carry a pistol and is mainly worn by senior military and police officers. The name comes from a British Indian Army officer who lost his arm in 1858 and found the belt helped him to continue wearing a sword.

Designer uniform
Hugo Boss, the founder of the eponymous fashion house, produced Nazi uniforms during the 1930s and 1940s. His company used prisoners of war and forced labor to produce the uniforms.

No umbrellas
Male United States Marines are not allowed to carry umbrellas while in

400

The number of pleats on the white kilts of the Greek presidential guards, to represent 400 years under Ottoman occupation. The uniform evolved from the outfits worn by the *klephts* (mountain warriors), who fought the Ottoman Turkish rulers of Greece until independence was won in 1829.

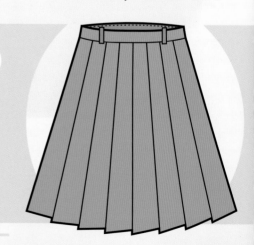

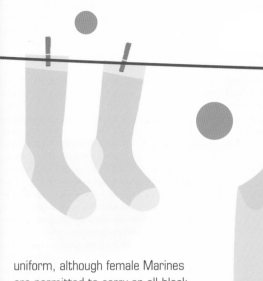

uniform, although female Marines are permitted to carry an all-black umbrella in their left hand during inclement weather.

Ax men

The dress uniform of the French Foreign Legion's sappers (combat engineers) brigade includes a leather apron and an ax. The Foreign Legion's Code of Honor, which all members have to learn by heart, compels them to take pride in their uniform.

Monster suits

The Australian Army calls the suits worn by its snipers "yowies," after the mythical Bigfoot-like Yowie said to roam the Australian wilderness. The outfits, called "ghillie suits" in other countries, are covered with shaggy scraps of cloth or twine to resemble foliage and aid camouflage.

$1,567.43 (MALE)
$1,798.42 (FEMALE)

The amount U.S. Army soldiers are issued to buy uniform. They then get $439 and $468, respectively, each year for replacements.

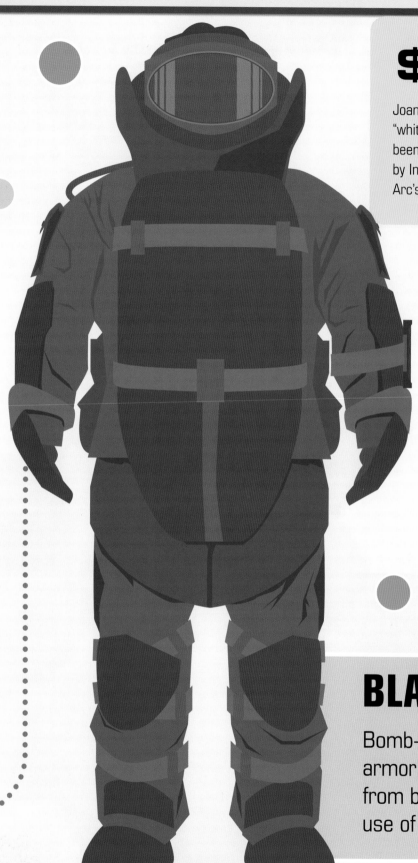

$61,500

Joan of Arc was said to have been given a suit of "white armor" by Charles VII in 1429, which has never been found. However, a recreation of the suit, as worn by Ingrid Bergman in the movie based on Joan of Arc's life, sold for this amount in 2011.

ARMOR

Late armor
As late as 1914, some French cavalry went to war in armor despite the fact they would be facing artillery and machine guns.

Strong silk
Ancient Chinese armies wore silk shirts under their armor, so that if an arrow pierced the armor it would drag the shirt into the wound without tearing it, and the arrow could be extracted cleanly by tugging on the shirt.

Hair helmets
Some ancient Egyptians grew their hair very long, then braided it tightly and wrapped it around their heads when going into battle. It is thought this may have helped to protect their heads.

BLAST PROTECTION

Bomb-disposal experts use special armor designed to give protection from blast waves while still allowing use of the hands.

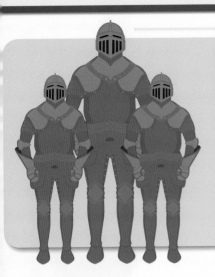

6 FEET 8 INCHES

(2.03 m) The height of the man who would have worn the largest suit of armor in the world. The 17th-century armor is housed in the Tower of London in England.

In the mesh
Mail armor features prominently on soldiers in the Bayeux Tapestry, indicating its prevalence in Europe by the 11th century. The practice of meshing small metal rings together for protection may go as far back as the Etruscans in the 4th century BCE.

Leather and steel
Armor was expensive, so medieval soldiers could opt for a cheaper and lighter version: "the brigandine." This leather or canvas doublet had steel riveted inside and was worn over mail.

Knights of old
By the second half of the 15th century, the suit of armor as we recognize it emerged. Improved steel manufacture made the material harder, and carefully worked shapes added strength while allowing relatively thin plates.

Samurai protection
Samurai armor was made of small plates laced together with silk and lacquered to protect it from the damp Japanese climate.

Colorful warriors
Babylonians wore brightly colored armor to look more impressive in battle around 1000 BCE.

Take the flak
Flak jackets became standard issue for American troops in the Korean and Vietnam conflicts. Pads of tightly woven fabric or ceramic plates provided some defense against bullets or shrapnel.

8,439

The number of individual pieces to make up the largest animal armor in the world. The 17th-century elephant armor at England's Royal Armories Museum would weigh 350 pounds (159 kg) if all the pieces were present, not including 22-pound (10-kg) tusk swords. War elephants were a feature of Indian warfare in the 16th and 17th centuries.

200,000

The number of pigeons who served Britain in World War II, carrying vital messages to and from the front line, ships, airplanes, and behind enemy lines.

ANIMALS AT WAR

Explosive dogs

During World War II, Russian tank regiments trained dogs to associate the undersides of tanks with food, planning to set the dogs of war loose on the advancing German Panzers, with explosives strapped to their backs. Unfortunately, the dogs, true to their training, associated only Russian tanks with food, and in 1942 the explosive hounds forced three brigades of Russian armor into retreat. They were successful in some battles, disabling 12 German tanks at the Battle of Kursk in 1943.

Bomb bees

Croatian scientists have trained honeybees to seek out landmines. The insects are trained to associate the smell of explosives with sugar, so they make a beeline for unexploded bombs. There are thought to be around 90,000 landmines in Croatia.

Marine mammals

The U.S. Navy's dolphin squad cleared a safe passage for ships in the port of Umm Qasr during the war in Iraq. Between March 24 and April 18, 2003, the aquatic mammals cleared 913 nautical miles (1,690 km), recovering 90 sea mines and destroying 11 more.

Daring donkey

Murphy, an Australian Army donkey, was posthumously awarded the RSPCA Australia Purple Cross in 1997 on behalf of all donkeys that served in the 1915–16 Gallipoli campaign. Murphy carried the wounded from the front on a hazardous journey down exposed rocky ravines to reach field hospitals.

Pigeon post

A World War I pigeon, named Cher Ami, received a medal from the United States Government for bravery. Cher Ami managed to get 12 vital messages through one battle in 1918. It also saved the lives of nearly 200 soldiers during another battle. Another pigeon, Gustav, was decorated for delivering the first message from the Normandy Beaches while serving with the British RAF on D-Day, June 6, 1944.

MORE THAN 16 MILLION

The number of animals that served in World War I. Used for transport, communication, and companionship, they included Togo, the cat mascot of the British battleship HMS *Dreadnought*, RAF No. 32 Squadron's fox-cub mascot, and the monkey mascot of the Third Army Trench Mortar School.

WARHORSE

Alexander the Great loved his warhorse Bucephalus so much he named a city after it when it died. Alexander is said to have tamed the supposedly untamable horse when he was 13, turning it toward the Sun so it would no longer be spooked by its own shadow.

Glowworms

Soldiers on the frontline during World War I used glowworms as lanterns. They collected them and kept them in glass jars so they could read maps, letters, and intelligence reports in the trenches.

1793

In this year, the French Chappe brothers demonstrated a visual telegraph, a system of semaphore arms that could be manipulated to form different shapes. A Chappe network spanned the whole of Napoleon's empire—the world's first telegraph network—and was still in use by the French military as late as the Crimean War, nearly 20 years after the electric telegraph had arrived.

COMMUNICATIONS AND INTELLIGENCE

Fiery message
The English navy was warned of the Spanish Armada of 1588 by a system of burning beacons on hills along England's south coast after the fleet was spotted off Cornwall on July 19.

Canine couriers
Dogs were used during World War I to deliver messages between the trenches when it was too dangerous for human runners. Dogs could cover 10–15 miles (16–24 km) in one or two hours.

Military Morse
Samuel Morse invented his Morse code for radio telegraphy in the 1830s. By the 1860s, President Lincoln was using it as a way of speedily being updated about the events of the Civil War and directing his generals. The Union forces used ciphers to ensure that the Confederates could not read their communications.

Navajo knowledge
The U.S. Army used Native Americans in both World Wars to deliver messages that could not be understood by the enemy. Around 400 Navajos, known as "code talkers," were enlisted in the Pacific war. The Japanese never cracked the code.

Innovative spy
Serbian spy Duško Popov, who worked as a double agent for Britain's MI5, is said to have been an inspiration for Ian Fleming's James Bond character. Popov spoke at least five languages and came up with his own formula for invisible ink. He also used microdots—photos shrunk to the size of dots. He tried to warn of the attack on Pearl Harbor, but the FBI did not act on it.

Beached body
In 1943, British intelligence landed a dead body on a Spanish beach as part of Operation Mincemeat, to convince the Germans that the Allies were going to invade Greece rather than Italy. A dead vagrant, given the identity of a naval officer, was planted with fake intelligence papers. The plan worked and is credited with saving as many as 40,000 lives.

183 miles

(295 km) The record distance for conveying a message by heliograph, achieved by the U.S. Signals Corps in 1894. The heliograph is a mirror that is used to flash Morse code many miles.

32 MILLION

The number of leaflets that were dropped over Iraq ahead of the Coalition invasion in 2003, warning Iraqis to avoid the conflict and promoting Coalition radio stations.

350 BCE

Greek writer Aeneas developed the hydraulic telegraph, a system that went beyond simple torch-based signals. Two distant parties would simultaneously remove a plug from a jar of water and replug it when signaled to do so. The level the water had descended to corresponded to one of an agreed series of messages, which could then be read.

Soldiers in a garrison eat up to 30 percent more calories per day than an adult civilian.

Stats

Adult male civilian
2,500 calories

Male soldier in garrison
3,200 calories

Male soldier in cold-weather field training
4,500 calories

Adult female civilian
2,000 calories

Female soldier in garrison
2,400 calories

Female soldier in training in cold weather
3,500 calories

LOGISTICS AND SUPPLIES

Time limit
Historically, battles generally took place in the summer, as the only way to keep troops fed was to allow them to pillage from local land. If the war had not been won by the fall the armies often had to return home.

Bonaparte's battalions
Supply was important to Napoleon, who said that an army marches on its stomach. His logistics infrastructure included 17 battalions of 6,000 vehicles, each of which would supply his troops for 40 days.

Twisted track
Railroads played a crucial role in the American Civil War, enabling quick and massive troop movements.

Union General Sherman destroyed thousands of miles of Confederate railroad, so much so that Southerners called the twisted rails left behind "Sherman"s neckties."

Blazing a trail
The People's Army of Vietnam developed a vast network of about 10,000 miles (16,000 km) of tracks and trails. The Viet Cong and North Vietnamese moved hundreds of tons of material along it every day, by bicycle, foot, and truck, to support their war effort between 1959 and 1975. It was known as the Ho Chi Minh Trail.

Gulf supplies
In 1990, the United States moved 2,000 tanks, 1,990 aircraft, 100

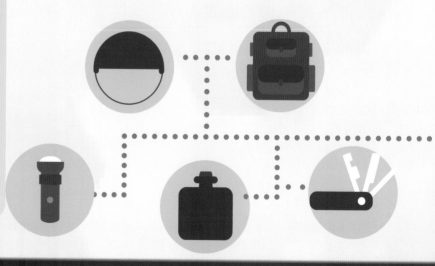

Soldiers in training in cold weather need almost twice as many calories.

warships, and 550,000 personnel to Saudi Arabia in a few weeks, ready to liberate Kuwait. In the first weeks of Operation Iraqi Freedom in 2003, U.S. military engineers built a record-breaking 220-mile (354-km) fuel pipeline from Kuwait to Iraq to ensure a supply of fuel.

Army catalog
Everything an army could want, from toothpicks to helicopters, has a 13-digit identification code. The codes are used by all NATO countries and some others, to make supply and requisition easier.

Soldiers around the world are issued with different ration packs when they enter conflict. These can include:

Britain
Mexican tuna pasta, chicken, sausage and beans, tea, lemon cake, chewing gum.

USA
Ratatouille with pasta, crackers, peanut butter, coffee, almond poppy seed pound cake.

Russia
Beef goulash, salted lard, meat with peas and carrots, vitamin pills, cheese spread.

Thailand
Yellow soup with fish, jasmine rice, beef with pepper and garlic, fish sauce, dried fruits.

Sweden
Yoghurt with breakfast flakes, chicken Rogan Josh with rice, nut cream, chocolate cake, meatballs with pasta.

Tanzania
Chicken stew, rice, porridge, mango drink, coffee, tea.

$244 BILLION

The predicted worth of the global private security market in 2016.

$138 BILLION

The amount the United States reportedly spends on "private security contractors" every year.

MERCENARIES

Foreign aid

The practice of hiring private soldiers to supplement an army is an ancient one. The Romans for example were not skilled at archery so hired archers from other countries. Most modern mercenaries work for private companies as security guards.

Scots abroad

One fifth of Scottish men in the 15th century went soldiering for foreign powers at some point in their lives.

Mercenary president

William Walker was an American mercenary who became President of Nicaragua in 1856 after helping out one of the sides in the country's civil war. As president he reinstated slavery, declared English an official language, and encouraged immigration from the United States. He was ousted by a coalition of Central American countries and executed by the government of Honduras in 1860.

Colorful soldiers

German *Landsknechts* fought for various European rulers in the 15th and 16th centuries. Renowned for their brutality on and off the battlefield, they wore distinctive multicolored tights and slashed doublets.

Failed coup

Former British Army officer Simon Mann was sentenced to 34 years in jail for his role in an attempted coup in Equatorial Guinea in 2004.

100,000

The estimated number of private security contractors working for the United States in Iraq in 2006.

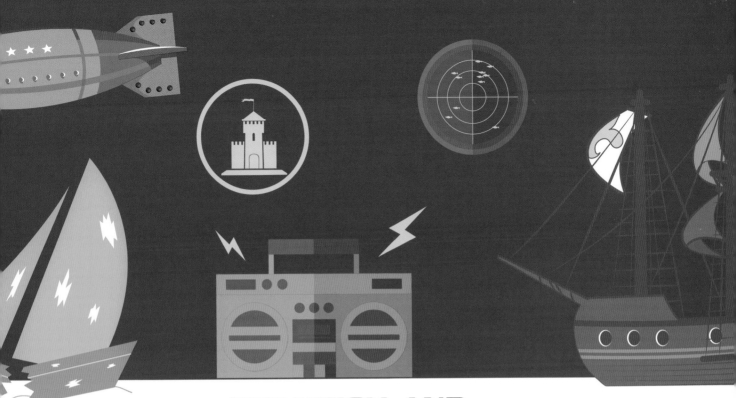

STRATEGY AND
TACTICS

16 miles

(26 km) The circumference of Ranikot Fort in Pakistan, believed to be the biggest fortress in the world. Its age and purpose are unknown.

CASTLES AND FORTS

Star shaped

Sébastien de Vauban, military engineer of French King Louis XIV, built more than 30 star-shaped forts because the traditional layout had become susceptible to artillery fire. His designs gave defenders excellent lines of fire and left no blind spots for attackers to exploit. He improved the fortifications of around 300 cities and conducted more than 50 sieges of enemy fortifications.

Murder holes

European medieval castles were often built with "murder holes" in the roof of the gateway. Popular imagination has it that castle defenders poured boiling oil on invaders, but oil would have been too expensive in most cases.

Although the holes may have been used to drop other missiles, their main purpose was to convey water to put out fires started by invaders.

First fortress

The stone walls of Jericho, which date from about 8000 BCE, were the world's first fortifications. At least 13 feet (4 m) tall and backed by a watchtower some 28 feet (8.5 m) tall, the walls were intended to protect the settlement and its water supply from intruders.

Line up

The Maginot Line, a series of fortifications built by France in the 1930s to defend its borders against attack from Germany, comprised 62

miles (100 km) of tunnels, 424 million cubic feet (12 million m^3) of earthworks, 165,000 tons (150,000 tonnes) of steel and 280 miles (450 km) of roads and railroads. It was built at a cost of 5,000 million francs. Unfortunately the Germans bypassed the line altogether, invading France through the Ardennes Forest in May 1940.

Earthquake survivor

Japan's largest castle, Himeji Castle, is made of wood and covered with white plaster. It has survived centuries of warfare—including World War II bombing—and earthquakes. When the rest of the city was damaged in an earthquake in 1995, it is said that even the bottle of sake

13,170 miles

(21,196 km) The entire length of the Great Wall of China. Begun in 500 BCE to protect the Chinese against attacks from the West, only 8.2 percent of the fortification remains intact.

placed on the altar at the top floor of the keep remained in place.

Body conscious

Fort Jesus, in Mombasa, Kenya, is built in the shape of a human body. It was constructed by the Portuguese in 1593–96 to protect the port and followed Renaissance beliefs that the most perfect proportions are found in the human body.

1,500,000

The estimated number of casualties of the 872-day siege of Leningrad (1943–44), one of the longest, costliest, and most destructive sieges in history. Most deaths were caused by starvation.

SIEGES

Roast camel

Parisians were forced to turn to unusual sources for meat when their city was besieged by Prussian forces for more than four months in 1870 and 1871. Zoo animals were killed and eaten, including elephants Castor and Pollux, camels, yaks, zebras, and antelopes. Top restaurants offered dishes such as Kangaroo Stew and Camel roasted à l'anglaise.

Hopeless cause

In the days of muzzle-loading muskets the soldiers in the first wave of attack during a siege were known as Forlorn Hope troops. It was likely that most of them would be killed or wounded, but those who survived would benefit from promotions and gifts. The French

47,400 TONS

(43,000 tonnes). The amount of iron fired during the siege of Sevastopol (1854–55)—the equivalent of six Eiffel Towers. The British fired 11,000 tons (10,000 tonnes) of iron shot, while the French fired 510,000 round shots, 236,000 howitzer shells, and 350,000 mortar shells. Some 100,000 Russians died defending the city.

Forlorn Hope soldiers, called *Les Enfants Perdu* (The Lost Children), were guaranteed promotion to officer rank if they survived.

Flaming pigs
The siege of Greek city Megara in 266 BCE was broken when the Megarians doused some pigs with combustible pitch, set them alight, and drove them toward the enemy's massed war elephants. Elephants are not keen on pigs at the best of times and they bolted in terror, trampling to death many of their own soldiers.

No surrender
In 73 BCE, the Romans besieged a group of Jewish rebels in the hill fortress of Masada by the Dead Sea,

constructing a massive ramp to get their siege engine up the mountain. The population is said to have committed suicide en masse rather than surrender.

Biological warfare
The 14th-century siege of Kaffa, in the Ukraine, is said to have introduced the Black Death to Europe. The besieging Mongol forces started catapulting the bodies of plague victims into the city. Ships carrying plague-ridden refugees then sailed to Constantinople, Venice, and other European ports.

Ship claw
Celebrated Greek inventor Archimedes provided the Syracusans, besieged by the Romans in 211 BCE, with

ingenious defense devices, including a lever-operated machine that could haul enemy ships out of the water. The Romans were apparently struck by terror whenever they saw a bit of wood peeking over the city wall, crying "There it is again!"

29 YEARS

According to ancient historian Herodotus, Azotus in modern-day Israel was besieged for 29 years by the forces of Psammetichus I of Egypt, making it the longest siege in history.

217 DAYS

The length of the Siege of Mafeking during the Boer War (1899–1900) in South Africa. Colonel Robert Baden-Powell negotiated that there would be no fighting on Sundays, allowing British troops to picnic, play cricket, and put on plays. Baden-Powell used psychological tricks on the enemy. His troops pretended to step over nonexistent barbed wire, planted fake landmines, and rigged up a fake searchlight. He became a national hero, as well as the founder of the Scout Movement.

FIGHTING ... ON LAND

Shield shell

Ancient Roman soldiers could adopt the *Testudo* (tortoise) formation to protect themselves from missiles. Troops in tight formation created a barrier on all sides using their shields, which allowed them to get closer to enemy positions safely.

Trench warfare

World War I frontline trenches could be a very hostile place to live—wet, cold, and exposed to the enemy. However, British troops actually spent little time there as the army rotated men continuously. Between battles, a unit spent perhaps ten days a month in the trench system and, of those, rarely more than three days were on the front line.

Biggest tank

The *Panzerkampfwagen VIII Maus* ("mouse") was the heaviest tank ever built. The World War II vehicle was completed in late 1944, only to be captured by Soviet forces. The Maus was too heavy to cross bridges and would tear up roads. However, it could cross rivers underwater, "breathing" though a large snorkel.

Ski patrol

The earliest recorded military use of skiing was at the Battle of Isen, near Oslo, Norway, in 1200, when the Norwegians undertook reconnaissance on skis.

Charge!

The largest cavalry charge in history was at the Battle of Vienna on

23RD

The 23rd Headquarters Special Troops were a U.S. Army division whose role was to confuse and deceive the enemy during World War II. Using props such as inflatable tanks, loudspeakers playing noise to indicate massing troops, and simulations of troop activity, the 23rd made the Allied forces appear more powerful than they were.

400 TONS

(360 tonnes) The amount of explosives buried in tunnels under German trenches during World War I by a group of British miners operating in total secrecy. The 21 mines at Messines Ridge in Belgium were detonated on June 7, 1917, creating explosions heard 140 miles (225 km) away in London.

September 11, 1683, when 20,000 Polish, Austrian, and German cavalry led by the Polish king, John III Sobieski, charged Ottoman lines.

Hidden danger

Although landmines can be dated back to the Middle Ages, their widespread use began during World War I and continued into World War II. As a cheap and lethal weapon, they proved popular with both sides. The 1997 Mine Ban Treaty banned the use, production, stockpiling, and transfer of mines. However, 35 states remain outside the treaty, and millions of mines remain active around the world.

£14,000

($55,500). The amount paid by the British government for salvage rights to the *Graf Spee*. The German warship was scuttled (in Montevideo) on December 17, 1939, to avoid capture. Using a Uruguayan company as a front, the British were able to obtain Germany's newest radar system.

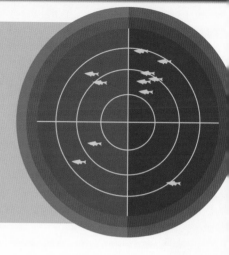

FIGHTING ... AT SEA

Chinese fortresses

Because of the country's large number of rivers and extensive coastline, the Chinese developed warships during the Neolithic period. Huge "floating fortresses" would approach another ship or palace, and crash into it, allowing hundreds of troops to stream aboard. Ancient Chinese inventors also devised snorkels, mines, and even torpedoes.

Biggest ever

The United States Navy's *Nimitz*-class nuclear-powered aircraft carriers are the biggest warships ever built. More than 1,000 feet (305 m) long, and displacing in excess of 100,000 tons, they have a crew of more than 5,000. Each ship can carry approximately

80 aircraft. The U.S. Navy has more aircraft carriers than all the other navies of the word combined.

Fire on water

Greek fire was used in defense of the Byzantine Empire. It was a liquid that ignited on contact with seawater, making it particularly effective in naval combat, and was first used against the Arabs at the siege of Constantinople of 674 CE. The ingredients of Greek fire were a state secret.

Back from the deep

English King Henry VIII's warship the *Mary Rose* sank as it sailed out of Portsmouth harbor in 1545. More than 400 years later, in 1982, the

ship was raised to the surface again and the remains are now displayed in the port.

Iron battle

The American Civil War saw the first battle between ironclad warships, the Union's *Monitor* and the Confederate *Merrimack*. Neither ship was destroyed in their 1862 battle, but *Monitor* did the most damage, and its turning turret became a feature of future fighting ships.

Speedy Skjold

The fastest operational class of warship is the Royal Norwegian Navy's *Skjold*-class stealth missile corvette, which can exceed 60 knots (69 mph/ 110 km/h).

1 IN 4

Of the 40,000 men who served on U-boats during World War II, only 10,000 returned. German U-boats sank more than 2,000 Allied ships at a cost of 781 U-boats destroyed.

77

Ships of the French fleet were scuttled in Toulon, France, on November 27, 1942, to prevent them falling into German hands. It was the largest scuttling ever.

Australia afloat

The Royal Australian Navy protects the world's seventh-longest coastline, at a length of 22,292 miles (35,876 km). It does this with 48 commissioned and four noncommissioned vessels, making it only the 51st largest fleet in the world.

Greatest maritime loss

The world's worst maritime disaster was the sinking of the MS *Wilhelm Gustloff* by a Soviet submarine in 1945 with the loss of 9,343 lives.

130

ships made up the Spanish Armada that sailed to invade England in 1588. As well as 22 fighting galleons, there were many smaller ships to supply the galleons and transport soldiers and supplies.

DECEMBER 20, 1989

The date of the first combat use of stealth aircraft, when two U.S. Air Force F-117s bombed a Panamanian Defense Force barracks in Rio Hato, Panama. In 1991, F-117s attacked the most heavily fortified targets in Iraq in the opening phase of Operation Desert Storm.

FIGHTING ... IN THE AIR

Flying French
The world's first corps of military balloonists was established by the French Army in 1794. The *Aérostiers* were a reconnaissance unit who used their elevated position to plot the location of the enemy.

Rising hemlines
Hot-air balloons were used by the Union side for viewing battlefields during the American Civil War in the 1860s. The hard-up Confederates requisitioned silk dresses to fabricate their own patchwork balloon.

Spy flight
The first time an aircraft was used in warfare was on October 23, 1911. Captain Carlo Piazza of the Italian Army flew a Blériot monoplane from Tripoli to Azizia, in Libya, to reconnoiter Turkish forces during the Italo-Turkish War of 1911–12.

Airship raids
Germany used Zeppelin airships to drop bombs during World War I. The earliest raid was on Liège, Belgium, on August 6, 1914. Zeppelins also attacked Britain, but by the end of the

352

German fighter pilot Erich Hartmann, known as "the Blond Knight" or "the Black Devil" depending on your allegiance, was the deadliest fighter ace of World War II, with 352 "kills."

6,184

The number of Londoners killed by V-1 rockets fired by the German Luftwaffe in 1944–45. Nearly 10,000 of the "doodlebugs" were aimed at Britain.

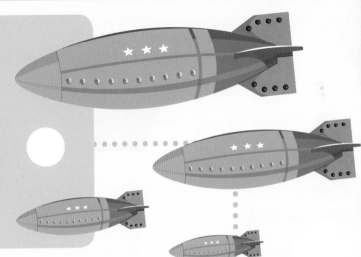

war this role had been largely given over to airplane bombers.

Jet attack
The Germans used the first jet fighters in World War II, among them the Messerschmitt ME-262. They could reach 540 mph (870 km/h) but were too late to change the course of the war.

Sky warriors
The Russian army was the first to have paratroopers in 1935. The Germans took note and started training paratroopers soon after, but the Allies did not catch up until 1940, when a test platoon was formed at Fort Benning, Georgia.

Long service
The Hercules C-130 has enjoyed the longest continuously operating production of any military aircraft. Manufactured by Lockheed Martin, it first flew on August 23, 1954, and is still being produced.

Highest flying plane
The greatest height achieved by a plane is 123,520 feet (37,650 m), set by Russian Alexander Fedotov in a MiG-25 fighter on August 31, 1977.

Big load
The gigantic Russian Antonov An-225 Mriya is the largest and heaviest plane ever constructed. It can carry four battle tanks, weighing in at nearly 275 tons (250 tonnes).

2,193 MPH

Despite first flying in 1966, the Lockheed SR-71 Blackbird is still the fastest-ever plane. The strategic reconnaissance aircraft achieved a speed of 2,193 mph (3,529 km/h) on July 28, 1976.

LARGEST EMPIRES FORMED BY MILITARY ACTION

BRITISH

14.1 million square miles
(36.6 million km²)

MONGOL

12.7 million square miles
(33 million km²)

RUSSIAN

8.6 million square miles
(22.4 million km²)

SPANISH

7.5 million square miles
(19.4 million km²)

INVASION

Neighborly disputes
Despite being a close ally today, Canada has been invaded on several occasions by its southern neighbor, including during the American Revolutionary War in 1775, and in 1812 due to disputes with the British government. Both times the American forces were unsuccessful.

Safe harbor
Two man-made temporary harbors were towed across the English Channel to allow unloading of cargo for the Allied D-Day invasion in 1944.

Panjandrum panned
Britain's Directorate of Miscellaneous Weapon Development devised a rocket-propelled rolling bomb to tackle

90%
The proportion of countries that have been invaded by the British at some point in their history. Only 22 countries have not experienced a military presence of some sort, including Andorra, the Marshall Islands, and the Vatican City.

$53 MILLION

This was the ransom in food and medicine exacted by Fidel Castro to release invaders captured at the Bay of Pigs in April 1961. The CIA had backed an invasion of 1,500 Cuban exiles who were attempting to overturn the Communist regime.

Hitler's Atlantic Wall fortifications when the Allies invaded. Called the Great Panjandrum, it carried 4,000 pounds (1,800 kg) of explosives and could travel at up to 60 mph (95 km/h). Unfortunately, steering was not a strong point and after continually veering off course the Panjandrum was shelved.

Ten years
The USSR invaded Afghanistan on December 24, 1979, to support the Communist regime against guerrillas. It was tied up in conflict for almost a decade and lost 15,000 troops before withdrawing on February 15, 1989.

Change of mind
Hitler postponed Operation Sea Lion, his plan to invade Britain, on September 17, 1940, after his airforce failed to dominate the RAF in the Battle of Britain.

Opening Japan
Japan had been an isolated country for more than two centuries before American Commodore Matthew Perry forced it to sign a treaty with the United States in 1854. Perry arrived in Japan the previous year demanding concessions for the USA and then returned with nine ships. The Japanese were no match for this military might and signed the first of many trading agreements.

180 PRIESTS

The number of Catholic priests aboard the Spanish Armada of 1588. The ships also carried 11 million pounds (5 million kg) of biscuits, 40,000 gallons (180,000 liters) of olive oil, 14,000 barrels of wine, and 600,000 pounds (270,000 kg) of salt pork.

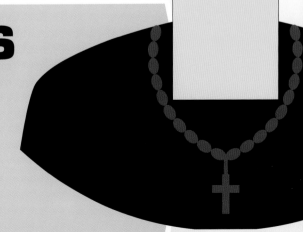

1990

Ahead of the invasion of Iraq, Saddam Hussein used so-called human shields to protect strategic Iraqi sites. Hundreds of Western hostages were held at power stations and military bases to dissuade the Coalition forces from attacking. The hostages were eventually released in December 1990.

UNDERHAND TACTICS

Straw men
Mongol warlords made use of disinformation tactics, spreading rumors about the size and effectiveness of their forces. They also used visual deception, such as mounting extra horses with straw dummies to create the illusion of more troops.

Fake letter
During the Crusades, Sultan Baybars is supposed to have captured the besieged Krak des Chevaliers castle in modern-day Syria. He handed the knights a forged letter from their commander, ordering them to surrender. The ruse worked and the knights gave up.

Superior force
In 1797, during the Battle of Fishguard, British commander John Campbell bluffed French invaders into surrendering to his much smaller force by informing them that reinforcements were on their way. The duped and demoralized French surrendered to his phantom force.

Double counting
During the Siege of Detroit in the War of 1812, British Major General Isaac Brock and his supporter, Native American chief Tecumseh, exaggerated the size of their forces by repeatedly marching the same men past American observers. Fearing the superior force, American Brigadier General William Hull surrendered the town and its fort.

Gas attack
Saddam Hussein used poison gas on his own people. In 1988, thousands died in the town of Halabja following a gas attack on the Kurdish occupants.

Hissing death
During Vietnam, the Viet Cong used venomous snakes as weapons. Bamboo pit vipers were hidden in tunnels or suspended at face height from trees, ready to bite unsuspecting GIs.

10 DAYS

When Panama's General Manuel Noriega sought sanctuary from U.S. troops in the Vatican embassy in 1989, they turned up the volume. The Navy Seals blasted deafening songs by The Clash and Guns 'n' Roses at the building for ten days, until Noriega surrendered.

16 miles

At Anzio, Italy, in 1944, U.S. troops maintained a 16-mile (25-km) smoke screen around the harbor for two months. The ancient Greeks used smoke screens as long ago as the Peloponnesian War of the fifth century BCE as a way of disguising military activity.

Losing faith

Americans got their own back with Project Eldest Son, when U.S. Green Berets secretly loaded exploding bullets into Viet Cong weapons hidden in arms dumps, causing them to doubt the effectiveness of their Chinese weaponry.

Vampire trick

During 1940s' operations against Communist guerrillas in the Philippines, CIA operatives preyed on local fears of vampires. They would abduct Communist troops, puncture their necks vampire-style, and drain the bodies of blood, then leave them to be found by terrified guerrillas.

Scorched earth policy

As part of Operation Alberich, a strategic withdrawal of German troops in 1917, water wells were poisoned, roads and rails were dug up, and a large number of booby traps and mines were left.

5 MILLION

The price in French francs the German Gestapo put on the head of New Zealand-born Resistance courier Nancy Wake in World War II. The Gestapo called her the "White Mouse" for her ease in escaping. She led attacks on German installations, killed an SS sentry with her bare hands, and once cycled 310 miles (500 km) in 72 hours, through several German checkpoints, to restore communications with London.

FIVE MILLION

SPYING

Monkey business

Legend has it that during the Napoleonic Wars in the early 19th century a French ship was wrecked off the coast of Hartlepool, England. The only survivor was a monkey, who was hanged by locals as a French spy. The local soccer team's mascot is a monkey called H'Angus the Monkey, and the mayor of the city from 2002 to 2013 campaigned for election dressed as H'Angus. He was elected three times.

Bridge of Spies

The Glienicke Bridge in Berlin, Germany, was known as the Bridge of Spies because it was used to exchange captured spies from the East and West during the Cold War. The largest swap took place in 1985, when 25 United States agents held in Eastern Europe were exchanged for four Eastern Bloc spies.

Head agent

The head of Mata Hari, the Dutch exotic dancer executed by the French government in 1917 for spying for Germany, was embalmed and kept in the Paris Museum of Anatomy. Some years ago curators were surprised to find that it had vanished from the museum altogether.

23 inches

(58 cm) The height of the smallest recorded spy, the Frenchman Richebourg (1768–1858). Richebourg was employed by the aristocracy as a secret agent during the French Revolution (1789–99), dispatching messages into and out of Paris while disguised as an infant carried by his "nurse."

BATTLES

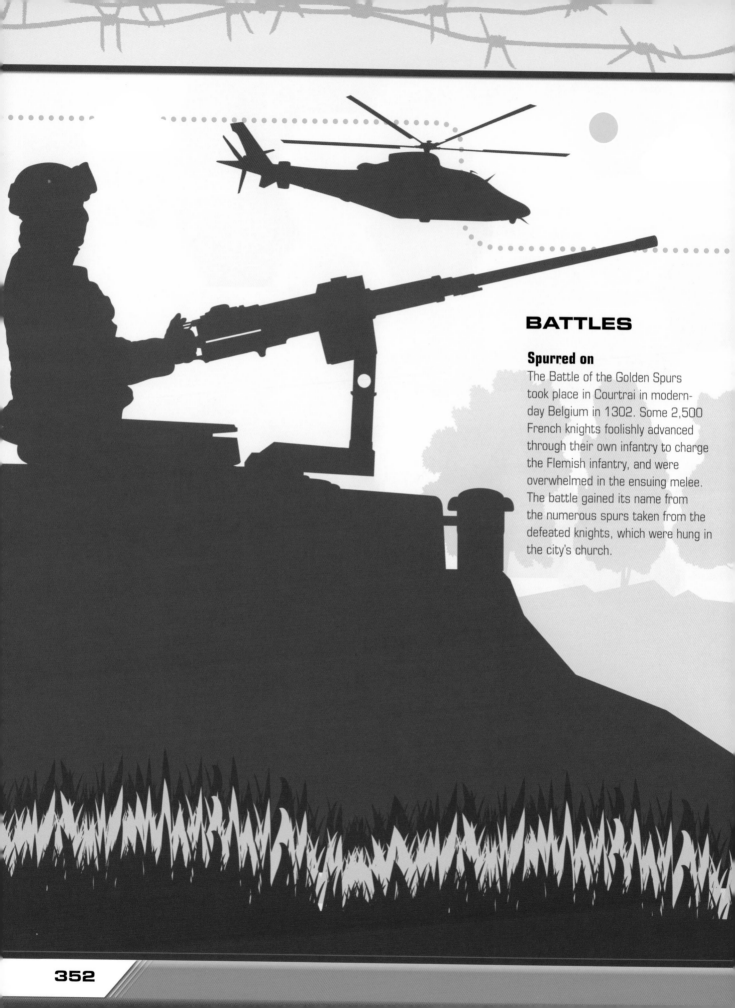

BATTLES

Spurred on

The Battle of the Golden Spurs took place in Courtrai in modern-day Belgium in 1302. Some 2,500 French knights foolishly advanced through their own infantry to charge the Flemish infantry, and were overwhelmed in the ensuing melee. The battle gained its name from the numerous spurs taken from the defeated knights, which were hung in the city's church.

14

The number of Dutch ships that were taken during the Battle of Texel in 1795, which is perhaps the only occasion when a fleet has been captured by men on horses. A Dutch fleet became stuck in the ice in the port of Den Helder, and after a charge across the frozen Zuiderzee a French cavalry detachment was able to defeat them.

Glowing wounds

After the Civil War Battle of Shiloh (1862), wounded soldiers lying on the battlefield noticed that their wounds were glowing in the dark. The cold damp conditions had encouraged the growth of a bioluminescent bacterium. Those whose wounds glowed eventually healed better than their non-shiny peers, as the bacterium inhibits pathogens.

Fairy flag

The Scottish Clan MacLeod owned a Fairy Flag which, when unfurled in battle, was said to have magical powers. The flag was unfurled in the Battle of Bloody Bay (1480) and the Battle of Glendale (1490), but legend stated if it were unfurled a third time it would either mean total victory or total extinction, and no one was willing to risk it. The flag is still at Dunvegan Castle in Scotland.

Leg it

Arthur Aston, the Royalist garrison commander at Drogheda in eastern Ireland, was beaten to death with his own wooden leg by Oliver Cromwell's Parliamentary troops after they attacked the city. The soldiers believed he had gold hidden in it.

Cab rank

Thousands of soldiers arriving to fight the Battle of Marne in the first year of World War I were transported to the front line by taxi. Paris police stopped cab drivers, turned out the passengers, and directed the vehicles to the Military College to pick up soldiers. Not all the cab drivers were happy about this.

Roll up

U.S. Marines taking part in the Battle of Chosin Reservoir in Korea in 1950 were mainly fueled by Tootsie Rolls. The candies were parachuted in to the 10,000 soldiers who had been trapped by the Chinese. Tootsie Rolls became such a symbol of the battle that the manufacturer sent a representative to the veterans' reunion.

Strange operations

Historically, battles have usually been named after the nearest town,

22,000 feet

(6,700 m) The altitude of the world's highest battlefield, the Siachen Glacier, in the disputed territory of Kashmir between India and Pakistan. Both countries maintain a military presence in the region, although reports suggest that most casualties (97 percent) have been a result of extreme weather rather than fighting. The temperature can fall as low as -76°F (-60°C).

20 PERCENT

The share of revenue that Pancho Villa, commander of Mexican rebels at the beginning of the twentieth century, was to receive from movies of his battles. He signed a contract giving an American motion picture company the exclusive rights to his combats, replacing his casual outfit with an imposing general's uniform and staging reenactments for the cameras.

but modern-day military operations are given names in advance. Some modern military operations with strange names include: Operation Grizzly Forced Entry (Iraq); Operation Elfin Cove (Iraq); Operation Toenails (World War II attempt to capture New Georgia); Operation Dracula (a planned invasion of Burma in World War II); and Operation Beaver Cage (Vietnam).

Cat shields

According to one chronicler, Persian conqueror Cambyses II won the Battle of Pelusium against the Egyptians in 525 BCE because he had his troops use cats as shields. The Egyptians saw cats as sacred and so could not fire on the troops. Other ancient writers describing the battle do not mention the cats.

Numerous Nelsons

There were eight Nelsons fighting the French at the Battle of Trafalgar. They included Vice Admiral Lord Horatio Nelson, a Danish soldier called Nelson, and three John Nelsons. All of them survived the battle except Admiral Nelson.

Brave woman

The Battle of the Rosebud, part of the Great Sioux War of 1876, is known by the Cheyenne as the Battle Where the Girl Saved her Brother. A Cheyenne woman, Buffalo Calf Road, rode on to the battlefield to save her brother, Chief Comes In Sight. The incident

$9,400

(£6,344) The amount fetched by a pressed poppy from a World War I trench in 1916, when it was auctioned in 2013. The poppy was picked by a 17-year-old British soldier a year after the poem, *In Flanders Fields,* was published, describing the flowers growing on the graves of the dead.

300

The number of casualties sustained by Allied Forces in 1943 as part of a battle against no one. The forces were retaking an Alaskan island that had been abandoned by its Japanese occupiers two weeks before. Injuries arose from friendly fire when United States and Canadian forces mistook each other for the enemy, as well as stray Japanese mines.

helped rally the Cheyenne forces to win the battle against the U.S. Army.

Banner bearer

English King Richard III's banner bearer, Sir Percival Thirlwall, kept the king's banner aloft at the Battle of Bosworth Field (1485) even after he had lost his legs, only dropping it when he was hacked to death. Richard was also killed during the battle. His body was discovered under a car park in Leicester in 2012 and reburied in 2015.

BATTLES IN NUMBERS

9

The number of times Lord Uxbridge had a horse shot out from under him during the Battle of Waterloo in 1815. Uxbridge lost his leg at Waterloo, where it was buried with its own tombstone and became a tourist attraction.

2.2 MILLION

The number of German and Russian soldiers that took part in the Battle of Kursk, the largest tank battle in history, backed by more than 6,000 tanks and 5,000 aircraft. The battle took place in 1943 and ended in victory for the Russians.

40 PERCENT

The proportion of casualties of the British Light Brigade lost at the Battle of Balaclava in 1854, made famous by Alfred Lord Tennyson's poem, *The Charge of the Light Brigade*. The brigade, led by Lord Cardigan, charged through a valley surrounded by Russian guns.

560,000

The number of troops engaged in the Battle of Leipzig in October 1813, the largest battle in European history before World War I. Napoleon's troops were defeated by an anti-French alliance in the three-day battle.

2

The number of English knights believed to have been killed at the Battle of Crécy in 1346. More than 1,500 French knights were killed.

10,000

The number of Ottoman troops who died while trying to escape Austrian forces across a river during the Battle of Zenta in 1697. Some 20,000 more were killed on the battlefield, in a victory that made Austria the foremost power in central Europe. The Ottomans lost all their artillery, plus the sultan's treasure box, to the Austrians.

700

The number of villages in Northumberland, England, that were burned to the ground by Scots patriot William Wallace and his army after his victory at the Battle of Stirling Bridge in 1297.

BLOODIEST BATTLES

302,000 dead
Battle of Salsu (Second Goguryeo-Sui War between China and Korea)
North Korea, 612 CE
The Chinese emperor invaded Korea with a million men.

200,000–1,000,000 dead (estimates vary)
Battle of Baghdad
Iraq, 1258
Hulagu Khan, grandson of Genghis Khan, destroyed the center of Islamic power with the largest army ever fielded by the Mongols.

Around 700,000 casualties
Battle of Verdun (World War I)
France, February–December 1916
The French resisted a major German offensive.

1,500,000 dead and wounded
Brusilov Offensive (World War I)
Russia, June–September 1916
A major Russian offensive against the Central Powers.

1,070,000 dead, wounded and missing
Battle of the Somme (World War I)
France, July–November 1916
Allied offensive against the Germans.

1,250,000 casualties
Battle of Stalingrad (World War II)
Russia, August 1942–February 1943
German attack on the city of Stalingrad.

600,000

The extortionate number of pesos demanded by the French government as compensation when a French pastry chef complained that his shop in Mexico City had been ruined by looting Mexican officers in 1838. The average daily wage was one peso. Mexico declared war on France in what was to become known as the Pastry War, but eventually paid up after losing a naval battle.

STRANGE WARS

Sacred stool

The Asante of Ghana revered their sacred golden stool, which was said to have descended from the sky and to contain the soul of the nation. When a British governor demanded to sit on it in 1900, war broke out, with the Asante side led by Yaa Asantewaa, the Queen Mother. The British defeated Yaa Asantewaa's forces but failed to capture the stool.

Bucket battle

In Italy in 1325, some soldiers of Modena, freshly victorious after fighting Bologna at the Battle of Zappolino, crept into Bologna's main square and stole a wooden bucket from the civic well. The Bologna authorities began the War of the Oaken Bucket to win back their bucket and their pride. The war achieved neither, although it did result in thousands of deaths.

Pig War

On the island of San Juan in 1859, a pig owned by a British settler wandered on to American-owned land and was promptly shot dead. The dispute over compensation for the pig grew into a full-blown military conflict, with 500 American troops facing 2,000 British soldiers and five warships. The pig was the only casualty as no shots were fired. Oddly, this is not history's only Pig War—in 1906, conflict arose around the ban on the export of live pigs from Serbia to Austro-Hungary.

The town that declared war

A Spanish town of 300 inhabitants, Lijar, declared war on France in 1883 after hearing that its monarch Alfonso XII had been insulted on the streets of the French capital. Local mayor Don Miguel Garcia Saez declared war and although no shots were ever fired, Lijar remained on a war footing until 1983.

3-2

The score of the soccer match that plunged El Salvador and Honduras into a bloody four-day conflict known as the Football War in 1969. Severe economic and social problems between the two nations boiled over after three bitterly contested matches during the 1970 FIFA World Cup qualifiers. The war resulted in more than 2,000 casualties.

Fish fight

The Cod Wars took place between Iceland and the UK in the 1950s and 1970s. After World War II, Iceland gradually extended its exclusive fishing zone from 4 nautical miles (4.6 miles/7.4 km) to 200 nautical miles (230 miles/370 km). The British were not happy and sent the Royal Navy to Icelandic fishing grounds to protect British trawlers. In 1976, the British recognized the Icelandic fishing zone and the conflict ended.

$35 BILLION

(132 billion gold marks) The war reparations that Germany had to pay under the Treaty of Versailles, signed on June 28, 1919, ending World War I.

PEACE TREATIES

No treaty

North and South Korea are technically still at war, more than 60 years after a ceasefire was agreed on July 27, 1953. Continuing difficulties in the relationship between the two parts of the Korean Peninsula have prevented the signing of a peace treaty between the two states.

Silver tablets

The earliest surviving peace treaty was drawn up on silver tablets in 1259 BCE and signed by Egyptian pharaoh, Ramses II, and Hattusilis III, king of the Hittites, in modern-day Turkey. Two copies were made, one in hieroglyphics, the other in the Mesopotamian language of Akkadian. A copy remains in the Karnak Temple, Luxor, Egypt.

38 WORDS

The length of one of the shortest peace treaties in history, which ended the war between Serbia and Bulgaria in 1885. It can be summarized in English as "The war between Serbia and Bulgaria is over as of now."

Carriage revisited

When the Germans forced the French to sign an agreement in 1940 to cease fighting against them in World War II, it was in the same railroad car used to sign the Armistice ending World War I, in which the Germans had been defeated. Adolf Hitler sat in the same seat that Marshal Ferdinand Foch, the French commander, had sat in 1918. The carriage was taken and exhibited in Germany, but was destroyed in 1945.

Long wait

Although the Treaty of Ghent, which ended the War of 1812 between the United States and Britain, was signed on Christmas Eve 1814, it took weeks for news of the peace to travel across the Atlantic from the Flemish city to America, where the fighting was actually going on. The treaty did not come into effect until February 18, 1815.

Sealed with a button

The Treaty of Versailles and the Covenant of the League of Nations, signed on June 28, 1919, were the first such international agreements ever signed by the Commonwealth of Australia in its own right. The Australian delegation had to hurriedly concoct a seal to use on the treaty as they didn't already have one. After scouring the antique stalls in a nearby Parisian street market, they opted for a tunic button from an Australian soldier's uniform.

190

The number of countries that have signed the Treaty on the Nonproliferation of Nuclear Weapons, which limits nuclear weapons to five countries—the United States, United Kingdom, Russia, France, and China. North Korea acceded to the Treaty but withdrew in 2003, while India, South Sudan, Israel, and Pakistan have not signed.

QUOTES

British Lieutenant Colonel Charles Hore's reply to the offer of surrender from Boers who besieged his position during the Battle of Elands River during the second Boer War in 1900.

I CANNOT SURRENDER. I AM IN COMMAND OF AUSTRALIANS WHO WOULD CUT MY THROAT IF I DID.

I KNOW I HAVE THE BODY BUT OF A WEAK AND FEEBLE WOMAN; BUT I HAVE THE HEART AND STOMACH OF A KING, AND OF A KING OF ENGLAND TOO.

Queen Elizabeth I of England, 1588. Addressing her troops in preparation for repelling a Spanish invasion, the queen wore a plumed helmet and steel armor over a white velvet gown.

General George S. Patton, 1944. General Patton's profanity-laden speech sought to motivate troops from the U.S. Third Army prior to the invasion of France. He later said: "You can't run an army without profanity, and it has to be eloquent profanity."

THE NAZIS ARE THE ENEMY. WADE INTO THEM, SPILL THEIR BLOOD OR THEY WILL SPILL YOURS. SHOOT THEM IN THE GUTS. RIP OPEN THEIR BELLY.

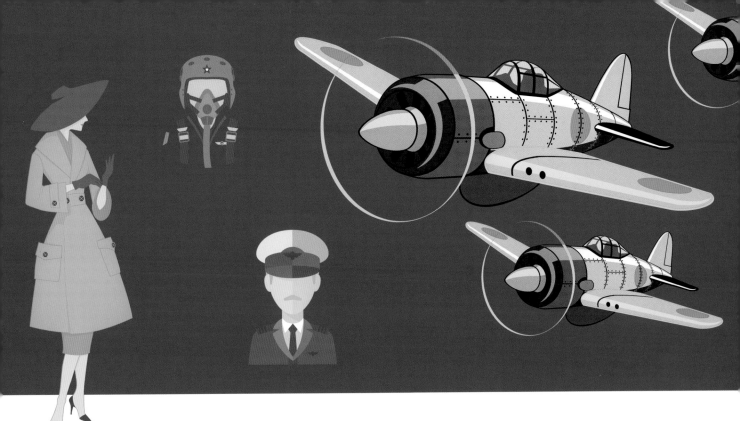

PEOPLE

8 PERCENT

The proportion of men in Asia who scientists have proposed are descended from Genghis Khan (1162–1227). That's 0.5 percent of all men in the world. The warrior leader was founder of one of the largest empires in history, including modern-day China, Russia, Turkey, Iran, South and North Korea, and Kuwait.

LEADERS

Fine romance

In addition to conquering much of Europe, military leader Napoleon Bonaparte found time to moonlight as a romantic novelist. He penned *Clisson et Eugénie*, the tale of a soldier's doomed romance, in 1795. Scientists have speculated that Napoleon, who died in 1821, might have been killed by his wallpaper—the dye used at the time could become poisonous when damp.

President's men

George Washington is the only U.S. head of state to lead troops to battle as President. He led a militia on a month-long march to put down a rebellion in 1794. Washington owned dogs called Sweetlips, Madame Moose, and Vulcan.

Fat king

William the Conqueror, the first Norman King of England, became corpulent in his later life—the King of France said he looked like a pregnant woman about to give birth. It is said that he decided to go on a diet consisting solely of alcoholic drinks. When he died after falling off his horse in 1087, his body exploded as the monks tried to stuff it into his coffin.

Ransom required

When Roman general Julius Caesar was kidnapped in 75 BCE, he was so insulted by the low price of the ransom set for his release that he insisted his kidnappers demand a higher figure. After he was freed he commandeered ships and men to hunt down the buccaneers and had them executed.

Know your onions

Civil War General Ulysses S. Grant was a great believer in the healthful benefits of onions. It is said that he

DRUM SKIN

Czech military commander and national hero, Jan Žižka, continued to lead his forces to victory even after he had been blinded in both eyes. He ordered his skin to be turned into a war drum after his death, so he could carry on leading men to battle from beyond the grave.

SEVENTEEN

The age of Joan of Arc when she arrived at the Siege of Orleans in 1429, a turning point in the Hundred Years War between England and France. The siege was lifted nine days after she arrived, giving her credibility as a divinely inspired strategist a major boost. Joan was 19 when she was burned as a heretic by the English.

wired the War Department saying: "I will not move my army without onions." Three trainloads of onions were then sent to the front.

Boer bounty
British Prime Minister Winston Churchill was captured as a young war correspondent in South Africa during the Boer War. He escaped from the prison camp in Pretoria and the Boers put a bounty of £25 on his head.

7-60

The ages between which males in ancient Sparta were required to be soldiers—no other occupation was an option. Separated from their parents at seven, boys lived in communal barracks where they studied warfare, hunting, and athletics. Warriors were required to remain on reserve duty until the age of 60.

DEADLY WARRIORS

High stakes

The warrior Shaka was the founder of the Zulu Empire in Southern Africa. When he came to power his first action was to seek out those who had bullied him as a child and impale them on the stakes of their own fences. When his mother died in 1827 he slaughtered thousands of cows, so the calves would know what it was like to lose a mother.

Hun dead

Attila the Hun, who led murderous hordes of mounted archers in raids against the Roman Empire in the fifth century CE, died on his wedding night of a nosebleed.

Head pyramid

Fourteenth-century conqueror Timur, known to history as Timur the Lame or Tamburlane, was renowned for his cruelty, building pyramids out of the severed heads of his enemies. One chronicler in 1388 counted 28 pyramids each made of 1,500 skulls while walking halfway round the walls of Isfahan, Iran.

1/3

DNA tests on 105 samurai warriors killed in the Japanese Battle of Senbon Matsubaru (1580) found that a third of them were female. Similar results have been found at other battle sites, suggesting there were more women samurai warriors than had previously been thought.

Pocket boat

The ninja spies and assassins of feudal Japan carried a number of tools to increase their success rate. These included rocket-propelled arrows, extending spears, and small collapsible boats.

War dance

Maori warriors from New Zealand performed a war dance or war "haka" before battles in order to intimidate their opponents. The New Zealand rugby football team has adopted the practice since 1905.

Gone berserk

The phrase "going berserk" comes from Viking warriors, or Berserkers, who would work themselves up into a rage before battle, in which state they could perform feats of superhuman strength and remain impervious to pain. The name came from the bearskins worn by the warriors in battle.

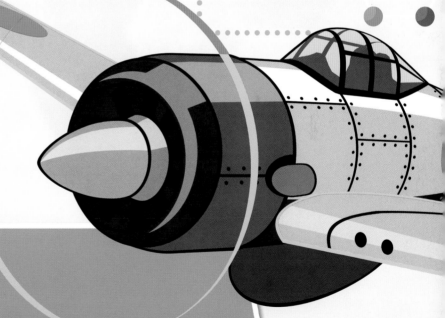

1,465

The number of Japanese kamikaze planes whose pilots died, crashing deliberately into U.S. ships in the Battle of Okinawa in 1945. The Japanese also employed suicide submariners, sealed into torpedoes known as "*kaiten*," which they would steer into American ships.

THE HOME FRONT

Railing against war

There were periodic drives to collect materials that were in short supply such as paper, metal, and rubber. During World War II, iron fences across Britain were ripped up for use in the war effort. However, legend has it that most were simply dumped at sea or buried as landfill, as too much metal was collected. To admit this would have been bad for morale.

Marriage ban

Serving Roman soldiers were banned from marrying because it was felt that this would split their loyalties. However, evidence has been found of women and children living alongside Roman forts on Britain's Hadrian's Wall, and inside forts in Germany.

The real thing?

Food shortages in Germany during World War I led to the production of substitute *ersatz* foodstuffs that used more easily available products. These included bread made using potatoes, cake made from horse chestnuts, and coffee made from barley and oats enhanced with coal tar.

Knit for victory

During World War I it is said that Herbert Kitchener, British Secretary of State for War, prompted the invention of a special stitch for socks to prevent chafing. It came to be known as "the Kitchener Stitch." Knitting was a patriotic duty, with socks, scarves, hats, and sweaters sent off to shivering troops.

3 MILLION

women in America entered the workforce in World War II, many for the first time. Government advertisements, such as those featuring the Rosie the Riveter character, encouraged them into traditionally male roles. One advertisement asked: "Can you use an electric mixer? If so, you can learn to use a drill."

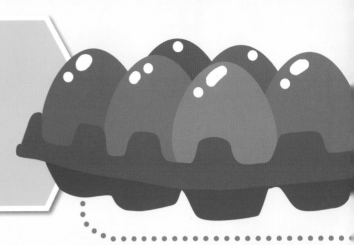

1942

Following its entry into World War II, the United States introduced rationing of tires, materials, and food. Gasoline was a worry too, and all automobile racing was banned.

War bonds

During World War II, $185 billion worth of war bonds were bought by 85 million Americans. This provided cash for the war effort and also helped prevent inflation that could have resulted from citizens driving prices up by chasing rare goods.

Sobering times

World War I saw a switch in attitudes to alcohol in Britain. By law, pubs could only open for a few hours at lunchtime and in the evening, beer was made weaker, and "treating" somebody else to a drink was a criminal offence.

Wartime light savings

Germany was the first country to implement daylight saving time (DST). Clocks were first turned forward on April 30, 1916, to minimize the use of artificial lighting and save fuel for the war effort. Other countries followed suit, only reverting to standard time after the war. DST made its return during World War II.

Propaganda textiles

Clothing became a way to show support during World War II. Japanese textile designers produced fabrics featuring patriotic icons, folk images, and military imagery. These were used to make kimonos, jacket linings, and children's clothes. Western nations also produced "propaganda textiles" such as headscarves for women.

47,783

European women married Canadian servicemen during World War II, the majority of them British. A total of 43,454 War Brides and 20,997 children were transported to Canada in an immigration scheme run by the Canadian government. Another 70,000 British women married GIs and moved to the United States.

HIGHEST MILITARY HONORS AND WHEN FIRST ISSUED

HONORS AND MEDALS

Movie star
Audie Murphy (1925–71) was the most decorated soldier in U.S. history, winning 24 medals including the Congressional Medal of Honor. He personally killed 240 enemy soldiers during World War II. The movie version of his autobiography, *To Hell and Back*, in which he played himself, was Universal Studios' highest grossing picture for 20 years until the release of *Jaws*.

Ace pilot
Hans-Ulrich Rudel (1916–82) was the most decorated German serviceman of World War II, and the only one to win the Knight's Cross of the Iron Cross with Golden Oak Leaves, Swords, and Diamonds—the highest military decoration a German could receive at the time. He flew some 2,530 combat missions and destroyed more than 2,000 targets, including the Soviet battleship *Marat*.

Five stars
The United States military ranks commanding officers in a star system. Five-star ranks are generally reserved for wartime use, and only nine people have ever held this position, including Dwight D. Eisenhower and Douglas MacArthur.

Aussie honor
The Victoria Cross for Australia was introduced in 1991 as a separate VC for Australian troops, distinct from the British honors system. The medal resembles its British counterpart and was first awarded in 2009 to Trooper Mark Donaldson for gallantry in rescuing an interpreter during operations in Afghanistan in 2008.

Cannon cross
Every Victoria Cross medal, awarded by Britain for valor in the face of the enemy, is cast from the bronze cascabels of two cannons that were captured from the Russians at the Siege of Sevastopol in 1854–55.

Serbian heroine
Serbian Milunka Savić (1890–1973) is thought to be the most decorated woman in history. She assumed a male identity to fight in the Balkan Wars in 1912, when she received

RUSSIA

GEROY ROSSIYSKOY FEDERATSII

(Hero of the Russian Federation)

1992

GERMANY

EHRENKREUZ DER BUNDESWEHR IN GOLD

(Bundeswehr Cross of Honor in Gold)

1980

ITALY

MEDAGLIA D'ORO AL VALORE MILITARE

(Gold Medal of Military Valor)

1793

FRANCE

ORDRE NATIONAL DE LA LÉGION D'HONNEUR

(Legion of honor)

1804

her first medal and was promoted to corporal. A wound revealed her gender, but she continued fighting in World War I. Her honors included the French Legion of Honor and the Russian Cross of St. George.

Reciprocal honors

The Unknown Soldier, chosen to represent all British soldiers who died in World War I but could not be identified, was given the U.S. Medal of Honor, America's highest award for bravery, in 1921. It hangs near his grave in Westminster Abbey, London. On November 11, 1921, the U.S. Unknown Soldier, buried in Arlington National Cemetery, was reciprocally awarded the Victoria Cross.

UK
AND COMMONWEALTH

VICTORIA CROSS

1857

INDIA

PARAM VIR CHAKRA

(Bravest of the Brave)

1947

UNITED STATES

MEDAL OF HONOR

1863

CELEBRITIES WHO SERVED

ELVIS PRESLEY

was inducted into the U.S. Army in 1958 for two years' military service. He served with the 3rd Armored Division in Germany, where he met future wife Priscilla, who was 14 at the time. While in the army Presley had ten Top 40 hits, his management having kept back a stock of unreleased material.

ARNOLD SCHWARZENEGGER

served in the Austrian Army for a year in 1965. The actor went AWOL during basic training so he could enter the Junior Mr. Europe contest and was thrown in military prison. He won the contest though.

QUEEN ELIZABETH II

joined the Women's Auxiliary Service in February 1945 when she was the 19-year-old Princess Elizabeth. She trained as a driver and mechanic, although she slept at home rather than in barracks with her fellow recruits. Her son Prince Andrew flew helicopters for the Royal Navy during the Falklands War, while grandson Prince Harry has served in the British Army in Afghanistan.

JIMMY STEWART

was initially rejected from the U.S. Army for failing height and weight requirements, but went on to become a bomber pilot during World War II, commanding missions deep into Nazi-occupied Europe. The American actor won medals including the Croix de Guerre and the Distinguished Flying Cross.

IAN FLEMING

creator of James Bond, was assistant to the director of British Naval Intelligence during World War II. In December 1943, he was put in charge of 30 Assault Unit, which became known as Fleming's Private Navy, and was tasked with capturing secret documents as the Allies proceeded through France after D-Day.

CHUCK NORRIS

the action-movie hero, joined the United States Air Force as an Air Policeman in 1958 and served in South Korea. While there he picked up his nickname *Chuck* (his real name is Carlos) as well as an interest in martial arts. When he left the Air Force in 1962 he opened his own chain of karate schools.

MARILYN MONROE

worked in a munitions factory during World War II while her then husband James Dougherty went into the Merchant Marines. She sprayed airplanes with fire retardant and inspected parachutes.

CHRISTOPHER LEE

volunteered to fight for Finnish forces in the Winter War—the conflict between the Soviet Union and Finland in 1939. He then served in the RAF as a flight lieutenant during World War II and helped track down Nazi war criminals. He was mentioned in dispatches in 1944.

JAMES BLUNT

served in the British Army after training at the Royal Military Academy, Sandhurst. Blunt rose to the level of captain and served in Kosovo where he took to serenading the locals with his guitar, which he carried strapped to his tank.

10

The number of times a young conscientious objector in Israel was arrested and imprisoned for refusing to join the army in 2013. The 19-year-old served a total of five and a half months in jail. Young men in Israel have to do three years' military service after finishing school, while young women serve for two years.

CONSCIENTIOUS OBJECTORS

May 15
is celebrated around the world as International Conscientious Objectors' Day. In London a white flower is laid on a stone for those remembered.

Objector hero
One of the most decorated U.S. soldiers in World War I was a conscientious objector. Sergeant Alvin York was a member of a church that opposed violence and claimed conscientious objector status, but this was denied. After changing his stance on pacifism during training, he eventually received nearly 50 medals, including the Medal of Honor.

Sassoon's despair
In 1917, as a soldier decorated with the Military Cross, war poet Siegfried Sassoon threw his medal ribbon into the River Mersey and refused to return to service. He did eventually go back to the trenches but was injured by friendly fire in 1918.

Forest duty
The Russian Empire allowed members of the Mennonite sect to run forestry units instead of serving in the army, owing to their religious beliefs. Some 7,000 took part in this work during World War I.

Ali takes a stand
U.S. boxer Muhammad Ali is one of the most famous conscientious objectors. He refused conscription in 1967, citing his religious beliefs and opposition to the Vietnam War. The U.S. Government refused to recognize him as a conscientious objector and he was arrested for draft evasion.

16,000

The approximate number of men who went through a British tribunal to appeal against their conscription during World War I on the grounds that fighting was against their beliefs. Only around 300 were granted absolute exemption, while around 3,400 joined the army but did not bear arms.

MODERN WAR:
THE FUTURE

DEFINITION

Cyber warfare—Internet-based conflict involving politically motivated attacks on information systems. Attacks can disable websites and networks, disrupt or disable essential services, steal or alter classified data, and cripple financial systems.

CYBER WARFARE

Attractions of cyber war

Cyber warfare may be an alternative to conventional weapons. It is cheaper and far more accessible to small countries and allows them to pull off attacks with less risk of getting caught.

Fake friends

The U.S. military is developing software that will let it secretly manipulate social media sites by using fake online personas to influence Internet conversations and spread pro-American propaganda.

Cyber war games

Britain and the United States are to carry out "war game" cyber attacks on each other as part of a new defense against online criminals. The first

exercise in 2015 was a staged attack on the financial sector. Money is also made available to train cyber agents.

Service denied

Following a spat with Russia over the removal of a war memorial in April 2007, Estonian government networks were harassed by a denial of service attack. Some government online services were temporarily disrupted and online banking was halted.

Pipe bomb

A 2008 explosion of an oil pipeline in Refahiye, Turkey, has been attributed to a cyber attack. The pipeline was superpressurized and alarms were shut off, to prevent the company reacting in time.

61398

The number given to the Chinese army's secretive hacking unit. Its 12-story HQ in Shanghai could hold up to 2,000 people.

New front in war

In January 2009, hackers attacked Israel's internet infrastructure during a military offensive in the Gaza Strip. The attack, which focused on government websites, was executed by at least five million computers. Israeli officials believed the attack was carried out by Soviet criminals, paid for by Hamas or Hezbollah.

Flamed

In May 2012, computer virus Flame affected computers in Lebanon, the United Arab Emirates, the West Bank, and Iran. It is said to have gathered intelligence by logging keyboard strokes, recording conversations, and taking screen shots. At Iran's oil ministry and oil-export terminal, the virus erased information on hard disks while gathering information. Many attribute it to the USA and Israel.

Nuclear blast

Stuxnet, a complex piece of malware designed to interfere with Siemens industrial control systems, was discovered in October 2010. Allegedly developed by the USA and Israel, the virus infected the computer system that ran centrifuges at the Iranian nuclear program, causing hundreds to self-destruct and setting the program back years.

WHAT COULD CYBER ATTACKS AFFECT?

- Power plants
- Water supply
- Air-traffic control
- Conventional traffic management systems
- Banking services
- Military systems

$110 MILLION

The amount the U.S. Defense Advanced Research Projects Agency invested in Plan X in 2012. This is a program to develop platforms for the Department of Defense to plan for, conduct, and assess cyber warfare. The U.S. Naval Academy is spending $120 million on building a classified cyber warfare center.

86 PERCENT

The proportion of battlefield deaths that occur in the first 30 minutes after injury, making rapid treatment essential. Researchers propose putting robotic surgeons on battlefields, which can be remotely controlled by doctors. Such telesurgery devices have already been used in hospitals—in 2001, a doctor in New York removed the gallbladder of a patient in France.

TECHNOLOGY AND WAR

Space bubbles
Terrestrial weather has always had an effect on battles, with armies and navies laid low by freezing temperatures or sudden storms. But now weather in space can also affect battle plans. Scientists say plasma bubbles in space may have been responsible for scrambling radio signals and endangering a U.S. rescue mission during Operation Anaconda, a 2002 Afghanistan battle.

Scary smell
U.S. military researchers are trying to isolate the smell of fear. They hope that tracking down the pheromones people give off when they are scared will allow individuals with a "sinister intent" to be targeted.

Electric armor
A UK designer has developed a material that is interwoven with electronic circuits, enabling troops to attach electric appliances to power points on their uniforms. This lightens a soldier's load by allowing electrical equipment to be docked directly into their clothes.

Dodging bullets
Future bullets will be able to change course in midair to follow their target. The Extreme Accuracy Tasked Ordnance system combines a maneuverable bullet with a guidance system.

Liquid uniform
Future military uniforms could be made from liquid. A new type of material is composed of iron particles suspended in silicone oil, which would harden within microseconds to create solid armor when a small current is supplied. The U.S. Army has been investigating such a material as part of its Future Force project.

TRICK SHOT

The Chinese have developed a gun that can fire around corners. The gun features a small high-resolution camera and monitor that allows the gunman to view targets safely before firing.

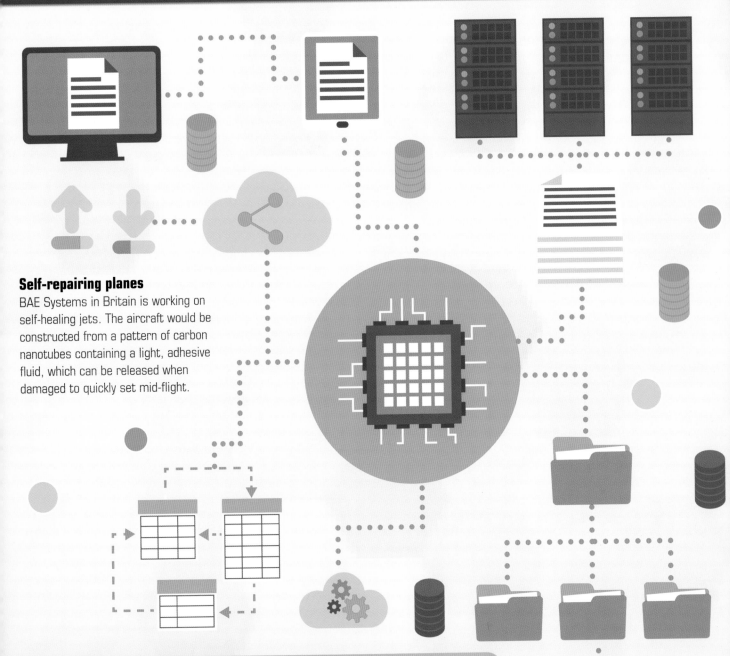

Self-repairing planes

BAE Systems in Britain is working on self-healing jets. The aircraft would be constructed from a pattern of carbon nanotubes containing a light, adhesive fluid, which can be released when damaged to quickly set mid-flight.

7 PERCENT

The proportion of countries who will be engaging in war in 2050, according to futurologists—that's down from 15 percent today. Scientists are able to mine data and predict trouble spots of the future—one Norwegian study claims that India, Ethiopia, the Philippines, Uganda, and Burma will be at the greatest risk of conflict in five years' time, while in 40 years, it will be China, Malawi, Mozambique, and Tanzania.

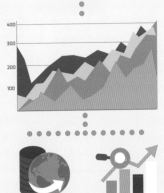

2013

The year a UN report called for a global moratorium on developing Lethal Autonomous Robots (LARs), which can select and kill targets without a human being directly issuing a command. Experts believe they could be a reality in the near future.

$12.9 BILLION

The estimated cost of the USS *Gerald R. Ford*, the U.S. Navy's newest aircraft carrier. New technology such as an electromagnetic launch system will allow 25 percent more flights per day than the *Nimitz*-class ships she replaces.

WAR MACHINES

Military machines
Robots were first used in ground combat during the war in Afghanistan in July 2002. Hermes was deployed ahead of U.S. troops to search a network of caves that was a potential hiding place for enemy personnel and weaponry. The other robots were called Professor, Thing, and Fester. They were long enough to carry 12 cameras, a grenade launcher, and a 12-gauge shotgun.

Robot pals
Soldiers' emotional attachment to military robots could affect their decision-making on the battlefield, according to research. The researcher

275 mph

(443 km/h). The speed of the Boeing V-22 Osprey, a vertical takeoff and land military vehicle that can go twice as fast as a helicopter. The Osprey can carry 24 combat troops, or up to 20,000 pounds (9,100 kg) of internal cargo, or 15,000 pounds (6,000 kg) of external cargo. More than 200 are in operation worldwide.

found that soldiers often named their robots after wives, girlfriends, or celebrities, and felt sorry for them when they were damaged.

Iron Man

Robotic suits can be used by soldiers to increase their agility, strength, and endurance. One exoskeleton, the XOS 2, uses high-pressure hydraulics to allow the wearer to lift objects 17 times heavier than usual.

Samsung sentinels

South Korean forces have installed a team of robot guards along its border with North Korea. Built by Samsung, the robots can identify

potential targets more than 2 miles (3 km) away, using heat and motion sensors, and each has a 0.2-inch (5.5-mm) machine gun and a 1.5-inch (40-mm) grenade launcher. Operators can use the audio and video features to communicate remotely before deciding to order the robots to fire.

Drone swarm

The U.S. military's defense research division is looking to build swarms of war drones that can work together in the sky without needing to be controlled individually by pilots on the ground. The swarms would collaborate to find, track, identify, and engage targets. The U.S. Navy

already has a fleet of robot boats that can escort and protect a main ship against possible attackers.

Lethal laser

Security firm Lockheed Martin has built a laser that can disable a moving truck or boat 1 mile (1.6 km) away. The 30-kilowatt Athena laser can precisely track moving targets at a range of more than 3 miles (5 km).

MARCH 23, 1983

President Ronald Reagan outlines the basis of his Strategic Defense Initiative (SDI) to the U.S. Congress. Popularly known as "Star Wars," Reagan's proposal envisioned an antimissile defense system that would destroy Soviet nuclear missiles in the air.

STAR WARS

Moon bomb

In 1958, the U.S. Air Force developed a top-secret plan to detonate a nuclear bomb on the Moon as a display of military might at the height of the Cold War. The Air Force wanted a mushroom cloud so large it would be visible from Earth—it would also have destroyed the face of the man in the Moon.

We come in peace

The Outer Space Treaty of 1967 prohibits placing weapons of mass destruction in orbit around the Earth, on the Moon, or on other celestial bodies. It does not, however, prohibit conventional weapons in space.

Space troopers

In the 1970s, the Soviets launched three secret space stations, known as the Almaz program, which were reportedly armed with space cannons to repel boarders. They were the only manned military space stations ever to have flown, but were eventually abandoned because satellites proved to be more efficient for reconnaissance.

Soviet space laser

The *Polyus* spacecraft was the Soviet attempt to create a space-based laser weapons system similar to that envisaged by the U.S. SDI program. A prototype of the space station was launched in 1987, but failed to reach orbit and fell back to Earth.

Satellite down

The Soviet Union, the United States, and China have all destroyed satellites in space, proving that orbital skirmishes are possible.

Asteroid alert

Scientists think we can use nuclear weapons to protect the earth from asteroids. Early warning systems would alert us to incoming asteroids, which could then be blasted to smithereens by a rocket-delivered nuclear warhead.

$60 BILLION

The estimated cost of the Strategic Defense Initiative (SDI) before it was abandoned in the early nineties.

1.4 MEGATONS

of TNT was the equivalent force of the 1962 explosion of a nuclear device 250 miles (400 km) above the Earth. The USA carried out the Starfish Prime test to determine the effects of war in space. The explosion crippled one third of satellites in low Earth orbit.

STAR WARS TECHNOLOGY THAT EXISTS

THE AEROFEX HOVERBIKE

Like the speeder bikes in *The Return of the Jedi*, this individual hovercraft will zoom over the ground at low level. It will be available from 2017.

LASER CANNONS

The U.S. Navy's USS *Ponce* has been fitted with a laser weapon. It has been used to shoot down drones and sink small boats.

FLOATING PROBE DROIDS

Seen in *The Empire Strikes Back*, a real world equivalent is the MLB Company's V-Bat, which can hover in position autonomously and use a robot arm to deliver a 1-pound (450-g) load.

... AND ONE THAT COULD SOON ...

LIGHTSABERS

Scientists at Harvard and MIT have managed to construct "molecules" out of light, which could allow them to build "objects" out of photons.

Dedicated to Jamie and Alex,
whose constant questioning
and search for knowledge
kept the authors on their toes.

This edition published by Parragon Books Ltd in 2015
and distributed by

Parragon Inc
440 Park Avenue South, 13th Floor
New York, NY 10016
www.parragon.com

Copyright © Parragon Books Ltd 2015

Written by Stuart Derrick & Charlotte Goddard
Internal design by five-twentyfive.com
Images courtesy of Shutterstock

ISBN 978-1-4723-9238-1

Printed in China